MW00489457

Ron,

Nice to have you join us.

Capt E

CAPTAIN ENERGY

CAPTAIN ENERGY

A TRUE STORY

BRUCE LEONARD

Published by Deeds Publishing in Athens, GA
www.deedspublishing.com

Printed in The United States of America

Cover design by Mark Babcock

Library of Congress Cataloging-in-Publications data is available upon request.

ISBN 978-1-944193-42-3

Books are available in quantity for promotional or premium use. For information, email info@deedspublishing.com.

First Edition, 2016

10 9 8 7 6 5 4 3 2 1

to Carol, the love of my life

AUTHOR'S NOTE

CAPTAIN ENERGY: A TRUE STORY IS MY "COMING OF AGE" STORY. IT chronicles a nine month journey triggered by a "peyote induced vision quest." As a 21-year-old recent college graduate from a conservative upper-middle class background, I travel to Hawaii where I find myself caught up in a series of bizarre escapades, fueled by drugs and the social upheaval my generation experienced in the '60s and '70s.

Alone in Honolulu, I'm faced not only with the specter of Vietnam and the issues of civil rights, women's liberation, and the war on poverty, but also the seduction of sex, drugs and rock and roll in the land of aloha.

The portions of the book that describe my nine-month odyssey contain flashbacks to events that precede my time in the islands. They reveal how unlikely it was that my life would detour so drastically into the realm of hippies and drugs. And why Captain Energy emerged, hell-bent on fulfilling a cosmic destiny.

Parts chronologically and order in book

1946 – 1968 – Growing up through college	(Part 8)
June 1968 – Dec 1969 – Hawaii VISTA	(Part 6)
Dec 1969 – Aug 1970 – Return to New York	(Part 4)
Aug 1970 – Dec 1970 – Return to Hawaii	(Part 2)
Jan 1971 – Peyote Vision Quest	(Part 1)
Feb 1971 – Return to Maui	(Part 3)
March 1971 – Makiki	(Part 5)
April – August 1971 – Maui, Honolulu and Mainland	(Part 7)

(Some names in the book have been changed to protect privacy)

PART 1

JANUARY 1971 VISION QUEST IN MAUI, HAWAII

1

THE PEYOTE INDUCED INTENSE VOMITING. MY EYES TEARED AND my nose ran as I stared at the clear ringlets of saliva circling the toilet bowl. I hadn't eaten in two days in anticipation of taking these powerful mind-altering cactus buttons. Another spasm erupted and I dry-heaved, leaving a bitter bile taste in my throat. After several hours, my nausea slowly vanished, my head cleared, and I was alert. My system was purged of impurities.

Marijuana had taken me to one level of introspection, and I'd felt ready to ingest another mind-expanding plant to launch me on this revelatory vision quest. The idea to try peyote had been reinforced by my reading of The Teachings of Don Juan by Carlos Castaneda, which relates his experience taking the powerful psychoactive plant while being mentored by a Mexican shaman.

After my internal cleansing episode in the bathroom, I sprawled on the cream-colored carpet of my Hawaii hotel room, listening intently to the lyrics of the Beatles' *White Album* on my cassette player.

Since returning to Hawaii, the dark sludge of gloom had receded, replaced by a burst of positive energy. I had spent nine months back home in cold, bleak New York, living with my father and struggling to avoid being drafted to fight in Vietnam. With the assistance of an attorney and letters from some sympathetic shrinks, I was able to convince my draft board that I was unfit for military service. It had been a paralyzing and depressing experience, but I was now liberated and was recapturing a feeling of optimism.

I had taken the peyote in this hotel on Maui to figure out how to channel my renewed sense of confidence and manic energy. The plan for this spiritual journey was to immerse myself in what I felt was the enlightened wisdom of the Beatles by listening to a methodically arranged progression of their music.

As a high school senior, I had watched with reserved curiosity the Beatles' American debut on the Ed Sullivan Show in the winter of 1964. There didn't seem to be anything special about "I Want to Hold Your Hand," and their long hair was just kind of weird. But as time went on, their music started to grow on me. Their self-deprecating, sarcastic wit appealed to me. They seemed to be amused and surprised by their growing fame. "What's the big deal? We're just a rock 'n' roll band." Then they released *Rubber Soul*, apparently recorded after Bob Dylan introduced them to marijuana, and their music took a distinctly new direction as youth culture began its seismic shift.

The four years I spent at Franklin and Marshall College in Pennsylvania before moving to Hawaii in 1968 drinking beer, playing cards, wrestling, and chasing women had delayed my exposure to society's chaotic cultural changes. I was a bewildered bystander, watching the protests, the hippies, and the drugs. My hair remained short and my drug of choice was alcohol.

It wasn't until after college that I smoked marijuana for the first time. Listening to music while stoned was a voyage into a whole different reality. Melodies and lyrics filled me with images, memories, and palpable emotions. I began to experience a rich inner life of euphoric dreams and fantasies.

With my return to Hawaii in 1970 after my nine months in New

York dealing with the draft, I had started taking yoga classes. Transitioning into a variety of yoga poses in that hotel room, I slipped into a trance as the Beatles' music flowed in and out of my consciousness. Balancing on the nape of my neck, I unfolded into a shoulder stand, and as I arched my back and pushed my feet toward the ceiling, blood and oxygen rushed into my brain. The music pulsated through my muscles and ligaments. My strength and flexibility had been enhanced by yoga and wrestling, and the extra pounds accumulated during my nine-month depression in New York were gone. Sitting in the lotus position, I meditated as the music flowed through my veins.

A parallel reality was revealed to the Beatles through their drug use, and the lyrics and mood of their music reflected this new direction. The *Sgt. Pepper* album was filled with songs that reflected their own personal artistic and spiritual growth. I closed my eyes and saw "Lucy in the Sky with Diamonds."

They had evolved as a result of their exposure to eastern religion and meditation during their trip to India, and this transformation could be heard in the sitar-accompanied "Within You, Without You."

The post-Beatles breakup albums produced by George Harrison and John Lennon were especially intriguing, exploring much more than romantic love. George's music reflected his spiritual quest, and John had become a social activist. Maybe this music could soothe my inner discord and enhance my drug-induced spiritual voyage.

With every trip to the toilet, I peered into the mirror, transfixed by the black void of my pupils and how my pores pulsated to Ringo's drum beats. Staring at the space between my eyes, my awareness became the whole room, and I perceived it not through sight or hearing, but from a place that transcended my senses. I was the room and I could experience it from anywhere.

In college, I had resorted to strict calorie reduction to compete at my wrestling weight of 160. I now weighed 145 through a combination of a vegetarian diet, regular wrestling workouts, and my marijuana-induced mania. The mirror reflected my gaunt, defined body. Rippled stomach muscles and sunken eyes morphed into the cream tiles of the wall. My body and mind were humming, and my eyes were clear. The cosmic energy searing through my being infused me with indescribable peace and serenity. The discord and noise were gone. Everything was stillness and light.

Starting with *Sergeant Pepper*, then the double *White Album*, *Abbey Road*, and George Harrison's *All Things Must Pass*, I finally got to *Live Peace in Toronto* by the Plastic Ono Band with John and Yoko.

By then, I was writhing on the floor. I had been on the peyote high for hours, smoking dope, gazing in the mirror, and staring into the toilet. Continually assaulted by emotions, images, and memories, I longed for some release, a final rapturous climax. Where was all this leading?

I had never heard the *Plastic Ono Band* album before and only later found out that Yoko Ono's track "John John (Let's Hope for Peace)" was influenced by her immersion in primal scream therapy. As I listened to her piercing wails, in my hallucinating mind I was transported to my mother's womb, floating in a warm pool of embryotic fluid. Breathing, moving, and restless to be reborn an innocent, blank slate, I could hear Yoko, my mother, pushing me out, experiencing the joy and pain of my birth. The sensation of being born again was overwhelming. I lay on the floor, surrounded by my loved ones, there to celebrate my arrival. I couldn't see them, but their presence washed over me. After Yoko finished howling, I lay on the floor for what seemed like hours, shifting to this new reality, about to embark on a journey I had been predestined to follow.

I turned the tape over and I was at the Live Peace in Toronto Festival. John Lennon was performing "Yer Blues" and the crowd was going wild. When they sang with one exuberant voice, "*All we are saying, is give peace a chance,*" it became clear why I was there in that hotel room and what I was meant to do. Weeks before, I had been playing music with some new friends and was christened "Captain Energy" by Billy Kim during an exuberant jam session. Woodstock had occurred several years earlier, and I recently experienced Santana at the Diamond Head Crater Rock Festival. I was profoundly impressed by the potential power of a large gathering of like-minded, enthusiastic idealists. Many in our generation craved love, peace, and happiness, but we were disillusioned and suspicious of our political and corporate leaders. We yearned for another Gandhi but had just lost Martin Luther King. Though the Beatles and Dylan were inspirational, what we really needed was a messenger with the talent of a musician and the credibility of a social activist.

Once I heard John and Yoko's performance at the Toronto Peace Festival, it dawned on me that I was that messenger; my band and I were slated to perform at the world's ultimate rock festival in the crater of Maui's Haleakala volcano that very weekend. My band, Captain Energy and the Electric Flesh, would surpass the Woodstock debut of Crosby, Stills, and Nash. The Toronto, Diamond Head and Woodstock festivals had demonstrated the ability of huge crowds to share provisions, problem-solve, and co-exist peacefully and harmoniously. And now, the world would witness the most spectacular display of peace, love, and rock n' roll anyone had ever seen.

What a delicious serendipity this opportunity had opened up to me, that I had been chosen, the one person equipped to handle this momentous undertaking. I figured the details of this rock festival and my particular role would eventually be revealed when I got to Haleakala. Which is why, on January 16, 1971, I ingested the peyote at the Wailuku Sands Hotel. I needed to be purified and primed for this historic and significant concert at Haleakala. This would be the long-awaited climactic trip of my life.

2

WITH MOUNTING URGENCY AND EXCITEMENT, I PULLED ON MY shorts, grabbed a T-shirt, and headed out the door. It was still dark, probably around 5:00 a.m. I felt an instinctual pull toward the ocean, and headed down the road, figuring if I ran far enough in one direction, with the slow light of day encroaching on the horizon, the ocean would reveal itself. In the distance was a clump of vegetation and just beyond, the water. The tangled brush in the early light took on a foreboding, primitive air. It was like a tropical jungle or the Garden of Eden. After maneuvering through a barbed wire fence, the ocean finally came into view and I pulled off my T-shirt and shorts. The cold water was invigorating and took my breath away.

I swam several hundred yards from shore and recognized Haleakala in the distance. As dawn approached, I could make out the summit surrounded by clouds. Pulling the water past my body, I cupped the coolness in my palms and breathed rhythmically. Completing this feat would be proof that I had the stamina to fulfill my new role as headliner of the world's greatest rock festival. But after a few more strokes, I began to wonder if swimming all the way to the crater was such a good idea. I concluded that it probably wasn't necessary to actually swim there, so I turned around and headed back to shore.

The trade winds had picked up as my feet touched sand and though the sun was climbing in the sky, it was still chilly. It had been several hours since I had eaten the peyote and its effects were wearing off. As I looked toward shore, I could see cars along the road and some structures I couldn't quite make out.

The notion of me performing at a world rock festival at Haleakala Crater that day was beginning to fade. Worse, I couldn't find my shorts, and I was naked a considerable distance from my hotel room.

Looking around, I found myself in what appeared to be an industrial park. The surface of the water was slick with luminescent, blue, red and purple oil, and the air was putrid. All along the shoreline was a scummy substance and white foamy bubbles. The structures I had been trying to make out turned out to be oil storage tanks.

Just a couple of hours earlier, I had learned I'd been cosmically handpicked to headline this epic rock festival, which would have launched a new age of international peace, love, and understanding. But here I was, wallowing in an industrial cesspool, totally naked, dripping with slime and chemicals, a significant distance from my hotel room. The euphoric, manic, drug-induced state had sadly worn off and a sober reality was setting in. It appeared that I was the butt of a sick cosmic joke.

Determined to retreat to the safety of my hotel room, I gingerly crawled back through the barbed wire fence and trudged barefoot up a hill covered in prickly kiawe bushes, all the while trying to protect my dangling genitals. I finally made it to the pavement and started looking for structures to hide behind, ducking between machinery and buildings.

It became apparent that I'd have to enlist the help of a stranger to get back to the hotel without being seen. I spotted a blue station wagon and figured I'd take my chances. This could be a like-minded hippie out for a Sunday drive. I darted out from behind an oil storage tank, waving my arms.

To put this scene into context, these had been interesting years for the local people of Maui. Many of the itinerant flower children from the mainland had descended on their tropical paradise. Maui was a treasure trove of isolated beaches, exotic fruit trees, lush gardens, and an intoxicating supply of locally-grown marijuana and psychedelic mushrooms. Makena Beach, on the leeward side of the island, had been transformed into a notorious hippie nudist hangout.

Needless to say, the driver of the station wagon, a middle-aged local guy, didn't exactly greet me with heartfelt aloha. His Sunday outing looked like it was about to be marred by yet another irritating hippie fruit loop. Having lived in Hawaii for a few years, I was familiar with this attitude and was committed to making a good impression.

He pulled up next to me and grunted in local Pidgin English, "Eh, where your clothes, brah? How come you naked?"

"I know, sir, I'm really sorry. Um, would you mind giving me a ride to my hotel? I'm staying at the Wailuku Sands."

"Get in da back and put on dis raincoat."

"Hey, thanks for picking me up."

"What happened to your clothes?"

"I know this may sound a little strange, but I got lost. I arrived here from Honolulu last night to spend the weekend. I woke up early this morning and decided to go swimming. It was pretty dark and I walked through the bushes over there to get to the ocean. I just had on a pair of shorts and they must have gotten washed away."

"But how come you went swim in dis oil storage place, brah?" he asked.

"It was so dark, I couldn't tell where I was. I figured I wouldn't bother anybody if I took an early swim. Believe me, I don't make a habit of walking around in public without my clothes on. I really appreciate you helping me out, man."

“Well, I’m off-duty police officer Lt. Sam Onaga and you undah arrest for indecent exposure. You cannot walk around wid no clothes, lolo. Put on da raincoat. We going to da police station.”

“What? Really, dude?” I was too exhausted to be indignant. “Whatever.” I wanted Onaga to know I wasn’t one of those drug-crazed hippies who’d been corrupting the youth of Maui and disrupting the tranquility of his town.

The Hawaiian Islands were originally occupied by Polynesians and were discovered by Captain Cook in 1778. They were subsequently settled by white missionaries who quickly gained influence and wealth and triggered the importation of labor from China and Japan. The Pacific basin immigration continued with Koreans, Portuguese, Filipinos, and other Pacific Islanders. Years of intermarriage resulted in a mix of ethnicities and cultures that had coexisted for generations. As in any other place, Hawaii had its share of racial tensions, which in 1971 translated to the animosity of locals toward young white hippies.

My arrival at the Wailuku police station was greeted with a mixture of amusement and disdain. It was a slow Sunday morning at the station and Onaga’s arrest had made for some welcome entertainment during the morning coffee and malasadas break. I maintained a cooperative demeanor, as I had no intention of revealing my outrage at what I considered to be police harassment. During the car ride, I inquired as to the seriousness of the offense and Onaga assured me that indecent exposure was a misdemeanor, no more serious than a parking ticket. At the police station, I answered questions about my home and my job, assuring the officer that I was a gainfully employed college graduate who didn’t live on the beach and didn’t support myself by selling drugs to his kids. Someone finally decided I should be driven back to my hotel room to get my clothes and that I would appear before the judge later that same day. Accompanying me to my room would also allow them to confirm their suspicions that this whole incident was drug-induced and they'd find a goldmine of illegal substances in the room.

I arrived at the hotel barefoot and clad only in the raincoat, escorted by two of Maui's finest. I was reasonably confident that all the marijuana and peyote had been consumed and there wouldn't be any incriminating evidence left. While I showered and dressed, the officers scoured the room and found nothing. My police escorts and I exited through the lobby, walking past the concerned hotel manager.

My hearing was held later that day before an amused but stern judge. After I recounted the innocent circumstances of my arrest, he scheduled an official court date and set bail for $30. He lowered it to $21 when I informed him that $21 was all the money I had on me. He said that since I lived in Honolulu, it would be understandable if I chose to forfeit my bail and not return for my hearing. Expressing my appreciation for his understanding, I requested that the details of this incident not be tipped off to the media, as it could jeopardize my job back in Honolulu. He shrugged and told me not to worry.

Upon my return to the hotel, I was intercepted by the manager, who abruptly handed me my suitcase. Having spotted me and my police escorts, he decided it was time for me to check out. He was unsympathetic to my protests and finally requested a courtesy van to return me to the airport. Drained and exhausted, I resigned myself to my fate and left Maui.

The bad karma continued when I returned to Honolulu. On Wednesday, a brief article appeared in the Honolulu Star Bulletin. "A young man by the name of Bruce Leonard was picked up stark naked on Hobron Street in Maui and when confronted by Lt. Sam Onaga, Bruce stated that he was 'lost'." When I got to work the following day,

I was summoned to the Program Manager's office, handed a severance check, and told that in light of recent media stories, it might be best for all concerned if I looked for a new job. I was shocked and embarrassed, but after some deliberation, I concluded that this was part of a cosmic plan and I was now free to pursue my new identity as Captain Energy.

Nude Stroll Lands Him in Trouble

WAILUKU, Maui — Bruce E. Leonard of 1712 Moani St., Honolulu, is to appear in Wailuku District Court Jan. 25 to face charges arising from a walk in the nude down a Kahului street.

Leonard, 21, was released on $21 bail following his arrest by police Lt. Sam Onaga on Sunday.

Onaga said he spotted Leonard walking "stark naked" on Hobron Street. He invited Leonard into his car and took him to Wailuku police station where he was booked on indecent exposure charges.

Onaga said Leonard told him he was "lost."

Honolulu Star-Bulletin

Published Daily Except Sunday at 605 Kapiolani Blvd.

Entered as Second Class Matter in Honolulu, Hawaii
Telephone 5367-222

SUBSCRIPTION RATES

DAILY INC. SUNDAY	Per Mo.
Daily Inc. Sunday, Oahu	$3.50
Neighbor Islands Homes Delivery	$4.00
Mainland ship Mail	$7.00
DAILY ONLY	
Oahu	$3.00
Neighbor Islands	$3.50
Mainland Ship Mail	$5.50
SUNDAY ONLY	
Sunday Star-Bulletin & Advertiser	
Oahu	$1.50
Neighbor Islands	$2.00
Mainland Ship Mail per month	$3.00

National and world news teletype service from Associated Press, United Press International and the New York Times. Special news services from the Chicago Daily News.
National advertising representation by Cresmer, Woodward, O'Mara and Ormsbee, Inc.
For further information please call or write Circulation Department (Phone 5367-222), P.O. Box 3350, Honolulu, Hawaii 96801.

Oronsay Due

The P and O Lines' S.S. Oronsay, from Vancouver, will arrive here Saturday at 9:30 a.m.

The ship, carrying 150 persons, will leave at midnight the same day for Pago Pago, American Samoa. It is scheduled to return to Honolulu March 10.

PART 2

—

FLASHBACK

—

AUGUST – DECEMBER 1970

3

BEING BACK IN HAWAII WAS FRIGHTENING AND WONDERFUL. I HAD just endured nine dismal months in North Tarrytown, New York, facing the military draft after having spent an exhilarating year and a half as a VISTA volunteer in Honolulu. VISTA (Volunteers in Service to America) was an anti-poverty program created by Lyndon Johnson's Economic Opportunity Act of 1964 as the domestic version of the Peace Corps. New York had beaten me up, and now here I was, back in Hawaii.

It was August of 1970 and Leo, a friend I had made over the last few months of my VISTA project, invited me to stay with him and his girlfriend Ann. I hoped he would tolerate this more subdued Bruce, who was nothing like the Juicy Brucie he'd known a brief nine months earlier. It turned out to be a comfortable transition that would, unbeknownst to me at the time, launch the emergence of Captain Energy.

Ann and Leo remembered me as an adrenalized VISTA volunteer who had developed an innovative project working with young Hawaiian drug users. Leo and I had met Ann, a divorced mother in her early thirties, when she was a graduate student in the School of Social Work assigned to our VISTA project in Palolo Valley a year earlier. She was now a graduate student in the School of Public Health. At Berkley, she had been involved with the Black Panthers and the free speech and anti-war movements, and was now an outspoken feminist. Strong, vulnerable, and a little neurotic, she hailed from a wealthy family and was supported by a trust fund. Her relationship with Leo seemed to work, probably due to an interesting tension between passion and conflict.

Ann was short, about five feet tall, with heavy breasts and ample hips. Her eyes had an Asian slant to them and her brown hair was soft and naturally curly. She often wore a stern, thin-lipped expression and approached most situations defensively. It was the start of the women's movement and she hid her vulnerability behind a tough, assertive mask. She was divorced with a two-year-old mixed-race son, Gregory. The boy was in the midst of his terrible twos, demanding independence and craving his mother's attention. His behavior was exacerbated by Ann's neuroses and the lack of a consistent male figure in his life. Ann, at 32, was six years older than Leo and working on her second master's degree. He was a high school graduate who had left the Coast Guard just before he and I met and was now taking courses at Leeward Community College on the GI Bill. Ann was from a venerable and wealthy Jewish family. Leo grew up in a blue-collar family in Massachusetts. He was a photographer and a light-hearted jester, quick to laugh, easy to engage with people, inquisitive but wary. She was intellectual and controlling, and her thinly veiled anger concealed a vulnerable, lonely woman. She valued having Leo in their lives — a handsome companion who accompanied her to social activities, took them to the beach on weekends, and provided a male presence in her son Gregory's life. Leo respected Ann's intelligence, affection and political sophistication and didn't have a problem with her picking up the tab. It was a volatile relationship, two independent, wary adults seeking their own identities and personal peace.

Ann was renting a spacious two-bedroom cottage in Manoa Valley, several blocks from the University of Hawaii campus. A comfortable front porch, scattered with flip-flops and sandals, overlooked the expansive front lawn. The grass was often strewn with overripe mangos and shriveled avocados, with clouds of fruit flies swarming over them. The porch opened onto a carpeted living room with a rattan sofa and matching chairs. The dining room led to the adjacent large kitchen, and Ann and Leo's master bedroom and a smaller bedroom bordered the other side of the house. I shared the smaller room with Gregory and his crib. Sunlight would stream into our room in the morning and I'd feel warm and comforted to be back in Hawaii.

Greg and I sized each other up. He'd watch as I tried to engage him, making faces and asking questions I thought a two-year-old could probably handle.

"How you doing, Greg?"

"Aren't you a big boy?"

"Wasn't that fun?"

He called me Roosh—his attempt at Bruce, and I called him Reg. As time went on, whenever I'd walk in the door, he'd run and jump into my arms, squealing, "Roosh! Roosh!" and I would answer, "Reg! Reg!" Ann was pleased to see we were bonding.

Despite the underlying tension between Ann and Leo, it felt good to be back in Hawaii. The sunlight, the fragrances, the craggy mountain ridges and the infinite blue horizon felt like home. The island breezes seemed to whisper *e komo mai*. Welcome.

One day, Ann announced her decision to become a vegetarian. Leo rolled his eyes, but I was pleased, as I'd always wanted to give the vegetarian lifestyle a try. Not knowing how to cook and never having been in a household where I had much control over what was served, it hadn't been a viable option. But now, with the three of us sharing the household chores, I was eager to learn to cook vegetarian meals for us.

Though Ann could be a bit uptight, she seemed comfortable with the status of my indefinite visit. I, in turn, was intrigued by her lifestyle. She was taking yoga, participating in group therapy (or "encounter group" as it was called), and had enrolled in the School of Public Health at the University of Hawaii.

On most days, Leo would attend class at Leeward Community College out in Pearl City, Ann would drop Gregory off at daycare before her classes, and I would coordinate a ride with someone to go hunt for a job. After a couple of weeks, I hooked up with some of my old VISTA contacts, who steered me downtown to an old building that housed a variety of programs under the Office of Economic Opportunity, including VISTA, Community Action Programs (CAP), Model Cities, and the Concentrated Employment Program (CEP). I reacquainted myself with some of the secretaries I had known as a VISTA volunteer and applied for the position of CEP Work Experience Coordinator.

4

ONE LATE AFTERNOON, LEO RETURNED FROM SCHOOL. THE SHAD-ows had lengthened, and the Manoa breeze was gently rustling the leaves of the large avocado trees in the front lawn. Greg's toy box was open, surrounded by cars, trucks, and stuffed animals.

"Leo, it's so great to be back. Thanks again for inviting me to stay with you guys."

"Dude, glad you're here. I've missed you."

We reminisced about the time we spent together the preceding summer and fall of 1969. Leo was about to leave the Coast Guard and I was in the midst of my year in VISTA. We met through mutual friends, and he became intrigued with my VISTA project, which involved my living and working with troubled Hawaiian juveniles in a low-income tenement. I developed the Palolo Youth Project to find educational and vocational opportunities for a group of school dropouts and drug users.

"After the Coast Guard, you gave me an opportunity to feel useful. I identified with those kids and loved working with them. It was therapeutic and rewarding."

"I never could've done it without you, Leo. You had a special rapport with them that I lacked and you gave me so much emotional support. Man, I'd get so down and discouraged, and you were there to pick me up."

"I couldn't believe you stuck with it. After all you did for those kids, they break into your apartment and rip you off, man? You never gave up on them. I learned a lot from you."

"Those were amazing times, but returning back east was such a complete downer. Living with my father, being unemployed, and with the fucking draft hovering over my head, I crashed and lost my confidence. The more I wallowed in self-pity, the more I started to think the whole Hawaii experience was some delusional fantasy."

"It wasn't a fantasy, man. Did you know about the school project report?"

"What report?"

Leo went to his room and returned with a document titled *Palolo Youth Development Project: Evaluation Report, School of Social Work, University of Hawaii, June 1971.*

"Remember Ted, the VISTA volunteer who was assigned to Palolo after you? Well, he gave me this report about a behavior-modification school pilot project that happened after we left. I know you were pretty discouraged about your Palolo project never being funded, but this school pilot project actually was funded and they got some pretty good results."

"Yeah, I was pretty bummed when I left."

"Me too, but the School of Social Work and the Palolo Community Council got some funding and started this small pilot project with about a dozen of some of the paint sniffers that were hanging around your apartment."

"Cool."

"Yeah, they used the behavior modification methods we were trying. You remember Daniel, Gary, Lisa and that kid with those nasty tattoos, what's his name?"

"You mean Larry?"

"Yeah, well, apparently after participating in this school project, they all got scholarships to Kapiolani Community College this past fall. Here's the report. They mention your name and how you laid the groundwork for this project while you were in VISTA."

"Man, you really made my day. Sometimes I think that was the coolest thing I've ever done, and other times I think I was on an ego trip and we just wasted everyone's time."

"Not true, Juice. I'll never forget you waking up at four o'clock every morning to write the Palolo Youth Project paper, talking to all those bureaucrats trying to convince them to let the kids go to that alternative school, or loosen up their fucking rules to let the kids into job training. Man, you were like a lawyer or something. I can remember Ann saying, 'This dude's going to be on the cover of Time magazine.'"

"Well, I'm just glad you convinced me to come back to Hawaii and gave me a place to stay."

Leo, let out a long sigh and stared at me.

"Living with Ann isn't easy. She says I don't clean the house well, I don't spend enough time with Greg, and I don't spend enough time with her. How've you been doing with her?"

"We're getting along fine. Obviously, I'm a guest so our relationship is different, but I think she appreciates my interest in her lifestyle and my willingness to help out."

Leo and Ann eventually had a huge blow-out and he left. I was a bit anxious about this new development. Leo was my close friend and the reason I was staying at the house, and now he was gone.

5

ANN AND I WERE SITTING AT THE DINING ROOM TABLE, SHARING A vegetarian meal she had prepared. Gregory was on the living room floor watching TV, quietly pushing one of his trucks. I took a sip of wine.

"Ann, I'm a little uncomfortable about this situation now that Leo's gone. As you know, I'm a bit low on money and I was hoping you'd let me stay here till the end of the month. By then, I'll hopefully have a job and can afford my own place."

"Hey, no problem. We like having you here." Ann smiled. "You're good with Gregory, and you do more around the house than Leo ever did."

"Well, I really appreciate your generosity, teaching me how to cook vegetarian, introducing me to your yoga classes. I think we share a lot of the same values and interests. Let me know of any other chores I can do around the house."

We lingered at the dining room table, drinking wine and discussing the new situation in light of Leo's departure. As the alcohol flowed and things loosened up, we talked about the nature of our past romances. I ventured that it might be nice to explore an open relationship that would allow the possibility of going out with other people without anyone getting jealous. I told her about a previous predicament where I'd found myself in love with two women at the same time. One had left for the summer, and in her absence, I got involved with someone else. I loved them each for different reasons and really wanted to continue to see both of them openly.

"And did they want to get to know each other?" Ann asked.

"Uh, no. They were both hurt. They were definitely not interested in exploring an open relationship."

I told Ann about some of the Robert Rimmer books I had been reading, like *The Harrad Experiment*, which explored free love in a college setting, *The Rebellion of Yale Marrat*, about a love triangle, and *Proposition 31*, which involved an open relationship between two couples. Ann seemed intrigued with the concept and admitted she'd often thought it would be nice to live in a small commune where everyone would pool incomes and share household duties, child rearing, and sleeping partners. We sat for several more hours, drinking and talking. After putting Gregory to bed, Ann reminisced about her previous two marriages, her other relationships, and about how possessive her partners had been.

By the time we got up from the dining room table, it was dark and the house geckos were loudly chirping. I headed towards Greg's room to crash on my mattress when Ann called me into her bedroom. I slept there that night and continued to share her bed for as long as I lived with her.

6

*ALTHOUGH WE LIVED TOGETHER AS A FAMILY AND SHARED AN INTI-*mate relationship, it was understood that Ann and I had the option to see other people.

One morning, Ann mentioned that she had invited the dean of the School of Public Health over to the house for a bite to eat. This was purely a social/political occasion, though she admitted she was open to whatever might come up. She described the dean as a handsome, brilliant scholar from Boston. Educated at Harvard, he had known the Kennedy family and was close to Bobby. He had previously served as Commissioner of Health for the City of New York.

When I came home, Ann told me all about their lunch together. She was smitten. She gushed about how handsome and clever he was. They had talked about a variety of things: national and local politics, school, and finally some personal issues. The dean admitted that he was in a troubled marriage and that he found Ann very attractive. He flirted with her, mentioned he'd like to see her again, and kissed her before he left. She giggled like a schoolgirl and speculated as to her next move.

Though I cared for Ann, I wasn't especially attracted to her and she admitted that I was not her type. She preferred her men built more like Leo.

She found me too rangy and sinewy. I was totally supportive concerning her pursuit of the dean, and felt no jealousy whatsoever. As a matter of fact, I was hoping their relationship would flourish, and I would get a chance to meet him.

About a week after I submitted my application for the position with the Concentrated Employment Program (CEP), I got a call to come in for an interview. I was hired the next day and started work the following Monday.

The job was perfect. I was a one-man employment agency, acquiring and providing free labor to non-profit organizations (NPO) in exchange for potential employment. The NPO would train someone, CEP would pay his or her salary for six months, and if all went well, at the end of the six-month period the NPO would officially offer the trainee a job. This arrangement benefited both parties. The trainees were grateful for the work and the NPO appreciated the six months of free labor. I served as coach and counselor for the trainees and a logistical problem solver for the NPOs. It afforded me a great opportunity to assess the non-profit community, which included the American Red Cross, the Heart Association, the Salvation Army, public schools, churches, and government agencies.

***

Ann informed me that Alex Lessin was going to conduct a weekend encounter group that would begin Saturday morning and take place at one of the participant's apartments. I didn't want to miss this. Alex was a politically liberal anthropology professor with a PhD from UCLA. He sported wire-rimmed glasses and wore his hair in a full, brown afro. Sixteen participants showed up Saturday morning: five couples and six individuals. The apartment was sparsely decorated with large pillows that we plopped down onto as we introduced ourselves and shared our personal goals for the weekend. Alex told us he would be putting us through a number of Gestalt exercises meant to break down our inhibitions and create trust within the group. In one case, we were randomly paired up and one partner was blindfolded. The sighted person would lead the blindfolded partner out of the apartment and down the stairs to the front lawn. We then returned to the group and shared with each other how we experienced leading and being led. We engaged in a variety of other physical and verbal exercises, exploring interpersonal and intrapersonal issues.

Alex knew me through my VISTA work with underprivileged paint sniffers and had invited me on several occasions to speak to his anthropology class about not just the underlying factors contributing to juvenile drug abuse, but also promising alternative activities that our project was trying to make available.

He was an experienced therapist and our group trusted him. Though we often dealt with painful issues, the encounters were typically positive. Not only was Alex adept at providing useful feedback, but the group was also supportive and occasionally insightful. With the session being twenty-four hours long, we had adequate time to explore issues in depth and develop the foundation for relationships that lasted beyond the weekend.

Camille and Roger were in a new marriage with an infant son. Roger had just returned from Vietnam and was trying to re-establish an intimate relationship with Camille. Bob and Nora wanted different things in their relationship. He wanted to be able to see other women and Nora was terrified of losing him.

Martha's husband had recently died of a heart attack and she was left angry and guilty. He was overbearing and had belittled her and tried to undermine her as she sought to change careers and go back to school. She was also angry because he had done the same thing to their kids. She blamed him for their grown son's inability to hold down a job or maintain a relationship.

Alex created exercises and techniques to address these situations. He led us in role-playing, where one person in each couple would take on the role of the other and engage in dialogue as their partner in order to better gain perspective and empathy. Then the roles would switch. Martha carried on a heated screaming session with a pillow representing her dead husband, which she punched and throttled to release her pent up rage. One of my issues was insecurity about my intelligence and my need for validation. I blamed the educational system and vented my frustration about my college GPA and having had to drop out of two graduate school programs. Alex's exercises helped me realize that as a VISTA volunteer, I had demonstrated a capacity to problem solve and an ability to document and articulate effectively, which resulted in my Palolo project laying the groundwork for a funded educational pilot program.

Ann and I left that weekend on an emotional high. I had alleviated some of my insecurities and dealt with my relationship with my father, and she and I resolved a number of personal issues, leaving with tools to improve our communication.

7

SEVERAL WEEKS LATER, LEO AND I MET UP AT THE GINGER MAN, A favorite bar near the University, to grab a beer and catch up.

"So how's life?" Leo asked.

"Actually, it's pretty great. Getting that job was really a boost to my self-esteem. There were fifty applicants, and many of them had graduate degrees. I was told I got it because of the work I did as a VISTA volunteer."

"You deserved it," Leo commented.

"How's school?"

"Pretty good. I'm digging this drama course and I've got a pretty decent political science professor."

"How's the social life?"

"It's cool, lots of great looking chicks on campus."

"You've never had trouble with the ladies."

"How about you and Ann?"

"Well, the other night, she and I were sleeping and the dean calls her around one in the morning. You know I told you she had the hots for him. He was drunk, got into a big fight with his wife and wanted to come see her. She tells me he's coming over, so I get out of bed and move into Greg's room. No problem."

Leo nodded. "Yeah, that's definitely a better arrangement for her. I could never have done that. Plus, I always felt uncomfortable with that whole university scene. I hated going to all those social events, making small talk with her professors and the other graduate students. I just felt out of place."

"Well, it's been perfect for me, especially since I'm considering applying to the School of Public Health. I'm not only getting to know some of the faculty, but shit, I'm letting the dean get laid... he better get me into the school."

Leo laughed out loud. "Man, that is a trip."

"I'll tell you about a trip. Several weeks ago, we went to a party in Hawaii Kai at her friend Carol's house. She lives in this great place with a wrap-around deck right on the lagoon. Well, I'm walking around schmoozing and drinking beer and Ann calls me over and introduces me to this straight-looking dude she's been talking to. Apparently this guy Bob is some kind of doctor who's in a residency program at Queen's Hospital. Ann's all excited and asks me to guess who Bob worked with during his internship." I paused for dramatic effect. "Freakin' Masters and Johnson, man."

"Masters and Johnson, who are they?"

"They recently wrote a couple of best-selling books about their sex research."

"Sex research?"

"Yeah, they were sex researchers and published all this shit on women's sexual responses and orgasms. They recruited these prostitutes and observed them having sex in their lab."

Leo was wide-eyed.

"Yeah, so this guy Bob says that he worked with them and is now an expert on women's orgasms. I said, 'Cool,' and we headed back to Ann's, where he and I proceed to help her with hers."

"See, this is way better for you. That would have totally freaked me out. The other shit I couldn't handle was her going to encounter groups."

"I love those groups, man. They helped me pull out of my depression. I got my energy and optimism back. Ann and I did a weekend with that guy Alex Lessin, the one whose anthropology class I spoke at."

"I hate that touchy feely shit."

"Well, that touchy feely shit led to some cool and unexpected situations, man."

"What do you mean?"

"One of the couples was having trouble with their relationship. The guy wanted to go out with other women and was encouraging his old lady to go out with other guys. She wasn't up for it, but when he suggested she go out with me, she said okay. So I took her to this party that was hosted by another couple from the weekend, and I wind up sleeping with the wife of the other couple and my date winds up sleeping with the husband. "

"Hmm, maybe I should reconsider that touchy feely shit."

"Yeah, you know the weekly group that we've been attending? I scored there, too. This chick Donna's father teaches at UH, and they have this amazing house in Aina Haina. It's on the side of a mountain and has this incredible view of Waikiki. So, there we all are, swimming nude in her pool, drinking and smoking dope. I'm sitting poolside with Donna and this beautiful chick, Barbara, kissing Donna and getting some attention from Barbara too. When Barbara announces she has to leave, she slips me her number and tells me she's available the following weekend. So I wander into the kitchen and find Donna and our group therapy leader, Chuck, in a lip lock. I grab a beer from the refrigerator and Donna grabs my hand and pulls Chuck and me into a bedroom for a threesome. Life is good, my man."

***

Yoga was held twice a week at the Church of the Crossroads, a haven for free thought and liberal expression, where deserters from the Vietnam War were offered sanctuary. This stirred up a lot of controversy that caught the attention of the national media in 1969. The church was located about a mile from the University of Hawaii campus and consisted of two buildings enclosing a large courtyard where the yoga classes were held, led by a soft-spoken young man. Ann and I went every Tuesday and Thursday night from 7 to 8:30. The teacher would light incense and we'd listened to Indian sitar music as we repeated the *Salutation to the Sun*. I eventually mastered the *scorpion pose*, balancing in a headstand on my forearms, lifting my chin and arching my back, feet dangling over my head. We'd transition through postures for about an hour, then practice a combination of rhythmic breathing, chanting, and meditation, in an attempt to reach harmonic bliss. The class would end with *savasana,* the corpse pose.

8

I RAN INTO ROB MOORE AT A STORE IN KAIMUKI, OCTOBER OF 1970. I had met him during my VISTA Molokai Project the year before, when I had brought a dozen paint sniffers to the island to spend the summer living off the land and getting away from what I thought was a toxic urban environment. Rob was spending the summer traveling around Molokai, living in a van with a friend. He seemed to be recovering from several life events, including a motorcycle accident and a drug arrest.

Rob was a University of Hawaii student and worked part-time at a surf shop. He was six feet tall with broad surfer shoulders, long brown hair, and spoke with a mellow "hippie surf" dialect. He was studying communications and television production at UH.

He would invite me to hang out at his pad in Makiki, an after work ritual that I would repeat many times that fall.

His room was in one of three houses located on a piece of property in Makiki Heights. The largest house held the communal kitchen. There were an assortment of interesting people living there, many of whom appeared to be alienated twenty- and thirty-somethings who'd dropped out of society.

Among the residents were an artist couple I had met camping one summer in Molokai, a few University of Hawaii students, several unemployed musicians, and an old wrestling partner of mine who I'd competed against and trained with during my VISTA year. Alan had wrestled at a college in Washington State and held an MA in psychology. We immediately made plans to meet at the YMCA the following week to work out. Alan was recently divorced from his first wife and living with an attractive strawberry blond airline stewardess. He was a good-looking, well-built guy with a dimpled smile.

We entered Rob's small room, which was decorated with an India Import bedspread on his wall. He lit a stick of incense, put on a Moody Blues album, sat crossed-legged on the floor, and pulled out a shoebox full of dried dark-green marijuana leaves. He took out two sheets of Zig-Zag rolling papers, licked the edge of one sheet, and stuck it along the middle of the second sheet. Reaching into the shoebox, he pinched some leaves, sprinkled them onto the paper, and expertly rolled it up.

"Light up this doobie."

I struck a match, inhaled deeply, held it until the heat in my lungs forced me to cough, and passed it to Rob.

After several rounds, Rob brought out a guitar. "Let's go to the big house and jam."

"Far out," I replied enthusiastically. "Primo shit, man."

After a few attempts, I managed to stand up and follow him out the door. "Hey, I brought along my tape recorder, a Beatles song book, some wine to lubricate our voices, and dope to invigorate our minds."

"All right, Juicie, you're getting into this."

"Dude, I got so high last time we jammed. I loved it."

We walked across the lawn to the main house. The sun was setting, casting an orange glow over everything. The evening breeze carried the fragrance of the plumeria and white ginger that were growing around the property. I was filled with gratitude, realizing I was stoned in paradise.

"Rob, sit down and pick a little," said Mike, a long-haired flamenco guitarist who was sitting at the kitchen table.

"What you got there, Juicie?" he asked as I entered the kitchen with my tape recorder, songbook, and wine.

"Dude, it's time to capture some of those amazing jam sessions on tape, and I brought along a little something to stimulate the creative process."

"Right on, man," chimed in Bobby Graham, the veteran musician in the group. He could play any instrument and at the age of forty-one, had performed with dozens of bands. His claim to fame was having played with blues legends Sam and Dave. His instrument of choice was the saxophone and his idol was John Coltrane. He was the dean and we all deferred to him. I handed Rob Moore one of the joints I had brought. He lit it, inhaled, and passed it to Bobby.

"All right!" Bobby coughed. With his deep-set black eyes and long graying hair, he had the demeanor and appearance of Rasputin. Those eyes were shining as he started playing his sax. Mike McCrillis's fingers danced on his guitar strings, accompanying Bobby. McCrillis, sporting a handlebar mustache and thick dark eyebrows, was a talented but unemployed flamenco guitarist. A motorcycle accident had left him with a limp and his speech was punctuated with random song lyrics. Rob pulled out his guitar and joined in. The music was infectious and I began tapping a beat on the kitchen table. Bobby laid down his sax and we both tapped away, grinning and rocking our heads to the beat.

Mark, the red-headed drummer, pulled out his sticks and Billy Kim plugged in his electric bass guitar.

I turned on my recorder, opened the bottle of wine, poured everyone a glass, and pulled out the Beatles songbook. Bobby Graham smiled, "That's what this group needs—a Captain."

"Right on," McCrillis agreed.

Another joint was lit and passed around.

Bobby pulled out a portable synthesizer. It was no bigger than a paperback book, but it projected well. We now had a keyboard. I opened the songbook in front of me and started singing,

"I get high with a little help from my friends."

We had two rhythm guitars, a bass guitar, drums, and a keyboard, with me as the lead singer. Bobby and McCrillis played off each other with their keyboard and guitar, while I provided the vocals. We exchanged smiles as we moved along on this musical ride.

We paused as Bobby played a haunting solo on his keyboard. Mark pounded out a beat while Billy and McCrillis faced off in a guitar-bass duel. Mark's hypnotic rhythm continued as we chanted to the melody and stomped along with the drumbeat.

We were all in the same creative zone, spontaneously sharing duets and exchanging leads. The jam went on and on as we continued to partake of wine and weed. In my substance-altered mind, this was almost like making love. I was in a timeless, effortless, orgasmic zone with five other beings. It was a pure connection I had never experienced before.

The beat got progressively slower and the music more subdued, then each musician gradually ratcheted it up toward a final resounding crescendo. When it was all over, we were sweating, eyes glazed, with euphoric grins plastered on our faces. Billy Kim grabbed the microphone and announced, "And that was 'With A Little Help from My Friends' performed by Captain Energy and the Electric Flesh!"

Bobby stood up. "That's it, man—we're Captain Energy and the Electric Flesh. I love it. Energy, we were there, man, we were in the fuckin' zone. Unbelievable, man. C'mon, play it back."

We passed around another joint, and exchanged relieved glances as we listened to the epic jam session. That moment in time really happened, and we captured it all on tape. "Too much, man...too fucking much," McCrillis repeated.

9

AFTER HAVING WORKED FOR SEVERAL MONTHS AT CEP, I WAS ABLE to save up some money and decided to return to New York for Christmas. My father, a successful partner at an architectural firm in New York City, re-married in 1970, five years after my mother died of cancer. To be closer to work, he sold the house my younger brother and I had grown up in, an hour's train ride from the city on the Hudson River. Jeanne, my new stepmother, was an attractive socialite from Dallas, Texas. She had two married sons who lived in Dallas and a 15-year-old daughter, Polly, who was enrolled at a private school in Connecticut. My brother Craig had dropped out of Miami Dade College in Florida and was about to join the Navy.

I wanted to show my father the emotional and physical transformation that had occurred since my return to Hawaii over the previous four months. I was looking forward to sharing my optimism and energy with old friends that I planned to visit. It had only been a couple of years since college and many of my friends were struggling to decide whether to dodge the draft or enlist and end up in Vietnam.

"Good to see you, son. You look tan and healthy," my father greeted me as I set my suitcase down in his spacious Park Avenue apartment.

"Thanks, Dad. Returning to the islands was a good move," I replied. "Hi, Jeanne, how do you like being in the city?" I inquired.

"It's great, lots of good restaurants. Your father loves going to the museums on the weekends."

"How's your new job?" my father asked.

"I love it. In some ways, it's sort of an extension of what I was doing as a VISTA volunteer, but more structured and the pay is better. I even have access to a government car that I get to drive all over the island."

***

After spending the afternoon and evening at home, I got a call from Dave Grayson, inviting me to his apartment. Dave had been one of my roommates my junior year when I lived at the Chi Phi fraternity house. He spent the previous year qualifying for a draft deferment by teaching at an inner city school in Harlem.

"Bruce, don't you look great with your Hawaiian tan! Wow, have you lost weight?"

"Yeah, I not only hang out at the beach, but I'm still wrestling. And thanks to my vegetarian diet, I'm ten pounds lighter than my 160-pound wrestling weight."

"You'd be in Clair's weight class." Jim Clair and I had been training partners and co-captains of the Franklin and Marshall wrestling team. Though I had a successful career and finished with a respectable winning record, Jim Clair was the star of the team and won the Eastern Championship his senior year.

"Yeah, he'd still kick my ass. You know he couldn't go to law school at Maryland because of the draft, but he did get his conscientious objector status and he'll be teaching math in Puerto Rico."

"I'm heading for Europe this summer," Dave said. "That is, after the school year is over and I've saved some money. Hey, Mendel's on the way over. He starts basic training in a couple of weeks with the Marine Corps reserves."

Mendel was another fraternity brother who was captain of the tennis team and a roommate with Jimmy Clair our sophomore year. When Mendy arrived, Grayson handed me a joint and we listened to George Harrison's *All Things Must Pass.*

"Look at you, smoking dope!"

"Yeah, I finally started."

"Man, you were so straight in college, I didn't think you'd ever turn on," Dave said.

"Yeah, I have a whole different perspective on things now. I really think it's mind-expanding."

"You want to have your mind expanded, try some acid," Mendel chuckled.

"You dropped acid?" I asked.

"We both have," said Dave.

"What was it like?"

"Intense...amazing...scary. I suggest doing it in a safe place, where you can experience nature. We tripped out in Central Park and I loved it. It's hard to describe and I think it's different for everyone," Dave explained.

"That's me and weed. I respond to it differently than most people," I said.

"What do you mean? It mellows me out. All I want to do is to sit back and listen to music. And eat."

"That's what I'm saying," I responded. "It makes me speedy. My mind starts racing and I talk nonstop. I try to analyze and explain all the stuff that's in my head. When I was in Hawaii, I was trying to process how I felt about Vietnam and poverty and everything I was experiencing. I'd smoke some dope and then go drinking with some of my VISTA friends and start talking a blue streak. My friends called me Rappin' Bruce."

"You've always managed to attract nicknames."

"Yeah, well, smoking dope not only helped me sort out my feelings about Vietnam, but it really helped me organize my thoughts so I could describe the project I developed in Hawaii."

"You mean the stuff you were doing with those Hawaiian kids?"

"Yeah, I told you I took a bunch of them to this outer island for a couple of weeks and then wrote a report about the trip. When I returned, I wanted to get some funding so I could help get them back in school or get them jobs. I'd hang out with friends and think out loud about possible causes for the kids' deviant behavior and paint sniffing, which is some nasty shit by the way."

"That's kind of ironic, you getting stoned to explain why the kids you're working with were getting stoned."

"True. But I could identify with them. I understood why they wanted to get stoned and I wasn't so judgmental."

"Well, when I'm stoned, I have zero desire to talk about what I'm thinking. I just turn into a vegetable and listen to music or watch TV." Grayson shrugged.

"That's another amazing thing about pot. When I'm stoned, music turns into a whole other experience for me."

"I can relate," Mendel agreed.

I put my tape in the player. "Get a load of this." The sounds of our jam session filled the room.

"Hey, that's pretty cool, what was that?" Grayson asked.

"That was Captain Energy and the Electric Flesh. When I got back to Hawaii, I started spending time with a friend I made while I was in VISTA. He lived with a bunch of musicians who were putting together a band. The keyboard player was this old guy in his forties who'd been playing music for years. I mean, he can play any instrument. After work, I'd hang out over there, and wound up joining in on some impromptu jam sessions. Well, this recording was one of the jam sessions."

"So who was playing the keyboard? That was pretty far out."

"Yeah, that was Bobby Graham, the old guy."

"And was that you singing?"

"Yeah," I responded hesitantly.

"Not bad, I didn't know you could sing."

"Well, as you can tell, I can't."

"It wasn't bad. Do you play anything?"

"Well, I played trumpet and the sousaphone in high school and Bobby lets me practice on his trumpet, but I'd really like to get into playing the congas."

10

AFTER RETURNING TO HAWAII FROM NEW YORK, I SHOWED UP AT the New Year's Day rock festival in Diamond Head Crater and experienced nirvana. It was a bright sunny day, and inside the crater were dozens of tie-dyed tents and tarps shading long-haired fans who were there for the music or to sell their macramé planters and handmade jewelry.

As I passed one of the tents, I heard someone call my name. "Hey Captain, over here."

I looked around and saw Bobby Graham waving for me to join him. He was surrounded by a group of fine-looking ladies.

"This is Captain Energy," Bobby announced as I sat cross-legged next to him.

"Hey Energy, I'm Darla." A smiling, buxom blonde with a dark tan passed me a joint.

"The Captain here is the leader of our band, the Electric Flesh."

"Wow, so this is the band you were talking about?" Darla asked.

I looked over at Bobby. "What've you been telling them?"

"It's time for me to make my move, man. I'm not interested in doing the top-twenty teeny-bop scene anymore. You know, Augie Ray's trying to recruit all of us to play in his band and do the Waikiki nightclub scene. I'm ready to play my own music."

"I'd love to join you, Bobby, but other than playing a sousaphone in my high school band, I don't have any musical experience and my singing gives even me a headache."

"Captain, you have energy and passion, man, and that's what we need. Anybody can learn to play music, but not everyone has a message. I've heard your social-change rap, man. It's heavy. You can communicate."

He turned to the others. "You know, Energy lived in Palolo Housing for two years with these paint sniffing Hawaiian kids, and took a bunch of them over and camped in Halawa Valley on Molokai."

"Dude, there's some rough kids in those housing projects," commented one of Bobby's companions.

"Yeah, that was a pretty powerful experience. Growing up in middle-class suburbia didn't exactly prepare me for life in a Hawaiian tenement. I realized that if I'd been brought up in that environment, I probably would have dropped out of school and sniffed paint, too."

"Our country has some heavy issues, man," agreed Bobby.

"I think our generation has lost all respect for the military and our politicians," I said. "We've lost our heroes. Because of the war and all the other shit that's going on, it seems like music might be the only catalyst for social change or revolution."

"That's why I love it. No bullshit, just raw emotion and truth," Bobby said.

I noticed everyone around me was smiling, something I had become accustomed to since I first got stoned two years before. It seemed as if there was an unspoken consciousness of shared values. We opposed the war and rejected materialism and judgmental morals. Many of these young people couldn't necessarily articulate their feelings, but I believed they passionately wanted change.

Music festivals created a sense of community for that generation. Not only did these gatherings allow us to dance and get stoned, but there were also a lot of new messages emanating from the music. We talked about the dawning of the Age of Aquarius. We were drawn to the "new age" style of spirituality that we experienced listening to "Jesus Christ Superstar" and George Harrison's "My Sweet Lord." It was easy for me to look at Jesus as a revolutionary radical.

Woodstock demonstrated that thousands of young concertgoers could cope with situations like inclement weather, poor sanitation, and scarcity of food, and manage to do it peacefully. In Diamond Head Crater that day, the music filled us with joy, and our bodies interpreted the sounds and rhythms in our own way, with an underlying, pulsating beat that brought us all together

When Santana started to play their synthesis of rock, jazz, and percussion, with Buddy Miles on drums, I sprinted to the stage, elbowing my way through throngs of fans headed in the same direction, until I was right up front. The music was joyous, tribal, and primitive. We swayed and moved together, singing, shouting, passing joints, and laughing. The feeling of community and joy was a transcendent experience. I danced to Santana for the entire two-hour performance, mesmerized by the sheer power the music had over the enthralled audience.

***

I left the festival in a euphoric, mind-altered state. Buzz Gilbert, my former VISTA leader who was enrolled at the School of Public Health with Ann, had invited me over to his apartment. When I got there, I was greeted by Larry Harrington and Art Tani, VISTA friends who had been assigned to the Big Island. Larry was teaching at a school in the same district where he had served as a volunteer and Art was working at the State Hospital in Kaneohe to fulfill his commitment as a conscientious objector. I hadn't seen them in months.

"Bruce, how was the festival?"

"Fucking amazing. Santana blew my mind. You guys missed out, man. Great music, beautiful chicks, awesome vibes. I feel like I just arrived from another planet. And there was plenty of this." I offered my friends a nice thick joint.

"We haven't seen you since we were in New York last summer. You look different," Art observed.

"I feel different, lots of good shit's been happening. I've lost a lot of weight from wrestling and yoga, and I'm a vegetarian now. Buzz, how's school?" I inquired.

"It's pretty cool. I'll be graduating in a couple of months with your girlfriend Ann," he replied.

"Actually, that relationship's taken a turn. I moved out a couple weeks ago. Ann can be intense."

"I hear that," he said. "How's working with CEP?"

"I'm traveling all over the island, finding job placements for trainees. I even got jobs for some of the kids I was working with in Palolo." As we sat around smoking and catching up, Buzz put a cassette of the Doors in his player.

"Didn't you go back to New York for Christmas?" Larry asked.

"Yeah, and I think I was able to make peace with my father."

"That's gotta feel good."

"He's pleased I'm gainfully employed, and you know he just got remarried. They're living in a great apartment on Park Avenue."

"Any political discussions?" Art asked.

"I think we've agreed to disagree."

"Good move."

"But it's such a relief he's not worrying about me. I think he's proud I have a good job and that we can enjoy being with each other."

"You sound like you're in a good place," Larry said. I agreed and got up to replace the Doors with another cassette tape.

"What's that?" asked Buzz as Captain Energy and the Electric Flesh began to play.

"Remember I told you I was playing music with some guys in Makiki Heights? Well, this is what we sound like."

"Far out, man," Larry said as he lit another joint.

"Yeah, I'm having a blast playing music, and it seems like smoking grass triggers that creative side of my brain. Larry, what was that acid trip like, the one you took a couple weeks ago?"

"The most incredible life-changing experience I ever had."

"Where'd you take it?"

"A bunch of us hiked into Haleakala Crater in Maui. I can't put into words what happened, but I'll never be the same. I highly recommend it."

"This woman I've been seeing gave me some peyote buttons. I've been trying to figure out what to do with them."

"Go to Maui and take 'em," Larry insisted.

"Hey, man, there's a dove sitting on the railing." He pointed toward the porch.

We slowly filed outside to get a better look. The dove sat there for a moment, then suddenly hopped onto my shoulder.

"What's the deal, Bruce? I think it loves you."

We heard a guttural growl coming from the apartment next door.

On the other side of a screened window sat a Siamese cat, glaring. The dove remained calmly on my shoulder, and as I slowly walked over to the window, the cat began to purr.

"Right on, man…that is a sign," Art declared.

Leo Dubois visiting Makiki Apartment, March 1971. Leo was the photographer for Palolo Youth Project

Dove arrives visiting Captain Energy

Hippie scene at Hawaii Crater Rock Festival

Hawaii Crater Rock Festival, June 1971

PART 3

FEBRUARY 1971
MAUI, THE BIG ISLAND AND GREENING OF AMERICA

11

I FLEW BACK TO MAUI TO CONTEST MY COURT CASE, GET MY $21 BAIL back, and later spend some time tripping around the island. With my newly purchased backpack and sleeping bag, I also planned to look up a friend from Sleepy Hollow High School who was teaching school in Hana.

Upon my arrival in Wailuku the morning of my scheduled court case, I learned that I had access to a public defender. I introduced myself to Phil Lowenthal and shared my situation. He informed me that no one had showed up for that morning's calendar of cases, and added that this particular judge would not be sympathetic to my case or, for that matter, any cases involving stupid young hippies. He said it would be in my best interest to forfeit the $21 and forget the whole thing.

Indignant, I explained that my arrest was completely unjust and I was sure I could get my $21 back by reasoning with the judge and pleading for the rights of all victimized hippies. Lowenthal rolled his eyes and reminded me that if I insisted on my day in court, Judge Wong would have to drive to the courthouse from his home, where he was probably comfortably ensconced in his easy chair watching his favorite show, and would not be amenable to hearing my one case, especially a case involving a hippie found walking around naked and lost.

I continued to demand my rights and Lowenthal finally notified the court that his defendant insisted on a hearing. It took about an hour for Judge Wong to arrive. The bailiff asked us both to rise and the judge entered the court in his long black robe, looking peeved. His dark hair was combed meticulously across his forehead and his lips were pursed tightly together.

"Counsel, please present your case."

"Your Honor, my client would prefer to present his own case."

"All right, Mr. Leonard, it appears that you were arrested on January 20th for indecent exposure. How do you plead?"

"Guilty, Your Honor. With an explanation."

"Proceed," he sighed.

"With all due respect, Judge, I flew in from Honolulu Saturday night to spend a nice relaxing weekend here in Wailuku. I had been under a lot of stress at work and I just wanted to unwind. I woke up early Sunday morning and couldn't get back to sleep, so I decided to go for a swim. It was still dark, and I wasn't familiar with the area, so I figured I'd walk around until I found the ocean. I made my way through some fences and bushes and finally reached water. Since it was so dark and there was no one around, I took off my shorts, put them somewhere, and went for a swim. When I got back, I saw that my shorts were gone, and that I'd been swimming in an industrial area. I waved down the first car I saw to try and get a ride back to my hotel. Well, that car happened to belong to off-duty officer Onaga, who promptly arrested me."

"Anything else?" he asked.

"Yeah, I was promised after my arrest that this information would not be made public, but when I returned to Honolulu, it was written up in the Star Bulletin newspaper. And as a result of this unwarranted negative publicity, I lost my job. I want to impress upon the court that this was an innocent situation. I was not being a public nuisance or intentionally exposing myself. I lost my pants and waved down the first car I saw to try to get out of public view and get back to my hotel. I don't believe that Officer Onaga, being off-duty at the time, was under any obligation to arrest me. He could have used some common sense and just helped me, instead of abusing his power as a policeman."

Judge Wong sighed. "Thank you, Mr. Leonard. The court finds you guilty, assesses a fine of $50, and sentences you to thirty days in jail." The bailiff called the court adjourned and Judge Wong promptly stood up and walked back to his chambers.

I looked over at my attorney, who was staring at the floor, shaking his head. I was sure I'd heard that wrong.

"What did he say?"

"I told you, you should have let it go. You've been sentenced to thirty days in jail and fined $50."

"What the fuck, this is crazy! I was just trying to get my $21 back and maybe have the court admit that Onaga's a jerk. How can he do this to me? The other judge told me I didn't even have to come back if I was willing to forfeit my bail."

Lowenthal asked the bailiff if he could speak to his client before I was taken to jail. We walked outside toward the courthouse steps and I suddenly remembered I had a couple joints stashed in my wallet. I quickly retrieved them and when we got to the top of the steps, discreetly dropped them over the railing.

"What can I do?" I pleaded. "This is insane! Where's the judge? Maybe I can reason with him."

"He's probably in his chambers, but if I were you I'd leave this alone. He doesn't appear to be sympathetic towards you or your case."

"Yeah, but this is blatant hippie discrimination and harassment, it's not fair, and I'm not even a hippie!"

"In Judge Wong's eyes, any haole with long hair is a hippie."

"I need to talk to him. He can't get away with this!"

"Bruce, wait…!"

I marched through the courtroom and was given directions to Judge Wong's chambers by one of the court employees. I knocked on his door.

"Come in."

I stepped in and was greeted by a startled expression. Judge Wong lowered his eyes to the document he was reading, shuffled in his chair, and after several seconds, raised his gaze to acknowledge my presence.

"What can I do for you?"

"Judge Wong, with all due respect, I would like to request that you reconsider your ruling. It is my understanding that the reason for incarceration is to prevent a criminal from harming the public and to teach a lesson so that he doesn't repeat the crime. I think it was clear from my testimony that my actions were not malicious or dangerous and I have no intention of running around naked again. Believe me, I've learned my lesson. Is there something I said that justified this harsh punishment?"

"Mr. Leonard, would you like to appeal my decision?"

"Yes, Your Honor, I would like to appeal your decision."

"All right, proceed to the desk outside my office and I'll have the bailiff set a court date for your appeal."

"You mean I don't have to go to jail?"

"Not yet. We'll see what happens in Appeals Court."

I quickly backed out of Wong's chamber, shocked at how close I came to spending a month in jail. I was exhilarated but furious at the injustice of it all. How could the system so arbitrarily punish someone because of the length of their hair and the color of their skin? I approached Lowenthal with a shit-eating grin and told him I convinced the judge to let me appeal my case. He shook his head.

"He never does shit like that."

"Well, thanks for your help, man. I'm outta here. This doesn't seem like a good place to get arrested."

I walked out of the courthouse with my backpack, retrieved the two joints I had tossed, and headed down the road, filled with relief and indignation.

It was a typical hot, breezy day in Maui. I set down my pack, stuck out my thumb and within fifteen minutes, a rusted-out gray Ford pickup pulled over. I tossed my pack in the bed full of tools, empty beer cans, and a couple of old tires and climbed in next to the deeply tanned, wiry haole. His hair was sun-bleached with dark brown roots.

He smiled and asked where I was headed.

"Out to Hana."

"All right, a mellow place."

"Yeah, I'm going to visit an old high school friend who teaches out there. Where are you going?"

"I can give you a ride to Paia."

"That's great man, thanks."

In Paia, I hitched another ride in the back of a van. I hopped in with two other guys and asked the couple driving where they were headed. They said they were on their way to a hippie commune known as the Banana Patch. I expressed curiosity about the place and was invited to visit. Most of the residents lived in tents, tree houses, and huts with corrugated metal roofs, plywood walls, and dirt floors.

The couple invited me to their one-room hut, which was furnished with a wood-burning stove for cooking, a small refrigerator, a mattress, and a dirt floor covered with Navajo rugs. An entire wall was dominated by a huge bookcase. After a couple of tokes of their hash, I browsed through their many books on eastern religion, astrology, numerology, Tarot cards, and the I Ching. This was 1971 after all.

After my visit to the Banana Patch, I got back on the road to hitch a ride to Hana. The mountains looked like a velvety green curtain rippling under its craggy rod. The sun's reflection turned the foliage almost fluorescent in contrast to the dark, dramatic slivers of recessed shadows.

12

HANA WAS AND STILL IS AN ISOLATED HAWAIIAN COMMUNITY LOCAT-ed at the eastern end of Maui, which is dominated by Haleakala volcano. The famed road to Hana is a winding 52-mile-long two-lane highway that borders the seacoast and passes numerous waterfalls with a constant view of the ocean. In 1971, it was a traditionally Hawaiian community with a population of around a thousand. Most of them worked at the Hana Ranch, an exclusive resort with a hotel and cottages.

John Stone was a year ahead of me in school. I didn't really know him too well, but we had a lot of mutual friends. I lived in Sleepy Hollow Manor, and John lived in Philips Manor, both upper middle class residential areas of North Tarrytown. He was a bit intimidating. I recall John hanging out in a certain hallway at Sleepy Hollow High School with Mike Murray, Bob McCoy, and a bunch of other members of the football team. There was always a perceived risk of being ridiculed as you walked past them. Fortunately, my high school girlfriend, Christine, was a favorite of the group and when I was with her, they'd usually leave me alone. John was a hockey star and we were both primarily bench sitters on the football team. He was average height with wavy, auburn hair and pale blue eyes. Popular with the girls, he was voted one of the best dancers, dressers, and heart breakers in his class yearbook.

"Hey John, its Bruce Leonard from Sleepy Hollow. I'm living here in Hawaii now. As a matter of fact, I'm here in Hana at the Hasegawa General Store."

"Wow, I'd heard that you moved to Hawaii. How you doing? You have a place to stay? You want to come stay with me and my wife Jean?"

"That would be great, man."

"Hold on, I'll come over and pick you up."

I hopped in his pickup and he took me to his cottage. He introduced me to Jean and another couple who shared their teacher's quarters, Linda and Doug. John offered me a beer and we sat down to catch up while Jean prepared dinner.

"After graduating from Sleepy Hollow, I went to St. Bonaventure University in upstate New York majoring in English, and earned my teaching degree. Jean was attending a nearby college, we dated, and then got married in '70, the year after she graduated.

"We both taught in upstate New York for about a year and then we saw these jobs in Hana posted in a teachers' journal. She and I were both tired of New York winters and were looking for an adventure, so we applied and we've been teaching since last September."

"So how do you like Hana?" I asked.

"Well it's beautiful and laid back, and the people are friendly, but it's frustrating teaching these kids. There's a real small town attitude here. Most of the kids never leave Hana and there's not much motivation to do well in school. But living here is a trip. We've done some amazing snorkeling and I've gotten interested in photography. Turned one of our bedrooms into a dark room. I'll show you some of my photos after dinner. How long can you stay"?

"Well, if it's ok, I'd like to stay for a couple days."

"That would be great. It gets kind of lonely around here and it'll be good to have some company. What brings you to Hana?"

"Well, it's sort of a long story, but I had a court case in Wailuku."

As I was filling him in about my peyote trip and the arrest for indecent exposure, John interrupted me.

"Wait... wait... wait... that was you?"

"What do you mean?"

"Last week I was running some errands in town and I heard on the radio about this guy that was arrested for indecent exposure in Wailuku. That was you?"

"It was on the radio? Here in Maui? Man, I can't believe this. They released me and told me to go back to Honolulu and all would be forgotten. When I got back there, it was in the paper, my boss saw it, and I got my ass fired. Can't believe you heard it on the radio. Anyway, I came back to Maui to contest that indecent exposure arrest."

"You came all the way back here to contest it?"

"Yeah, when they arrested me, the judge released me on $21 bail and said that since I live in Honolulu, I should just forfeit the money and not come back for the court case. I told them I had a job and they assured me there would be no publicity about the arrest. So when I got back to Honolulu and got fired because of all the publicity, I was pissed. It's not like I was going around flashing people. When I couldn't find my shorts, I flagged down a car to get a ride back to my hotel and, of course, the driver was an off-duty policeman."

"Dude, the locals don't like hippies. They were sending a message."

"Well I guess I got the message." I filled him in about my thirty-day jail sentence, $50 fine and my appeal.

"Wow, like I said, they don't like hippies around here," John said, shaking his head and smiling at Jean.

"Hey, does the high school have a wrestling team?"

"Yeah, as a matter of fact, we have the 185-pound state champion."

"Maybe I could work out with the team tomorrow?"

"Anthony, the state champ, is in my English class. I'll mention to him that you're here and see when they have practice. Let's go have dinner."

As the evening progressed, we continued to reminisce about Tarrytown and compared notes about old friends. We talked about the war and current events and I was pleased to find that John shared most of my progressive views. He was into Maui Wowie, but was extremely paranoid about smoking it around Hana. The community was conservative and he knew if anyone ever found out he smoked dope, he'd probably lose his job.

John and I woke early the next morning and we walked down to the beach where he snorkeled. The water was crystal clear, with a coral reef not far from shore. He showed me where I could snorkel amid schools of multi-colored tropical fish. I spent the morning there, snorkeling and reading while they taught class.

John came home during his lunch break and pointed out the school annex building where wrestling practice was held. He said to meet him there at 4:00 p.m.

I wandered over to the annex after school. Half the floor was covered with tumbling mats and a couple of large blue 40' x 8' wrestling mats joined together with tape. John introduced me to Anthony who was about 5'10", probably close to 200 pounds. It appeared he had to lose a bit of weight to get down to the 185-pound class he wrestled at. He had broad shoulders and a thick neck, a dark Polynesian complexion, short wavy black hair, and arms that hung out due to bulging lats. In contrast to his thickly muscled body, I was a scrawny 155 pounds at six feet.

"Hey, Anthony."

"Howz'it," he replied shyly. John had told me there was no official practice today but Anthony wanted to work out.

I had been warming up for a while and a thin film of sweat covered my arms and back.

"You want to roll around?" I asked. We got down on the mat. I put my right arm around his waist, with both of us facing the same direction and pulled on his left arm with my left hand. He started to stand up and I drove forward, breaking down his left arm support, and scooped and trapped his back left ankle into the cleft formed by my left thigh and calf. As he lifted his right leg up again and tried to stand, I applied pressure at a slightly different angle, which caused him to lose his balance and fall to his right hip. Anthony was strong and quick, but I was able to use my reach and experience to control him on the mat. Slipping my left leg around his, with my left foot hooked around his calf, I arched my back, keeping my left hip higher than his, and forced all my weight onto his hip. He struggled as he lay on his stomach and tried to regain his balance on his hands and knees. I continued to drive my weight across his hip and forced him onto his side as he fought to stay off his back.

Though he was heavier and stronger, my height gave me the ability to exert leverage and, along with my leg wrestling ability and sense of balance, I was able to keep him off his base. As he flailed on his side trying to stay off his back, I cradled his head in the crook of my left arm to force his shoulders to the mat. As he struggled to push my arm away and arch off his back, I locked his upper left arm and forced my elbow towards his left ear, the palm of my hand on his shoulder blade, forcing the left side of his back to the mat and pinning him.

As we continued to work out, the practice room filled with other wrestlers. I spent the rest of the afternoon demonstrating wrestling techniques and working out.

That evening, we enjoyed another delicious dinner, then sat in the living room chatting and listening to music.

"How was wrestling practice?" Doug asked.

"He not only manhandled Anthony, he took on the rest of the team," John bragged.

"You manhandled Anthony? He must outweigh you by thirty pounds," Doug remarked.

"I wouldn't exactly use the word 'manhandle,'" I chuckled. "Luckily, it takes more than brute strength to wrestle well. I have four years of college experience so I was able to use my height and leverage to hold my own. John would probably be able to manhandle the Hana High School hockey team if they had one."

"Good analogy," John said.

John asked about the jam session I had mentioned during the previous evening's conversation. I played the Captain Energy tape for them and they seemed politely impressed.

The next morning, I went for another swim, did some hiking and returned to the cottage, where I put on some Led Zeppelin and proceeded to get wasted. My visit with John had exceeded my expectations. Though I hadn't known him well in high school, I felt we had really bonded and that I had finally found a real friend in Hawaii. I was dancing around to Zeppelin's "Whole Lotta Love," tripping in my head about how lucky I was to be there, smoking Maui Wowee in paradise, listening to great music. The synapses in my brain were sparking and I was in bliss, imagining myself producing these sounds and getting others to feel what this music was making me feel.

"Hey, turn down the fuckin' music!" Doug's voice jolted me out of my reverie. He marched into the living room, turned down the stereo, and stomped back down the hall to his unit. John asked me to join him in the bedroom.

"Bruce, it's time to go. I'll give you a ride to Wailuku."

"Ok, is there something wrong?"

"We'll talk in the car."

I grabbed my pack and thanked Jean, Doug, and Linda for their hospitality. No one would look me in the eye.

I hopped in John's pickup. "What happened in there?'

"Bruce, I loved having you here. It was a great visit. But you blew it this morning by smoking weed and playing Zeppelin too loud. It wouldn't have been so bad if it was just the music, but when our class smelled what you were smoking… that was too much. I told you, man, we could lose our jobs if anybody suspected we smoked marijuana."

"I am so sorry, John. I screwed up. I hope we can remain friends."

"Sure man, don't worry about it, be cool."

John drove me over to Wailuku, I repeated my apologies and hitched a ride to Lahaina.

13

LAHAINA WAS THE ORIGINAL CAPITAL OF THE KINGDOM OF HAWAII in the 19th century and was the center of the global whaling industry. I had attended the Lahaina Whaling Spree the previous year when I'd been a VISTA volunteer. It was the first rock festival I had ever been to and the Steve Miller Band was the headline act. Lahaina continues to host sailing ships anchored at its waterfront and is one of the most popular tourist destinations on Maui.

I had been picked up in Wailuku by friendly hippies who took me to see their dealer friend in Lahaina. Roger handed me a baggie of marijuana, which I examined carefully. I opened it and sniffed, inspecting the ratio of leaves to twigs and seeds. He told me it had been grown in the hills above Kula and was pretty powerful. I asked if they wanted to smoke some.

"Sure, man, cool."

Sharing a joint was a sort of bonding ritual that assumed a common set of values. It seemed to unite us in some sort of underground fraternity, being that it was illegal, but it also relaxed certain inhibitions and allowed for easy conversation and a friendly, open social atmosphere. Roger put on a Crosby, Stills, and Nash album, handed me some rolling papers, and we sat around his wooden phone company spool table. Jim, the guy who had brought me over, lay back against the wall with a contented smile and accepted the joint I passed to him.

The longer we smoked, the more subdued and relaxed they became. I, on the other hand, just got more hyper and I proceeded to interview them, trying to establish common ground, asking where they were from, what they did, or anything that would allow us to connect beyond the dope. We sat around for a while after finishing the joint, then Bob announced he had to go downtown to meet his ol' lady, so we all dispersed.

I contently drifted down Front Street with a lid of weed in my backpack, headed toward Banyan Tree Park. I spotted some people sitting under a shady tree, listening to a black dude with dreadlocks play his bongos. I joined them and listened for a while, and eventually lit a joint and passed it to the woman next to me, glancing at her breasts, barely covered by her macramé top. Her eyes widened and she smiled as she took a deep drag. The joint was passed around, with appreciative nods toward me. A smoky haze enveloped us as we grooved to the guy's bongo rhythms. I went over to introduce myself when he stopped to have a toke.

"I'm Bruce. You sound great, man."

He exhaled and nodded his thanks. "Fred."

After the brief jam, I began my usual interview. Fred said he was from back east, outside of Philadelphia. I told him I grew up in North Tarrytown, New York and graduated from Franklin and Marshall in Lancaster. As our conversation progressed, we shared our interest in music. He introduced me to his partner Joe, who wore thick wire-rimmed glasses and was covered in freckles with reddish, shoulder-length hair. Joe had graduated from Temple University in Philadelphia a couple of years earlier with a degree in biology, and Fred had dropped out with a year to go. He said he wanted to go back, but for now was more interested in playing music.

As the afternoon progressed and another joint was passed around, the group eventually dispersed, leaving the three of us.

"How about if I buy you guys lunch," I offered.

We walked over to a health food restaurant, where I ordered a passion fruit smoothie and a tuna sandwich with avocado and alfalfa sprouts, the quintessential hippie meal. I told them I'd come to Hawaii a couple of years earlier as a VISTA volunteer and, after dealing with the draft for nine months in New York, returned to Hawaii in September. I admitted I had little musical training but was drawn to playing music.

Fred listened intently and asked questions. He seemed impressed that I'd worked with young paint sniffers. Joe, on the other hand, remained quiet. His thick glasses made it difficult to read him.

Fred told me he had played in a couple of bands in high school and college and was a bass player. He mentioned that Joe played keyboard.

"Well, I played trumpet and sousaphone, but I think I want to switch to drums and write my own music. There's a group I've been jamming with back in Honolulu and I sort of sing with them." I told them about some of the jam sessions we held in Makiki and played them the Captain Energy tape.

"Far freaking out! Well, Captain Energy, we should start a band here in Maui. All I need is a bass guitar. I feel like this is the right place and time, man."

"Well, is there a music store around here? I'll get you a bass guitar."

Fred looked at me and chuckled, "Energy, you're a trip."

I paid for our lunch, picked up my pack and we headed over to the music store at an adjacent strip mall.

"Which one do you want?" I asked Fred as we stood in front of a wall of electric basses. Fred grinned and shook his head, wondering if I was for real. A local sales girl approached and asked if we needed help.

"Fred, up to you?"

He smiled as if to call my bluff and pointed to a jet-black electric bass that hung on the wall.

The saleswoman handed it to him, and he strummed a few chords, grinned at Joe, and said, "This is the one."

"Do you take personal checks?"

She paused briefly, gave me a quick once over, and asked if I had identification. I showed her my Hawaii drivers' license, lied that I was employed at the Hawaii Concentrated Employment Program and that I was in Maui for a brief vacation. I gave her the CEP phone number, my home number, and told her confidently that the check was good. She said, "Let me call your bank and check your balance."

"Cool," I replied.

Fred and Joe stood with their arms crossed, watching this exchange.

"I'll have to add the phone charge to your bill."

"No problem," I smiled.

She verified things with the bank and we walked out of the store with Fred's bass. Our relationship had moved to a deeper level of trust and appreciation. I felt I had earned some credibility and maybe now we could play music together.

Joe invited me to camp with them in an old abandoned house on the edge of town.

I was impatient to make things happen. We had to grab the moment. If I was meant to play music, maybe it was supposed to happen here in Maui, instead of Honolulu, and with these two instead of the group in Makiki. I was convinced that there were forces moving me in this direction and I was willing to trust the flow.

Over the next couple of days, we were inseparable. We wrote songs, smoked grass, and slept on the floor at the abandoned house. Fred wanted to keep the place a secret, wanted us to be careful about where we smoked dope, and was cagey about how much to say and who to include in our interactions. I, on the other hand, was totally uninhibited and open to anything or anyone. Joe served as a neutral arbiter, and whenever Fred and I couldn't agree on something, we deferred to him.

After a while, after having paid for the bass guitar, the dope, and several meals, I started to expect some reciprocity. These guys could at least pay for their own meals. Fred was secretive about his money. I knew he had some, but he never divulged how much and he spent as little as he could get away with.

I started having trouble cashing a check. We were walking down Front Street at about 3:00 in the afternoon and I had spent all of my cash. Fred started to goad me.

"Come on, Energy, I bought dinner last night, it's your turn."

"Listen, man, I've tried cashing this check at three different places with no luck. Here's the check and my driver's license. You try to cash it, then meet me at the Banyan Tree Restaurant with the money. I'm starved." The fact that Fred was black and the face on my driver's license was white hadn't occurred to me.

"All right, no problem, be right back," Fred replied as he took off down the street with Joe.

I went to the restaurant, sat down and ordered a salad, some stir-fried vegetables with tofu, and a glass of Chablis. I hadn't eaten all day and was famished. My waitress was a young haole woman with long brown hair and an easy smile. She took my order and responded to my flirtatious questions with brief, evasive answers. My bloodshot eyes and rapid speech probably hinted at how wasted I was. Fred, Joe and I had smoked some powerful hash just before our frantic attempt to get some cash.

I was in a good mood, as I usually was when I was stoned. I was ready to savor the moment, flirt with the waitress, enjoy my meal, and bask in my hash-induced daydreams. All that was missing was some music. There was a jukebox over in the corner, but I had no money.

"Kathy, would you lend me a quarter for the juke box?" I asked as she served me my salad and wine.

She looked at me with narrowing eyes.

"I'll pay you back when I pay my bill. I just don't have any change on me at the moment."

She shook her head and finally handed me a quarter. I thanked her, sauntered over to the jukebox, and pressed the buttons to select the Moody Blues, Jefferson Airplane, and the Mamas and Papas. I then headed to the men's room. When I glanced back, I saw Kathy and the restaurant manager over at the cash register, conferring and glancing in my direction. I returned to my seat as the manager approached the table with the tab.

"Sir, will you please pay for your bill?"

"What do you mean pay for my bill, I barely started eating."

"I prefer that you pay now."

"I'll pay when I finish my meal, thank you," I responded calmly.

She glared at me and seethed, "I'd like you to pay now or we can't serve you."

"I plan to eat my meal and pay when I'm finished, like all of your other customers, thank you." I replied slowly and emphatically, hoping to terminate the exchange as we were getting looks from the other diners. I kept glancing over at the entrance with mounting anxiety, willing Fred and Joe to appear with my money.

With an exasperated sigh, she walked back to the register.

I ate my salad with as much dignity as I could muster and calmly ignored the nervous stares of the other customers.

After several minutes I asked Kathy how my dinner was coming and she mumbled it would be ready soon.

Suddenly a grim-looking Hawaiian cop appeared at the cash register, talking with the restaurant manager. They both looked at me, and the officer walked over to my table.

"Sir, would you please step outside."

"I haven't finished my meal," I protested.

"I need to speak with you," he insisted.

"Sure." As I got up, my stomach churned and I prayed my money would arrive soon so I could put this incident to rest.

"I understand you refused to pay for your food."

"I am more than happy to pay for my food, but I'd like to be treated like any other customer and pay for it after I've eaten."

"Can you pay?"

"Of course I can pay."

"Then pay," he demanded.

"Not until I finish my meal."

He grabbed my arm and pulled me over to his patrol car and cuffed me. After a heated exchange, he arrested me for disturbing the peace. Having no ID on me, I insisted my name was Howdy Doody.

I was brought to the police station and booked for disturbing the peace. What the heck was going on? I had never been arrested in my life and now, in just the last two months, I found myself in jail twice. At the station I repeated that my name was Howdy Doody. I was still pretty stoned and since I didn't have identification, they had no way to determine who I actually was. They cuffed me and took me to the county jail, where I spent two nights in a stark concrete cell.

When they finally let me out, I hitched back to Lahaina and went looking for Fred and Joe, I checked the abandoned house where we had been staying. Everything was gone. My pack, my clothes, my sleeping bag, and all of their possessions. I felt sick to my stomach. After my recent ordeal, I wasn't ready for this shit. I ran down to Front Street and scoured the town for Fred, asking anyone who looked familiar if they'd seen him. There weren't many black guys with dreads wandering around Lahaina.

They were gone. The bastards not only bolted with my possessions, but stole my license and my fucking check book.

I sat on the wharf, exhausted and emotionally drained. Blond, spacey Jerry sat down next to me. When I met him for the first time a few days earlier, I nicknamed him Joey after a childhood friend he reminded me of. His laughter would get caught in the back of his throat and his eyes would water every time I spoke in my WC Fields voice. He'd squeal with glee whenever I'd greet a passing babe with, "Hello, my little chickadee."

"Hey, Captain Energy, how's it going?" he asked as he plopped down and handed me a nice fat joint.

I glanced around for any unsavory characters or cops, took a deep drag, and exhaled, "My fucking compadres, Fred and Joe, took off with my pack and my check book." I pondered my plight for a minute, held the joint in the air, looked at it, and took another long drag. "Fuck it, who gives a shit. Don't sweat the small stuff, right?"

Jerry's face turned from sympathy to glee. He started giggling like he was my 6-year-old playmate. I was back in control and I had an appreciative audience, an attentive little doggy, his tail wagging, waiting for a pat on the head and another opportunity to laugh.

"Energy, you are a trip."

I took another drag, "Yes, Joey, life's a bitch. You're born, you get stoned, you get laid, you get ripped off, and then you die."

"What are you going to do now?" he asked.

"I'd like to get laid," I responded.

Jerry started to giggle again.

One of Maui's golden-tanned sultry maidens sauntered by, her perky breasts bouncing softly to her hip-swaying seductive walk.

I pulled out my best WC Fields. "Ah, my little passion fruit, would you care to imbibe in some of Maui's finest loco weed with two lonely space cadets?"

She smiled and kept walking.

"Well, Joey, it doesn't look like my prospects for getting laid are improving. I already got ripped off, so guess I'll just die."

"Why don't we go up to Gino's Café and see if anyone's seen Fred?" Jerry suggested.

"Paramount idea, my good man. If you play your cards right, I might even let you buy me lunch," I said out of the side of my mouth in my W. C. Fields voice.

"Okay." Jerry smiled.

I didn't feel quite so bad. The magic of the pakalolo and a fan club lifted my spirits.

I continued to entertain Jerry as we walked up Front Street, providing a running commentary about everyone we passed.

We walked by Kimo's Pool Hall and I spotted a beefy young Samoan slouched in the doorway.

"How's your pool cue?" I quipped.

"What you said?" he asked.

"I say, how's your pool cue, my good man?" I repeated in my W.C. Fields voice.

As I turned to grin at Jerry, the Samoan clubbed me on the side of my head with his meaty fist. My knees buckled and I went down, grabbing hold of his pants to keep from falling over. As he pounded my back and shoulders, I instinctively grabbed his leg and lifted it, trying to trip him. He danced on his opposite foot and proceeded to pummel me in the face with his right fist. After several punches, I finally dropped his leg and staggered away.

Jerry watched it all go down with bloodshot, horrified eyes. He put his arm around my waist and helped me down to the beach, where I washed my bloody face and trembled, more in shock than pain.

"I guess he didn't care for my W. C. Fields impression," I finally joked.

Jerry's face brightened with a relieved grin.

We continued on to Gino's, a local bar that was owned by a big, friendly black dude who played the drums. Inside was a small stage where he had his drum set and an electric piano. On those afternoons when the bar wasn't busy or sometimes when it was closed, he used to let Fred, Joe, and me practice.

"What happened to you, Energy?" he inquired when he saw me shuffle in with a red welt on the side of my face.

"One of the locals didn't appreciate my W.C. Fields impression and cold cocked me."

"Gotta be careful around here, man, the locals aren't crazy about all the hippies showing up in town."

"Gino, have you seen Fred or Joe?"

"Yeah, a couple days ago. They said you got arrested for not paying a bill or something."

"Well they were supposed to cash a check for me and meet me at the Banyan Tree Restaurant with the money, but they never showed up. When I couldn't pay, the manager called the cops."

"Bummer, man."

"Yeah, I gotta find Fred or Joe. They have my license and they took off with my sleeping bag and pack."

"They were talking about going to the Big Island."

"Can't believe those fuckers would rip me off and just bolt like that."

"Well I guess they didn't know how long you'd be in jail."

I walked out of Gino's, shaking my head, stomach churning with despair and self-loathing.

"I can't believe how bad I misjudged those guys. We were friends, man. We were going to put together a band. I'm so freakin' stupid."

"What are you going to do?" asked Jerry.

"I need to call my roommate back in Honolulu and have him send me my unemployment check so I'll have some money."

"You can stay with me while you're waiting for your check."

"Joey, you are a savior and a prince," I replied as I slipped back into W. C. Fields.

Maui was like some sort of forbidden fruit. Every time I showed up there, I got my ass handed to me. By the time my check arrived, I decided to go to the Big Island to visit my VISTA friend Larry and try to find Fred and Joe.

14

THE ISLAND OF HAWAII IS THE YOUNGEST AND LARGEST OF THE eight Hawaiian Islands and referred to as the Big Island.

Larry Harrington picked me up at the airport in Kona.

"Shows, how's life? Glad you're here," he greeted me, using the nickname I'd been given in college.

"Glad I'm here too, LH, but life has been challenging of late," I said, referring to him by his initials, a nickname he had acquired as a VISTA volunteer.

Back at his cottage, I recounted the stories of the Maui arrests, losing my job in Honolulu and finally being ripped off by my erstwhile musical partners.

"That sucks, Shows. What are you going to do now?"

"Well, besides hanging out with you, I'm going to try to find them," I replied grimly.

"Here, why don't you light this while we come up with a strategy. I have an incredible ability to solve problems," LH characteristically boasted as he handed me a joint. He put the Beatle's *Sgt. Pepper* album on his turntable.

"That's comforting. I guess that's why I came to you, LH the problem solver. How are you doing?"

"Teaching is a trip, man. Hookena is a small school where they group kids of different ages in the same classroom. I'm teaching math and science to kids in the fifth to eighth grade. The administration loves me and pretty much leaves me alone."

"You'll probably be running the place soon."

"Wouldn't doubt it. You look like you're still in pretty good shape."

"Yeah, when I smoke pot it makes me hyper, so I've been running, doing yoga, and I can usually find a high school where they'll let me wrestle with the team. When I was in Maui, I worked out with some kids in Hana and I wrestled with the high school team in Lahaina."

"Tomorrow you should come to my school and you can show my PE class some wrestling moves."

"I'm there, man."

"Later on, let's go over and see my friend Larry who's the editor of the *Hawaiian Harpoon*. He might know how we can find those assholes, maybe even post a notice in the paper."

"Right on, man. You are a problem solver."

After a visit to the *Hawaiian Harpoon* office, Larry Ketchum and his wife Linda, an elementary school teacher, invited us over for dinner. They were sympathetic to my search for Fred and Joe, especially after hearing how they ripped me off and disappeared with all my possessions. We also discussed some of the social issues his paper was addressing, and I shared with him my VISTA experience.

"More and more kids are dropping out of school here, and I've heard of a growing problem with paint sniffing just like Honolulu," Larry said.

"Well, it's like some of the other issues you address in the paper. The educational system alienates the local kids, unemployment is high, so there aren't that many employed role models. The kids end up influenced by their peer group."

The Ketchums were hosting Linda's sister Karen and her friend

Sally, both on vacation from Kansas. Though Linda and Larry had been full participants in the excesses of the '60s and smoked a fair amount of grass, Karen and Sally were newcomers to the hippie lifestyle. Eager to learn, they were getting pretty stoned.

As we gorged on Linda's manicotti, salad, generous quantities of Chianti, and spumoni ice cream, Larry and I continued our conversation about local politics. LH mentioned that the *Hawaiian Harpoon* had helped him with his VISTA efforts to change the land leasing laws for local Hawaiian farmers.

During dinner, Linda began playing footsie with me under the dining room table.

"LH claims you're a rock and roll star," Linda said as her foot landed in my crotch.

"I don't know about that, but I'm try...YOW...uh...trying to start a group." I squirmed as Linda's foot caressed its target.

"Play them the Captain Energy tape," LH suggested.

I pressed play on the cassette player.

"That's not bad." Sally nodded approvingly.

"He's also a yoga guru," offered LH.

"LH has a tendency to exaggerate, but I *have* been practicing yoga for several months."

"Show us!" requested Karen.

"Well, there's different types of yoga. You can do postures, breathing, chanting, and ultimately meditation."

"Show them that pose where you stand on your head," LH encouraged.

"Ok, but I need to go to the bathroom." I stood up and quickly turned away from the table to hide the effects of Linda's fancy footwork.

After peeing and waiting long enough for things to settle down, I zipped up and returned to the kitchen.

I showed them the scorpion pose, which involved getting into a headstand balanced on my forearms, face towards the ceiling, arching my back, and letting my feet hang above my head.

"Whoa, that's pretty amazing," Karen murmured, her eyes wide and bloodshot.

"Is there any more pot?" she asked after she regained her composure.

After I delivered a detailed discourse on the techniques and benefits I experienced during my yoga training, LH announced, "Thanks guys, but I gotta go home. I teach tomorrow."

"Bruce, you're welcome to stay here tonight. You can show us some more of that yoga and I'll drop you off at LH's tomorrow," Linda suggested.

We chatted for a while after LH left. Karen and Sally eventually staggered upstairs and passed out from the wine and dope.

"Hey, come on in here." Linda invited me into the master bedroom as she put George Harrison's *All Things Must Pass* album on and gestured for me to join Larry and her on their queen-sized waterbed.

"Show us some of the breathing and chanting you were talking about."

I led them first in rhythmic breathing exercises. Once our breathing was synchronized, I added chanting and then some guided imagery. We sat cross-legged with eyes closed, holding hands, our knees touching.

After several minutes of guided imagery, we remained seated, inhaling deeply, experiencing the ensuing calm. Larry eventually dropped my hand and slumped over on his side, asleep. Linda and I shifted so that we were facing each other. Our breathing deepened as we caressed each other's hands and fingers, and she eventually wrapped her legs around my waist, writhing on my lap.

Larry's breathing got more rhythmic and he began to snore. The louder he snored, the bolder we became. We eventually slid onto our sides and continued to grope and grind. Just as she was slipping off her panties, Larry suddenly awoke.

"No! No! Get the hell out!"

I jumped off the bed as Linda attempted to sooth him. "It's all right, Larry, nothing happened."

I backed out of there and darted upstairs, where Karen and Sally invited me to join them in their bed.

The next morning, Linda drove me to back LH's cottage.

"Hey, how's Larry? I think we may have upset him last night."

"He'll live, we've been having problems… give me a call anytime," she replied as I got out of the car.

LH had left me a note instructing me to phone him at school. He planned to pick me up so I could show his gym class some wrestling moves.

"When's the class?"

"At eleven, right before lunch."

"Where did you say your school is?"

"Go out the door, turn right and it's about five miles down the road."

"You don't have to pick me up, I'll just run over."

By the time I arrived at the school, I was covered with sweat. At 11 a.m. the temperature was already in the 90's and oppressively humid.

"Shows, nice run. Let's go to the gym."

"This is Mr. Leonard, he was a college wrestler, and he's agreed to teach you guys some wrestling moves."

"Gross. How come he's all wet?" asked one of the students, cringing.

"He ran from my cottage…he's in good shape."

I proceeded to teach some wrestling.

***

That evening Larry drove me to visit Bill and Carol Sutkus. Bill had been one of our VISTA leaders and was now working for one of the VISTA-sponsoring agencies, Queen Liliuokalani Children's Trust (LT), as a community organizer in the Big Island.

Bill had not only been a VISTA leader but also a personal mentor and supporter of both my Molokai and Palolo Projects. He grew up on a farm in Minnesota and received his BA from a Catholic Seminary, with the intent of studying for the priesthood. During an extended break from seminary, Bill abandoned his plans of becoming a priest and enrolled as a VISTA volunteer in 1965, the year of its inception.

After his first year working with migrants in Michigan, he was recruited as a VISTA leader and eventually hired by LT to serve as a program officer in Honolulu. During my VISTA year, he and Carol got married. After work, he'd kick my ass in a series of handball games at the local YMCA, then we'd return to their home for dinner. As a newlywed, Carol was trying to broaden her cooking repertoire, mastering a few of the appetizing new recipes she found in the cookbooks she had received as wedding gifts. I was an enthusiastic guinea pig, and enjoyed many wonderful evenings of fine food, much wine, and stimulating conversation.

Bill was four years older than me and an experienced community organizer. As I tried to sort out my political feelings about poverty and our roles as VISTAs, Bill was always able to put into perspective what was actually going on. In addition to his intellect, I admired his diplomacy and ability to work with people. He was highly respected and could maneuver within the VISTA bureaucracy and at the same time maintain working relationships with local Hawaiians in the community. He had also sent my draft board a compelling letter supporting my application as a conscientious objector the previous year. I treasured my relationship with him.

"Showman, welcome to Puna, how you doing?"

"I've had some adventures."

"Let me get you a beer and you can tell us all about it."

I once again related the saga of my peyote trip, the arrest, losing my job, my court case in Maui, my second arrest, and ultimately the relationship with and rip off by Fred and Joe.

Carol sat back in her chair. "Wow, Shows, that's some story."

"So let me get this straight, during this peyote trip you were convinced that you were going to perform at a rock festival in Haleakala, which was going to usher in the Age of Aquarius. Sort of the dawning of a revolution...?" I could see Bill was struggling to wrap his mind around this.

"Yeah," I admitted. "I was hoping this peyote-fueled vision quest would help me figure out how to focus all my pent-up energy. Depending on who I'm with, I feel like I have something to contribute. Sometimes I'm thrust into sort of a leadership role. Like these musicians I've been hanging around with. They made me Captain Energy."

"What's with this Captain Energy deal?"

"Well, let me play my tape and you tell me if it's got potential."

While we listened to the tape, I gave him an overview of the players and why I was interested in exploring a future in music.

"Well with your enthusiasm and discipline, I have no doubt that if this is what you want to do, you'll probably be successful. You know, your prediction of a revolution isn't all that far-fetched. Carol and I just finished reading this book, *Greening of America*, by this Yale professor you might find interesting. Let's get some sleep and I'll show it to you tomorrow. I'm working out of the house, so I'll be around."

The next morning, after an early morning swim, we sat around and continued our conversation over breakfast.

"Shows, here's the book."

I sat comfortably in an easy chair, facing their picture window. The rental property was perched on a rocky shoreline overlooking the Pacific.

From the first paragraph of the first page of *Greening of America*, I was transfixed. After about an hour of reading, I jumped up and declared, "This is fucking amazing! He not only articulates everything I've been predicting, but his theory of the levels of consciousness explains why there's so much tension between the generations!"

The Greening of America was written by Charles Reich, a law professor at Yale, and made the *New York Times* bestseller list in December of 1970. He claimed that we were in the midst of a social and cultural revolution, unlike any other we had previously experienced. The revolution would only change the political structure as its last act and would not require violence. Its ultimate creation would be higher reason and a more humane community. He felt that the logic of the new generation's rebellion must be understood in light of the rise of the corporate state, and the way in which the state dominates, exploits, and destroys both nature and humanity. Reich challenged the one-sided viewpoint that had dominated American policy. According to him, our society was founded on the belief that life was essentially an economic problem, and the best solution to this problem was extensive organization for production. But how could increasing production aid us in finding answers to the crucial problems of race relations, environmental damage, and the war in Vietnam?

The book's argument rested on three separate types of consciousness. "Consciousness I" was the world-view of rural farmers and small businesspeople that arose and was dominant in 19th-century America. "Consciousness II" represented the viewpoint of "an organizational society," featuring meritocracy and improvement through various large institutions. It informed the New Deal, World War II, and the 1950s. "Consciousness III" represented the worldview of the 1960s counterculture, focusing on personal freedom, egalitarianism, recreational drugs, and rock music.

Though I love to read, I'm pretty slow at it, and I don't have a long attention span. But I spent the entire day engrossed in the book, pausing only to refill my coffee cup, hit the bathroom, and rave about what I was reading with Bill and Carol. I kept reading until I had finished all 399 pages.

I was beside myself, and somehow concluded that this book confirmed all the thoughts and ideas that had been percolating around in my head. I spent another day on the Big Island with Bill and Carol and then decided to abandon my hunt for Fred and Joe and return to Honolulu.

PART 4

FLASHBACK

DECEMBER 1969 – AUGUST 1970

SELECTIVE SERVICE SYSTEM

NOTICE OF CLASSIFICATION

This is to certify that

BRUCE E. LEONARD

(First name) (Middle initial) (Last name)

Selective Service No.

30	10	46	2016

is classified in Class 4-F

until ____________

by Local Board unless otherwise checked below:

☐ by Appeal Board

vote of ________ to ________

☐ by President

FEB 9 1972

(Date of mailing)

W. Zemnick

(Member, ~~Executive Secretary, or clerk~~ of local board)

(Registrant's signature)

(Fold along this line)

15

MY LOTTERY NUMBER OF 129 GUARANTEED THAT I'D BE DRAFTED. I returned to New York in December of 1969 with the plan to submit a Statement of Religious Training and Belief as a conscientious objector (CO). If accepted, it would require committing two years of acceptable alternative service, but I would ultimately be exempt from serving in Vietnam. Convincing my father that this was a reasonable and viable path to avoiding the draft was very important to me.

My eighteen months in Hawaii and serving as a VISTA volunteer had been the most exhilarating and intellectually stimulating time of my life. It felt like my values and belief system had been turned inside out. In contrast to my previous political assumptions that led me to vote for Nixon and support the Vietnam war a year earlier, I was now strongly opposed to the war and becoming more comfortable with a variety of liberal positions that were being championed by many in my generation. The success I experienced with my VISTA projects fueled my confidence in my ability to solve problems, speak in pubic, and write. It also gave me a potential career path toward public service. The most gratifying facet of the experience was the release of energy that came with encountering an activity that I was committed to. In the past, I pursued Boy Scouts and competitive wrestling with a passion and energy tempered by discipline and determination.

My objective in joining VISTA was to find a direction and a potential career. It turned out to be an arduous journey. The focus it took to create, implement, and evaluate my Molokai and Palolo VISTA projects required a complete overhaul of my pre-existing values. In order to develop strategies for working with troubled juveniles, I had to reassess my previous assumptions about our economic and educational systems. This in turn allowed me to reexamine my feelings about my own intelligence after having graduated college with dismal grades and an insecurity about my academic abilities. With my new-found career dreams, I enrolled in several graduate classes in psychology. My confidence and self-esteem were lifted by the support I'd received from a new set of friends, especially Leo and the relationships I'd had with girlfriends Mary and Judy. I also felt I could resolve my draft situation by applying as a conscientious objector.

Some of the confidence and enthusiasm dissipated with a series of setbacks that seemed to come all at once. A grant that would have allowed me to continue with the Palolo Youth Project wasn't funded. The extension of the lease on my VISTA apartment, which served as a halfway house for the kids I was working with, was not granted. The faculty I encountered in the psychology department were unsupportive and indifferent and I ended up dropping two courses. Judy, Mary, and my father attended a meeting where several Palolo residents confronted me about my project, blaming me for enabling the kids I worked with to continue abusing drugs and for making their community look bad in the media.

My low draft lottery number provided me a convenient escape from this escalating series of disappointments and led me to return to New York to explore a new start. I hoped that with my newfound energy and confidence, I could redirect my commitment to a similar social problem in New York, re-engage with old friends, spend some time with my father, and get my draft situation resolved.

***

I walked into the kitchen with my bags and shook my father's hand.

"Hi, Dad."

"Welcome home, good to see you."

"Nice to be home, though I'm already starting to miss the warmth and sunshine of Hawaii."

"Yeah, we've already had a couple of snowstorms. That tan probably isn't going to last. How long are you home for?"

"Well, probably indefinitely, until I can resolve my draft situation."

"What do you mean?"

"Well, my lottery number is 129, which means I'll probably get a notice to report for my physical in a couple of months."

"What have you decided to do?"

"I want to file as a Conscientious Objector."

"You do?" Dad looked a little shocked and disappointed. "Well, let's talk about this later. In the meantime, why don't you go upstairs and say hello to your brother. He's back from Miami Dade and is threatening to drop out."

"You don't look too happy."

"Well, I'm pleased to see you both. But I was hoping you two would be squared away by now. I'm in the process of getting this house sold and moving to the city. But we can talk about all of this later."

My brother Craig is four years younger than me. As we were growing up, in our respective attempts to get our parent's attention, I became the straight-arrow and Craig defaulted to cute and naughty. I worked hard in school and got reasonably good grades. Craig was an underachiever. Goal oriented, I became an Eagle Scout and worked hard to excel in sports. Craig was indifferent to scouting and a lackluster participant in sports. We had the same fourth and sixth grade teachers, Mrs. Thomas and Mr. Fiala, and unfortunately they let it be known that Craig wasn't as conscientious as his older brother, which Craig understandably resented.

My mother was diagnosed with breast cancer when I was a sophomore in high school. In light of her illness and with the hope that Craig might improve his academic performance and avoid being compared with me, my parents decided to send him away to private school. Craig felt abandoned and soon started acting out, smoking and cutting classes. He managed to get himself kicked out of several of the schools.

Both my parents were heavy Camel smokers. I hated smoking from my earliest memory. We drove for five days to Denver, Colorado from New York when I was six and Craig was two, and my parents smoked the entire distance in the car. I got carsick many times. I was not only repulsed by the smell, I developed a revulsion not just to holding a cigarette but also to touching the package. My distaste for anything smoking-related was solidified by my mother's cancer, and by the fact that she kept smoking until her death at the age of 43.

Craig took up smoking in elementary school. Our parents caught him and punished him many times before they eventually sent him off to private school. In those days, private schools had zero tolerance for smoking and he ended up being expelled from several of them.

His participation in sports was pretty casual until he discovered skiing. Our parents sent him to a couple of New England prep schools that offered competitive skiing, hoping that would give him some direction, improve his grades, and involve him with a healthier group of friends. Though he did ski competitively for one of the schools, his smoking and fraternizing with the other disaffected students continued until after our mother's death. Our father finally had to pull him out of private schools and enroll him at Sleepy Hollow High School.

At Sleepy Hollow, his tendency to associate with the school's troublemakers continued, and they were among the first group of kids in our community to be arrested for smoking marijuana. He was suspended from school and my father hired a tutor so he could eventually earn his GED. During a winter vacation in Jamaica, Craig was introduced to and fell in love with scuba diving. He subsequently enrolled at Miami Dade Junior College in Florida, where he expressed an interest in pursuing oceanography.

"Hey, Craig."

"Brucie, welcome home."

"Thanks, how's school?"

"It sucks. I wanted to take oceanography, and Dad enrolled me in all these other boring courses."

"Well, to get a degree, you have to take those prerequisites. But I know how you feel. I was in some prerequisite graduate psychology classes last semester, and they were terrible."

"Yeah, I don't know if I want to go back."

"I hope you do. You're really going to hurt Dad if you drop out. Come on, man, here's your chance to do something you love."

"Yeah, well, I'll think about it. What are you going to do?"

"I have to stick around and figure out how to get out of the draft. I got a low lottery number so I'll probably get called for my draft physical in a couple of months. I'm planning to apply as a Conscientious Objector."

"How do you do that?"

"I need to write a statement that answers a bunch of questions about how my religious beliefs support my conviction of non-violence. It needs to be submitted to the draft board with some support letters."

"How does Dad feel about this?"

"He seems pretty skeptical. I know he doesn't want me to go to Vietnam, but he still supports the war. He's preoccupied with getting on with his life, and would like us to be squared away. I'm gonna be around for a couple of months dealing with this. I know he'd be a lot happier if you were committed to getting your college degree."

"Yeah, I know," Craig responded with resignation.

"Well, I'm leaving next week to go to Dyke's wedding in Memphis."

"Oh yeah, Dyke. Wasn't he the college roommate who did VISTA in Hawaii like you?"

"Yeah, he asked me to be his best man."

***

Dyke had left Hawaii after his two years as a VISTA volunteer. He decided to enroll in the Berkeley School of Theology to study to be a minister, but more importantly to get another draft deferment. On December 1, 1969, Dyke's spiritual calling suddenly evaporated when his lottery number of 331 was announced, thus eliminating his draft problem. A randomly selected number assigned to your birth date would determine in what order your draft notice would be issued. Every day of the year was designated a number from 1 to 366. If your number was under 200, it meant that you would probably be drafted. Dyke immediately withdrew from the seminary and returned home to New Jersey to prepare for his wedding, which would be held in Vickie's family home in Memphis. Vickie, who Dyke had met working at a resort in Maine the summer between his junior and senior year in college, moved to Hawaii and lived with him during his second year in VISTA.

I was flattered to be asked to serve as his best man and looked forward to fulfilling my obligations, despite the fact that this would be the first wedding I'd ever attended. I also looked forward to visiting my college friend, Rick Mesard, who lived outside of Washington, D.C.

***

I called a high school friend, and a Dartmouth graduate, Roc Caivano, for advice about applying for Conscientious Objector status. My father had served as his mentor and encouraged him to pursue a career as an architect and apply to Yale's school of architecture.

"Hey Roc, how's it going?"

"Hey Bruce, are you back from Hawaii?"

"Yeah, I got a low lottery number and now I'm dealing with the draft. I hear you applied to get a CO."

"Yeah, but fortunately I was rejected before I ever sent in the CO statement."

"What do you mean?"

"I refused induction. When I was asked to step forward, I stepped back. They took me to a room to talk to some shrinks. I told the military guy that I'd rather go to prison than kill someone. He explained that I could get sent somewhere other than Vietnam. I told him it wasn't the Vietnamese I was concerned about. I didn't want to kill the person who would teach me to use a gun. They declared me something like "mentally incompatible with military life" and kicked me out of the building. I feel bad about not standing beside guys who are being sent over and risking their lives. They're good men. But this is an immoral war and I hate the politicians and bureaucrats that are responsible for these needless deaths."

"Wow, what a trip. That took some balls. So how sympathetic do you think this draft board is with CO applications?"

"Since I didn't appear before them, I can only tell you what I've heard. Our draft board is pretty screwed up. They tried to draft a blind guy last year. Westchester County is one of the most affluent counties in the country. There are lots of college-educated, upper middle class guys all trying to avoid getting drafted. Consequently, the board is having a difficult time filling their quotas. To get a CO you almost have to have been raised a Quaker or Mennonite. They aren't interested in "born again" conscientious objectors. If your application is denied and you refuse induction, you could end up in jail. However, while serving time you can appeal their ruling. I was not going to Vietnam, and was willing to go to jail."

"That's pretty sobering news. Thanks for the information. So what are you up to?"

"Well after I graduated, a classmate and I started Elephant Trak Construction."

"Elephant Trak?"

"Yeah, we wanted to make a statement about our competence. An elephant track is the mark a hammer makes on a piece of lumber when you miss the nail. In other words, this is sort of a seat of the pants company. What we lack in skill we try to make up with enthusiasm. My partner and I are reluctant at this point to enter the corporate world of architecture. We've got a few small contracts, but we might have a pretty good project this summer. Let me know if you want to move over to New Haven and I'll put you to work."

"Thanks, Roc. Once I'm able to get things squared away with the draft, I might take you up on that."

***

After reflecting on my conversation with Roc, I sat down to talk with my father.

"Bruce, thanks for speaking with Craig. I think you motivated him to return to school."

"I'm surprised. He doesn't take advice very often."

"Unfortunately, you're right. So now that it's just the two of us, what are your plans?"

"Well, I'm not completely sure. I obviously need to take care of the draft before I can really do anything. I'm planning to apply as a conscientious objector. That will involve writing a statement, submitting it to the draft board, and waiting for them to determine its merit."

"Bruce, I supported your decision to spend a year as a VISTA volunteer and I think under the circumstances, that was a good choice. It seems like you had a meaningful experience. I understand your reluctance to join the Army and possibly be sent to Vietnam, but I'm not so sure about you being a conscientious objector."

"Dad, I've thought about this a lot, and I don't believe in killing people in order to resolve conflict."

"I don't either. I served in the Second World War and fortunately wasn't put in that position, but I believe in defending my country.

Sometimes we have to do things we don't want to," he replied impatiently, raising his voice.

My stomach tightened and my head was reeling. I sat there trying to collect my thoughts without losing my temper. I so wanted my father's approval and thought he would understand. I desperately wanted him to respect my point of view.

"Dad, I'm not going to participate in this war. It's immoral and unjust. My year in VISTA not only opened my eyes to our twisted addiction to war, but I learned a lot about myself and my values," I said trying to control my emotions.

"I think that I'm a true Christian. I believe in the Golden Rule, in turning the other cheek, and trying to make the world a better place. Christians should follow the commandment *Thou Shalt Not Kill* in every circumstance, not just when it's convenient." My voice was trembling. "I hoped you would be proud that I want to follow my convictions and not be a hypocrite." I bolted from the kitchen in tears and retreated to my room, slamming the door.

My concept of Christianity evolved during my time in Hawaii. Not only had I read extensively, but I engaged in discussions with numerous clergy and fellow VISTAs. I met several Christian ministers who served as community activists. Larry Jones was one of them. He headed a ministry that addressed the social problems facing the young street people in Waikiki. He also hosted a social activist radio talk show and was on the faculty at the University of Hawaii. Robert Lovelace not only ministered to his church but served as director of the Palolo Community Council. Ed Brantz was an ordained minister who managed a poverty outreach employment program. Reverend Ron Ching assisted me in Palolo, counseling some of the addicted kids I was working with. He used the "Transactional Analysis" technique popularized by Eric Berne's 1964 book, *Games People Play.* These ministers were actively applying Christ's teachings to the community. Their lives were about helping the poor and resolving conflict with love and understanding. Fighting in wars seemed un-Christian to me. *Thou Shalt Not Kill* was a commandment that came with no conditions or exceptions.

The next day, my father and I tip-toed around each other, barely speaking. He eventually asked me to join him for a drink at the dining room table.

"Bruce, I'm sorry about our heated discussion. I want you to know I'm proud of you and love you. These are tough times. I know Vietnam is not the same as the Second World War, and I'm trying to come to terms with that. All I want is what is best for you. The World War II conscientious objectors were considered to be cowards and traitors. There was little sympathy for anyone who avoided serving, and it wasn't much different during the Korean War. I don't want you to make a decision that is going to jeopardize your future. I'm concerned that having that on your record might hurt your chances for future employment. Maybe these are different times. If you want to apply, go ahead."

"Thanks Dad, that means a lot. This wasn't an easy decision. I don't want to hurt you and I know you want what's best for me. I just want you to know I'm not an irresponsible coward. A lot of responsible, thoughtful guys in my position are doing the same thing. You know my college roommate, Jimmy Clair, and a fellow VISTA volunteer, Art Tani, applied for CO status."

"Well, what do you plan to do while you're preparing your application? How long should all of this take?"

"It's hard to say. It'll be several months before I'll be called for my physical and if I pass, then the board will rule on my application. In the meantime, I'll look for a job. The problem is, most employers won't hire me if my draft status is 1-A. While I'm looking for work, I can make some money substitute teaching. I'm sort of in limbo for the time being. I'm sorry to have to be living at home and depending on you at this stage in my life."

"Don't worry about it, son, I'll enjoy having company. I know these are difficult times."

***

My parents married immediately after the Second World War and my Dad's honorable discharge as a captain in the Army. He had always been my hero. He served as the peacemaker in the family, as my mother was moody and always seemed to be creating drama in their marriage and in our lives. Though they loved each other and were devoted to my brother and me, my mother often found something to fight about with each of us. I was grateful and amazed that my father never ridiculed or blamed her for what Craig and I felt was completely irrational behavior.

He was the managing partner in the highly successful architectural firm I.M. Pei and Partners. The firm earned significant prominence when they won the highly coveted competition to design the John F. Kennedy Library after his assassination. Soft-spoken, poised, and dignified, he was an impressive presence at six feet three inches tall, and he earned respect by his actions, not necessarily his words. His self-assuredness and the professional confidence he exuded permeated his personality. I aspired to be as passionate and disciplined in my endeavors as he was.

With his calm demeanor and rational judgment, I can barely remember a time growing up that I ever disagreed with a decision he made. When my mother was diagnosed with breast cancer, I was a sophomore in high school. She spent four years struggling with this disease before she died my sophomore year in college. Throughout her illness, my relationship with my father evolved into a friendship as we struggled with our loss and tried to guide my brother, who continued to misbehave and bounce from school to school. While I was at Franklin and Marshall, he would travel to Pennsylvania to watch my wrestling matches. My senior year, we would even double date. We both supported Nixon and became increasingly annoyed at the long-haired, drug-addled protestors who seemed to be disrupting the country. But my values evolved during my eighteen months in Hawaii, and it was painful for me when my dad and I began to disagree about political and social issues.

16

I WENT TO NEW YORK CITY TO SEE BONNIE HAYES, A SHAPELY BRU- nette who had been a grade ahead of me in high school. Bonnie had gone to Russell Sage College in Troy, New York, with my high school girlfriend, Christine. I began casually dating her in college after Christine broke up with me, and we maintained a correspondence during my eighteen months in VISTA. She ended up dropping out of Russell Sage and was now working for a book publisher and living in an apartment in New York City.

"Bruce, how do you like being back?"

"Well, it's nice seeing you, but overall being back sucks. I miss Hawaii. Mainly, I'm feeling trapped here. I'm living back home with my father. The draft's hanging over my head, and I don't think I'm gonna get my conscientious objector classification."

"Why not?"

"Well, I've been calling around trying to get advice and found out our draft board is extremely tough and unsympathetic to CO applications."

"You know, my dad's a shrink. Maybe he could write you a letter."

"That's not a bad idea, I'll keep that in mind. What are you up to?"

"I'm taking some art courses at the New School of Social Research."

"Well, I took some graduate-level psychology classes at the University of Hawaii last semester and the whole experience was disappointing."

"You should consider the New School, it's very progressive."

I proceeded to enroll in two graduate psychology classes at the New School, which required commuting into the city by train twice a week. I reconnected with Marty Pine, who had been a couple of classes ahead of me in college and was now in his last year of medical school. Several times over the spring, I would stay overnight with him and his wife Debbie so I wouldn't have to commute to school from home. Once again, I found the whole experience disappointing. One of the classes was held in a huge auditorium packed with students. The professor would stand in front of class and babble a stream of consciousness mumbo jumbo for an hour straight. Faced with boring textbooks and incomprehensible lectures, it looked like I was headed towards another ill-fated academic experience.

***

As time went on, it became more and more difficult to formulate my conscientious objector statement. After the conversation with my father, my resolve was badly shaken. Roc's warning about how tough my draft board was further chipped away at my confidence. Worse, I couldn't come up with the words to even start writing the statement. I would sit and stare at the four questions I needed to address and wind up writing and rewriting one sentence until I gave up and went to go watch TV. When I first saw the questions, they didn't look too difficult to deal with. But as I sat at my bedroom desk and tried to formulate my thoughts and express my convictions, I ran into severe writer's block.

Composing what I considered to be the most important statement of my life was turning into a nightmare. I spent most of my time procrastinating and dealing with the subsequent guilt. The sight of my desk cluttered with notes and papers left me with a knot in my stomach and a throbbing headache. The task of formulating this statement hung over me like a dark, heavy blanket. Rarely was I able to escape the guilt, and it was starting to turn into self-loathing.

I had left Hawaii with confidence and drive and now my sunny optimism was replaced with despair. In Hawaii, I felt equipped to pursue a future full of possibilities. Now I just felt trapped and hopeless. It didn't help that I was there during an oppressively cold and miserable winter. I daydreamed constantly about sun-drenched Hawaii.

The Statement of Religious Training and Belief listed four instructions.

1. Describe the nature of your belief that is the basis for your claim, and state why you consider it to be based on religious training and belief.
2. Explain how, when, and from whom or from what source you received the religious training and the religious belief, which is the basis for your claim.
3. To what extent does your religious training and belief restrict you from ministering to the sick and injured, either civilian or military, or from serving in the Armed Forces as a noncombatant without weapons?
4. Have you ever given expression publicly or privately, written or oral, to the views herein expressed as the basis for your claim? Give examples.

When I was in Hawaii, I was certain that my statement of opposition to bearing arms was going to be an eloquent and formidable treatise that might even serve as a model document. In the months that I sat trying to write it at my desk overlooking our neighbor's house and their large oak tree, the words wouldn't come, the conviction wavered, and all I wanted to do was sleep. This piece of paper required that I describe not just my feelings or opinions, but how over the course of my entire life, non-violence had been the foundation of my values and religious belief.

***

Enzo, who was my best hometown friend, had joined the Army Reserves, was in basic training in Alabama, and wouldn't be back until May. Being stuck in North Tarrytown without my best friend really sucked. Another friend, Gary Greenbaum, who had been a year ahead of us in high school and also graduated from F&M, was teaching at Washington Irving Junior High School.

Gary had gone through an interesting metamorphosis after graduation. As a high school nerd, he'd worn thick black-rimmed glasses, was in most of the advanced academic classes, played on the tennis team, and hung out with other brainy nerds. I had very little contact with him in high school. When Enzo and I went off to visit F&M as high school seniors, Gary met us and showed us around campus. He had morphed into a fast-talking, chain-smoking party animal. He was now a disc jockey at the campus radio station and had the rapid-fire clever banter of Cousin Brucie Morrow from WABC, NYC's rock 'n' roll radio station.

Though we hadn't pledged the same fraternities, Gary became a friend and would occasionally attend our frat parties. After Enzo and I entered F&M our freshman year, we would visit Gary at Dietz Hall, his dormitory. There we met a cohort of freshmen: Rick Mesard, Stu Magee, Dave Grayson, and John Haas. We all became friends and eventually pledged at the same fraternity, Chi Phi. They liked Gary and enjoyed his outrageous persona. He had pledged Sigma Pi, a strange group of characters. Gary brought his St. Bernard, Molson, to the fraternity, and the lovable sloppy dog was raised on beer and table scraps. Gary had been a strong supporter of my wrestling and we shared an affection for the comedians he physically resembled: Groucho Marx and Woody Allen. He was often "on" doing routines, dropping puns, and joking around.

Gary not only taught at Washington Irving, but moonlighted as a bartender at the Huddle Bar. He encouraged me to substitute teach, and I filled out an application for both the junior high and elementary school.

It was pretty weird teaching at schools that I had attended. At North Tarrytown Elementary School, I taught alongside my former 6th grade teacher John Fiala, my first male teacher, who had boosted my self-esteem by noting my intelligence and encouraging me. Several of my other junior high teachers were still there, including William McCloud, who had been my favorite English teacher.

Gary failed his draft physical due to a hernia. Consequently, we spent a good amount of time either at his apartment smoking grass and listening to music, or hanging out at the Huddle Bar, which was frequented by guys from high school who had returned to Tarrytown after college or had never left. There were also girls there from some of the local colleges, such as Marymount and Briarcliff. Aside from Gary, trying to converse with these people was a mind-numbingly lonely waste of time in comparison to my social life in Hawaii, where I was usually engaged in political discussions and reflecting on social issues.

***

One evening at the Huddle Bar, I spotted one of my close friends from high school, Charlie Smith. We had been teammates on both the football and wrestling teams and in the same high school social group.

"Charlie, how you doing?" I greeted my old friend as we sat down at a booth with our beers.

"A lot better since I got out of the service, how about you?"

"I'm home dealing with the draft."

"Let me give you a piece of advice. Don't go!!!"

"I intend to apply as a conscientious objector."

"I'll help you write it."

We spent the evening catching up. He told me he had dropped out of college and got drafted and served as a medic. Though he didn't go into detail, I gathered that it had been a pretty traumatic experience. He intended to hitchhike out west to visit some of his army buddies, but didn't have a clue about his future.

"This war has fucked up a lot of lives, man. Even if you manage to not get yourself killed or injured, most guys are not the same when they return," he said.

"Yeah, one of Craig's friends, Ron Manca, was killed last month."

"Did you hear about our football teammate Frannie Burns? Apparently, he hung out around town for a few months after he got out of Nam, started drinking heavily, and finally jumped off the Tappan Zee Bridge."

Suddenly we heard bellowing from the back of the bar. Greenbaum came over to our booth and explained that it was Steve McClean. He had been a high school classmate who returned from Nam the year before. After several beers, he would start screaming and keep it up until he'd inevitably pass out and a group of his friends would carry him home.

***

The war was still raging and the news was filled with numbers of U.S. troops killed each day and anti-war protests around the country. Eventually the results of the Chicago Seven Trial were broadcast. The defendants had been indicted for conspiracy to incite riots during the 1968 Democratic National Democratic Convention in Chicago. Abbie Hoffman, Jerry Rubin, Bobby Seale, and others had been tried the previous fall with considerable media coverage. They were found not guilty of conspiracy, but were convicted of crossing state lines with intent to incite riot. Their convictions were eventually overturned and they were set free.

Their actions reflected much of the anti-government sentiment of my generation, but I couldn't identify with that cast of characters. They were ridiculing the hypocrisy of the establishment, but they offered no solutions and they provided no leadership. The government sucked, but what was it going to be replaced with?

Also during the spring of 1970, the SDS turned violent with the emergence of the Weathermen, and three members died in a bomb that was accidently detonated in Greenwich Village.

While in Hawaii, I was encouraged and optimistic that my generation was going to change society and make things better. But my lethargy and pessimism worsened with every violent and pointless event I saw on the news. The prospect of a peaceful, enlightened society was becoming a pipe dream.

***

This was the spring after the summer of Woodstock. Greenbaum and I got tickets to attend some concerts at Bill Graham's Fillmore East in the city, a companion music venue to his infamous Fillmore West in San Francisco. Among the more memorable acts we saw was Joe Cocker. Though he'd received a lot of attention after his performance at Woodstock, I'd never seen him perform. The Fillmore East was always a spectacle with all of the outrageously costumed hippies that attended the shows. We had consumed some extremely potent hash on the way to the city and by the time we entered the auditorium, I was totally wasted.

We were grooving on the evening and enjoying Cocker's opening act. Finally, it was time for the main performance. Mad Dogs & Englishmen was Cocker's band, a group of more than twenty musicians, including pianist and bandleader Leon Russell, three drummers, and backing vocalist Rita Coolidge. The band seemed to keep growing as the musicians' kids and even dogs wandered onto the stage.

When Joe Cocker approached the microphone and started to sing, his arms started flailing and he looked like he was about to have a seizure. I kept looking around to see if anyone else was disturbed by his strange writhing, but everyone seemed to be enjoying the concert and his performance. I remained transfixed, anticipating that he'd be flopping on the floor momentarily. Since none of the Mad Dogs or Englishmen seemed alarmed by his physical antics, I finally decided that this was actually his singing style and settled back to enjoy the spectacle.

17

AS MY VISTA PROJECT HAD EVOLVED IN HAWAII, I'D DEVELOPED AN unexpected but close friendship with Leo Dubois. He'd been at loose ends because he was leaving the Coast Guard and looking for something to do. We'd met through a mutual friend at the Gingerman, a local University of Hawaii watering hole. I'd shared with him my project working with teenage dropouts and drug abusers in Palolo Valley, and he'd become quite interested. He'd started showing up at my VISTA apartment and had begun to form relationships with the kids I was working with.

Leo was an artist and into photography, and he'd begun photo-documenting the Palolo Project and mentoring several of the kids who'd showed interest in drawing and artwork. We had soon become inseparable and Leo not only helped with the project, but his support had imbued me with confidence and resolve.

The project had required a lot of resource hustling, bureaucratic maneuvering, and marketing. I was constantly networking to obtain advice and assistance. I worked hard to create opportunities for these kids, many of whom had dropped out of school and were on drugs. They needed alternative educational opportunities and employment training. I had moved out of my VISTA apartment in order to turn it into a halfway house for those kids who wanted to go straight. I'd tried to juggle all the various responsibilities of this project and found myself on an emotional rollercoaster. I 'd been disappointed by bureaucratic setbacks in dealing with community, governmental, and educational institutions. But even worse, I'd been constantly tested and undermined by the kids I was trying so hard to help. Leo had always been there, bolstering my confidence and helping me resolve the unending issues we had to deal with.

After I left Hawaii, we kept in touch. He announced that he was coming east to visit his family and would be coming to New York to visit me.

"Leo, welcome to dreary North Tarrytown, New York! I'm thrilled you're here. It's great to see my ol' partner in crime from Hawaii."

"Juicy, great to see you, too. I'm here to drag you back to Hawaii."

"Man, that would be great. I'm ready to get out of here. The draft is freaking me out and I can't seem to be able to write my CO statement."

"What have you been doing?"

"Well, I'm taking a couple of extremely boring graduate-level psychology courses in the city, making a little bread substitute teaching, and getting stoned with some friends from high school and college that live around here. Mostly all I do is think about Hawaii and feel sorry for myself."

"Perfect, pack your bags, your driver has arrived and it's time to get back to paradise. You can ride with me to deliver this car I'm being paid to drive back to California. Great deal, they pay for gas and per diem. I could use the company."

"Let me think about it, it sounds tempting. What've you been up to?"

"Living with Ann, and taking some courses at Leeward Community College."

Leo stuck around for a couple of days. I introduced him to my friends and we spent some great evenings reminiscing about Hawaii. I declined the opportunity to return to Hawaii with him, but told him that as soon as I got my draft situation resolved, he could expect to see me and he assured me that I would have a place to stay.

Leo's visit reminded me of how trapped I felt and after he left, my mood continued to spiral downward. I'd wake up and realize that instead of being in Hawaii, I was in cold, gray New York with nothing to look forward to, no one I wanted to be with, and nothing I wanted to do. All I wanted to do was sleep. Then when I tried to sleep, all I could think about was having to write my CO statement, which paralyzed me, or having to do my psychology readings, which disheartened me.

I was racked with guilt knowing how my situation was affecting my father. He knew I was depressed, and he was unable to improve my situation. I knew he was disappointed to see how lethargic I was. He heard me refuse offers to substitute teach on mornings when I was too depressed to get out of bed. All I wanted to do was pull the covers over my head and go back to sleep, but the dark thoughts wouldn't let me slip into the blissful void of sleep. Once I managed to get out of bed, I was faced with the very issues that were depressing me. In this case it was invariably the draft, which required that I sit and write my CO statement, something that was becoming increasingly more difficult.

The months dragged on. I had arrived in December and my notice would probably show up in April. I was fortunate to have the sympathy and support of friends back in Hawaii. In addition to Leo, I maintained correspondence with several VISTA contacts. They all sympathized with my dilemma and encouraged me to return to Hawaii. In desperation, I applied to the Peace Corps, thinking it might be an interesting experience to look forward to once the draft nightmare was over.

At the beginning of April, I knew the draft notice was coming. Waiting for that envelope to arrive was hell. Every day, I'd open the front door to the porch, reach into the mailbox, and pull out an assortment of envelopes, looking for the government document. In mid-April, it finally arrived. I had thirty days to prepare my statement and return it by registered mail. Now that I had a deadline, it was a huge relief. I knew what I needed to do. My conscientious objector statement was due May 15 and I would finish it. With a week left, I brewed a pot of coffee, sat down and finally cranked out my statement.

In addition to sending it in, I explored a variety of fallback options. Following up on suggestions I had gotten from friends, I went to a couple of sympathetic psychiatrists I had hoped would provide documentation declaring me unfit for duty. The first shrink had me lay down on a couch just like in the movies. He sat with his pad on his lap and wrote non-stop as I answered his questions.

"How long have you been depressed?"

"For several months."

"What about?"

"The prospect of getting drafted and all the issues involved. But now it's even more than that. I don't know what I'm going to do when this is over. I don't have the energy or ambition to do anything. My father isn't happy with his life, he's disappointed in me, my brother's a mess and taking drugs, and my mother's been dead for five years. Life pretty much sucks."

The other shrink wanted to know more about my relationship with my mother. She loved me, adored me even, but she thoroughly annoyed me. I carried a lingering guilt that I never lived up to her lofty expectations. I rationalized it by telling myself she had tried to live vicariously through me in an attempt to elevate her own fragile self-esteem.

Both psychiatrists wrote medical statements to be presented at my physical. One implied that I was bipolar and the other that I was a latent homosexual. They suggested that under duress of war, I would either kill myself or kiss my sergeant.

I also got the name of a good attorney. We met and planned my strategy. He read my CO statement, examined my physical and psychological documentation, and sent it all by registered mail to the commanding officer of the examination station.

When I took my physical exam at Whitehall Street, I was given a 4F with no explanation. I suspected that I had hit a home run with my attorney, and that when the board received my stack of documentation, they concluded that I would be too much trouble to deal with. An enormous burden had been lifted, but I was still emotionally drained, confused and lethargic. What now?

18

I WAS FINALLY FREE OF THE DRAFT AND TRYING TO FIGURE OUT what I was going to do next. Enzo was back from his six-month Army Reserve basic training and was feeling energized. We decided to work for Roc in New Haven. Elephant Trak Construction was renovating an old mill that the head of Yale's school of architecture wanted to turn into an office and living space. Enzo and I stayed at an apartment owned by one of Roc's classmates, John Krantz, and his wife, Laurie.

Enzo was going out with Michele, who lived in Connecticut and was graduating from Skidmore, where my college girlfriend Lenna had gone. Committed to staying in the east, he began applying for jobs in Boston.

The work was good therapy for me. It kept me busy. We would get up early each morning, go over to John and Laurie's kitchen to make our lunches. Roc would pick up the construction crew in a green van and drive us to the project site. Many of the crew members were Yale classmates. Enzo and I were relegated to non-skilled tasks such as painting, scraping, and carrying supplies. The work was boring, but provided me with income. And it was nice to spend time with Roc and Enzo. It took us a month to complete the renovation.

John and Laurie lived in a huge three-story home that he was renovating. He had been tearing down walls and overhauling much of the house. Enzo left to pursue some job leads in Boston, and I remained in New Haven to paint John's house, which required scaffolding. For the next month, I spent eight to ten hours a day listening to Sly and the Family Stone and Three Dog Night on the radio while scraping, priming, and painting this monstrosity of a house.

John and Laurie welcomed me into their home and their lives. We ate meals together and I would sometimes babysit their two-year-old daughter, Pebbles. Our discussions were often political. They were very liberal, well informed, and opinionated. We opposed the war and were critical of Nixon as he began to dismantle the programs that supported Johnson's War on Poverty. It was a good summer to regroup, save some money, and try to recover from my five-month draft-induced depression.

I wound up immersed in a John Steinbeck marathon, reading *The Grapes of Wrath, Tortilla Flat, The Red Pony, Cannery Row, The Pearl,* and *East of Eden*.

In August, the Peace Corps invited me to a three-day screening/orientation at Pomona College in Pasadena, California for an assignment in Fiji. The weekend would allow the Peace Corps to evaluate whether the candidates were suitable for the two-year placement, and we would determine if we wanted to commit to an assignment on this remote Pacific island.

I had started dating Mary Oshiro during my year in VISTA. She was the younger sister of one of Enzo's VISTA roommates, and we met when her family invited Enzo and me for dinner during his visit to Hawaii. We dated in the spring of 1969. I spent several weeks that summer camping on the Island of Molokai with a group of a dozen local kids in what I called the Molokai Youth Project. My VISTA year obligation would end in July, and I was scheduled to return to New York. However, with the success of the Molokai Project and the subsequent development of the Palolo Youth Project, I was granted a three-month extension. Mary spent the summer with her brother Bill in Oakland and it was assumed that our relationship had run its course.

During her absence, I had begun dating Judy, a hairdresser I had met at a Waikiki night club. When Mary returned from Oakland, I suddenly found myself in a love triangle. For the remainder of the summer and fall before I returned to New York, I dated both Mary and Judy. This caused a good amount of stress and wasn't satisfying to any of us. I maintained correspondence with both women during my ordeal in New York and we continued to declare our affection for each other. In the midst of my depression, I couldn't choose one over the other, and found it difficult to conceive of a long-term relationship with either of them.

Judy expressed compassion and patience in her letters and said she was there for me regardless of my mental state. In May, she decided to return to the mainland and take a bus trip across the country to visit me in New York. I had mixed feelings about it. In my state of mind, I was in no position to commit to this relationship. But I hoped she might be able to help lift my spirits so I was willing to see what would happen.

She arrived in late June and, after a brief visit with my father in New York, we returned to New Haven to stay with John and Laurie as I continued to paint their house. We got along, but she soon realized that the energetic and optimistic VISTA volunteer she had been dating in Hawaii was a shadow of his former self. She was faced with a lethargic, insecure, and confused house painter. By this time, I had decided that I would attend the Fiji Peace Corps training in California and try to return to Hawaii.

We spent most of the time hanging out with John and Laurie, going out to dinner, watching movies, and occasionally babysitting Pebbles. We spent a lot of time talking things over, but despite Judy's patience and understanding, it was apparent that for the time being, there was no future in this relationship. After her month-long visit, Judy hopped back on the Greyhound bus for her return to California. We committed to stay in touch and reevaluate our relationship once I determined if I was going to join the Peace Corps or return to Hawaii.

***

As I was painting one afternoon, Laurie told me I had a phone call.

"Shows?"

"Larry? Where are you?"

"I'm in Boston visiting my family on my way to New Haven."

"What?"

"Yeah, me and A.T. are here to rescue you and bring you back to Hawaii."

"Amazing."

I gave him the Krantzes' address and Larry and A.T. arrived the next day.

"You would have been proud of A.T. We were driving past the Honolulu airport and I asked him if he wanted to go visit Showman in New York, and A.T. said, 'Let's do it' so I pulled into the airport, grabbed my American Express Card, bought our tickets, and here we are."

I stared at them. "A.T. you have evolved, man. What's with the spontaneity?"

"You gotta capture these moments when you can. When's the

last time you were offered an expense paid cross-country trip to visit the Showman?"

I leaped across the room and gave A.T. a kiss on the cheek, which he immediately wiped off on his sleeve.

Once I had finished painting the house, Larry, A.T., and I drove down to North Tarrytown and made a couple of trips into New York City to show A.T. the sights. I shared with them that in a couple of weeks I would be heading to California to participate in a three-day Peace Corps orientation in Pasadena. The Peace Corps trainers explained that everyone would return home after the three days of orientation, and those who were selected would be sent to Fiji in October. I convinced them to change my return New York ticket for one to Hawaii, which was the same price. I explained that I wanted to return to the islands, visit some friends, and consider whether I wanted to become a volunteer. If I decided to go to Fiji, I persuaded them that a ticket from Hawaii would be cheaper than having to send me from New York. Larry and A.T. went back to Boston to visit Larry's family and we made plans to get back together once I had returned to Hawaii.

19

*THE GROUP OF ABOUT THIRTY PEACE CORPS CANDIDATES GATH-*ered on the Pomona College campus on the first day of orientation. We stayed in college dorms and attended meetings and presentations for the next two days. The orientation was conducted by administrators, volunteers from existing projects, and Fijian project officers and personnel. We watched slide shows describing the country of Fiji and its political and cultural traditions, and attended presentations about the respective projects that we'd potentially be assigned to. We passed around a coconut shell filled with the traditional ceremonial Fijian drink, kava. It looked and tasted like muddy water. We were told it had sedative effects. All I felt were numb, tingly lips.

Though the majority of projects were school-based teaching assignments, one of the Fiji volunteers approached me and described a project with Fijian youth that he thought I would be uniquely suited for, considering my VISTA youth experience. He had organized rock bands with some of the Fijian kids who had dropped out of school and were vulnerable to delinquent behavior and possible drug use. Our conversations continued over the three days, and at the conclusion of the orientation, the administrators offered me a job working with the music group project. I told them that I was interested, but would like to return to Hawaii for a couple of weeks to make my final decision.

Along with attending the Peace Corps training, I also intended to visit my cousin Jack Leonard and my college roommate, Dyke Hendrickson. Jack was one of three sons of my father's oldest brother Adolphe. My father was the youngest of four, with an older sister, Louise, and another brother, Leroy. Adolphe's sons Joe, Jack, and Bob were the star cousins of the family, all good students and Eagle Scouts.

Jack graduated from Harvard with a degree in chemistry. He was four years older than me and attended Harvard while I was in high school, and would occasionally stay with us in North Tarrytown on long weekends. He was in a doctoral chemistry program at Cal Tech, and had recently wed his high school sweetheart, Karen Kay, a graduate of Boston College. They were also new parents of an adopted half-black daughter, which had completely freaked out the conservative side of the family. I appreciated Jack's intellect and his liberal Christian views. He had supported my application as a conscientious objector.

After the Peace Corps training weekend, Jack picked me up at Pomona College, which wasn't that far from their apartment in Pasadena. We spent a couple of days visiting and catching up.

I left the majority of my traveler's checks and clothes with them and hitchhiked from Los Angeles to San Francisco, where Dyke picked me up and drove me to his small rental cottage in Petaluma, about an hour north of San Francisco.

After getting married in December, Dyke and Vickie had driven across the country to Petaluma, where he got his first post-VISTA job as a newspaper writer. While Dyke was at work, Vickie and I tended to her garden and listened to Joni Mitchell, Cream, and a variety of other contemporary artists. Dyke had a dry sense of humor and we spent time catching up and making each other laugh. They were among the first of my friends who seemed to be settling down. Though Dyke had been a history major at F&M, he was finally pursuing his dream of being a journalist. Vickie, after graduating from college, had followed Dyke to Hawaii and lived with him there for a year. She was attractive, with dark blond hair, pale blue eyes, and a dimpled smile. Along with gardening, she pursued water-color painting and macramé.

"So, Shows, this war has managed to disrupt most of our lives."

"Yeah, Enzo, Grayson, and Mendie all went into the reserves," I said, recounting the plight of our fraternity brothers.

"Well, you know Jeff Nixon, Koehneke, Sawers, Haas, and Pokul are all officers."

"And then there were the dodgers—you, Mesard, Enzo, and I all went into VISTA and Magee, Druck, and Sarnoff joined the Peace Corps. Clair got his CO and is teaching in Puerto Rico."

"Yeah, and it's still not over, fucking Nixon."

"Yeah, and you voted for him!" Dyke chided me.

"Well that was before I attended the Hendrickson social education seminar," I said, recalling the books Dyke suggested I read and the discussions we had while I was a VISTA volunteer.

"And now with no draft to worry about, are you seriously considering going to Fiji in the Peace Corps?"

"I don't have a clue. These last few months have really screwed with my psyche. I don't know what I want to do. I felt reasonably confident after VISTA that I wanted to continue to work in some social service capacity, but I'm realizing that to get a decent job, I'd probably need a master's degree. I got pretty discouraged after taking graduate psychology courses that turned out to be a waste of time.

"I'm not sure about Fiji anymore. It seems like a cool adventure, but I still haven't processed my change in values after being in VISTA. If I do end up on a remote third-world island for two years, I might not want to come back. It's nice to have the option of returning to Hawaii, maybe getting a job and just bagging the Peace Corps."

"Yeah, I know what you mean. I envy you going back to Hawaii. We really miss it."

***

After a great visit with Dyke and Vickie, Dyke drove me down to San Francisco so I could hitch back to Los Angeles and eventually catch my flight to Hawaii. He dropped me off at a strip of road used by lots of hitchhikers headed for Southern California.

I struck up a conversation with a bearded, bespectacled guy who said he was hitching to Los Angeles, so we decided to hitch together. Before long, a couple of black dudes in a dark green, two-door Mustang pulled over, rolled down their window and asked where we were going. When we told them we were going to Los Angeles, they told us they were headed there too and invited us to hop in. We were psyched to get a ride all the way to LA. The guys engaged us in friendly conversation and my hitchhike partner revealed that after visiting a friend in LA, he was headed home to Kentucky. I mentioned that I was flying out of LA and going to Hawaii.

"Hey, I need to make a quick stop to pick up some pot. Either of you smoke?" the driver asked.

"Sure."

The car pulled into an alleyway near a housing project. The dude in the passenger seat turned around and pressed the point of a switchblade to my companion's throat. I thought my heart would jump out of my chest. Blood drained from my head and I felt faint.

"Empty your pockets and give me your wallets and money," he ordered menacingly.

We emptied our pockets. I handed him my wallet, my $25 in traveler's checks, and $5 in cash.

"What's this shit?" he screamed as he turned around and backhanded me across the face with his closed fist.

"You're going to Hawaii and this is all you got?"

"I left the rest of my money and clothes with my cousin in Los Angeles," I blurted, my eyes tearing and ears ringing. I was terrified and convinced that if he didn't kill us, he was going to carve up our faces. My hitchhiking partner sat whimpering next to me. As I cowered in the backseat, trapped in the two-door car, I felt a fragment of tooth on my tongue.

"Maybe we should keep your friend in the car while you go to a store and cash these traveler's checks." Then he and the driver engaged in a prolonged whispered conversation. They finally drove out onto the highway and stopped the car.

"Get the fuck out!" the driver barked. Amazingly, though he kept our cash, he gave us our wallets and traveler's checks back.

As we stood on the side of the road, my traveling companion and I looked at each other, relieved to be alive. It took a while for the shaking to stop and for my stomach to stop churning. I knew I had just narrowly escaped with my life.

After a while, my partner decided to regroup back in San Francisco and I resigned myself to continue hitching to Los Angeles. I caught rides with drivers I tried my best to screen before hopping in, and spent an uncomfortable night sleeping behind a gas station. I finally arrived in Los Angeles relatively unscathed.

"So how was your trip?" Jack inquired after picking me up.

"Eventful," I replied and proceeded to share with him the harrowing details.

After having my molar repaired by my cousin's dentist, I flew to Hawaii.

PART 5

—

FEBRUARY 1971
MAKIKI

20

AFTER A SQUABBLE WITH ANN, I SAID GOODBYE TO GREG AND MOVED out of her Manoa cottage. With nowhere to live, I went to hang out at the house in Makiki after my return from the Big Island.

Rob Moore, my friend from Molokai who had introduced me to the group who inspired my Captain Energy persona, lived here with a motley crew of interesting and creative dropouts. There was guitarist Mike McCrillis, and Alan Johnson, my wrestling partner, also lived there. He had a master's degree in psychology and lived off his stewardess girlfriend's income while taking flying lessons and selling grass. The quiet, stand-offish artists I had met in Molokai, Willow and Don, with their matching long blond hair and tie-dyed shirts, were also residents. Finally, there was Roger, who had been a VISTA volunteer in Chicago, was my age, wore wire-rimmed glasses, and whom I called Clarence Darrow because he was a first-year law student at UH.

They all lived in this sprawling Makiki estate, nestled among the banyan trees. The main house had several bedrooms that connected to the centrally-located kitchen, living room, and dining room. There were also three small guesthouses on the property. We'd occasionally gather around the large kitchen table, drinking wine, smoking dope, and regurgitating our cynical opinions about The System. We vowed never to "sell out" or fall for the materialistic capitalist game.

This house also attracted several musicians who were contemplating forming a band with Augie Ray, a Waikiki entertainer who had arrived in Honolulu in 1970 from New York City.

The musicians would set up their amps and electrical instruments in the living room and practice top-twenty cover tunes they intended to perform at Waikiki nightclubs. Saxophonist and multi-instrumentalist Bobby Graham was resisting recruitment into Augie's band.

McCrillis told me they had been given a week's notice to vacate the house because the landlord was selling the property.

"Where you guys going to go?" I asked.

"I don't know but we have a week to decide."

"What a drag, man, this was a great house."

I had been sleeping on a couch in the living room since returning from the Big Island, hoping one of the rooms would open up. McCrillis's news forced me to start scouring the newspaper for furnished apartments. I eventually found one several blocks away, on Wilder Avenue. It was on the fourth floor of an apartment building with a small patio that overlooked the lush grounds of the nearby Catholic Church. The floor was covered with a thick, red shag carpet and there was a black leather couch with matching chairs in the living room. A long Formica counter separated the kitchen from the living room, and one of the bedrooms had a sliding Japanese screen panel.

I went back to the Makiki house and announced that I had found an apartment and anyone who wanted to move in with me was welcome. Bobby and McCrillis followed me on my motorcycle to the new place.

"All right," McCrillis said approvingly after a brief look around.

I tossed a baggie on the coffee table. "Let's christen the place."

I sat on the floor next to McCrillis and rolled some joints. Bobby sprawled next to us on the couch. We passed around a joint while

Santana's *Abraxas* played on my cassette player. I opened beers for everyone.

"You sure it's cool for me to crash here, Energy?"

"Long as you teach me to play your trumpet."

"No problem."

McCrillis smiled, his dark, nervous, darting eyes finally slowing down.

"What about you?"

"I don't know, Energy, I want to leave my options open, but I'll stay tonight if that's okay."

"So what went down in Maui?" Bobby asked.

"Well, you heard I got busted."

"What happened?"

I related my story about taking peyote in Maui.

McCrillis looked at me and nodded. "Far out man."

Bobby chortled. "You thought the Flesh was going play at Haleakala?"

"I know. Believe me, I know. But remember the Diamond Head festival? I thought the whole peaceful vibe was mind-blowing. Hundreds of us there and we all got along. A few days later, I took the peyote and listened to the Toronto Peace Festival with everyone singing "Give Peace a Chance" and I thought, 'That's it. There's going to be another festival and it's happening at Haleakala, and this time our band will be the next messengers for world peace.'"

Bobby took another toke. "Similar thing happened to me, except it wasn't peyote."

"What do you mean?" I asked.

"Acid changed my life, man. I was up in Connecticut, graduated from college, met someone, started teaching. Before I knew it I had a wife, a mortgage, and car payments. I got a promotion, but we were spending all this money, and my needy ol' lady was driving me nuts. I could barely sleep with all the bullshit I was dealing with at school. Playing music on the weekends was the only thing that kept me from flipping out. One day, my guitar player and I said fuck this, let's go camping and drop some acid.

"It blew me away, man. I was talking to John fucking Coltrane. He was as real as McCrillis sitting there. After that, I knew I had to play the sax. I decided this is it, man, life's too short. I quit my job, got out of that shitty marriage, and moved to Florida. Five years ago… never looked back."

"Freakin' Bobby. I didn't know you taught school."

He chuckled. "They promoted me, remember? I was the principal, son."

With his long black hair, scraggly goatee, and deep-set eyes, Bobby looked nothing like the principals I knew. He reminded me of Rasputin. It was always a relief to see him smile, because he normally just looked pissed-off and dangerous.

"So then what happened?" Bobby could be a good listener.

I related my court case, the subsequent arrest, getting burned by Fred and Joe, and my visit with friends on the Big Island.

"Here, this'll blow your mind." I handed him a copy of *Greening of America*. "Started reading it on the Big Island."

"Cool. Well, I'm thinking we need to play music. That jam session in Makiki was phenomenal. And you made it happen, Energy."

"Are you going to join Augie's band?" I asked.

Bobby took a long drag. "I don't want to play that tired nightclub shit. The hell with Augie Ray. It's Energy and the Flesh, man."

I sat back against the wall, my heart in synch with Santana's percussion. Buoyed by Bobby's endorsement, I wallowed in fantasies of leading the band. We already had a set of congas, a saxophone, keyboard, trumpet, and guitars. I could wing it on the congas and maybe even sing. We'd be unique, a multi-ethnic group with a sound and a social message that would appeal to all ages and ethnicities. Drifting into euphoria, I sipped my beer.

"Hey Energy, so what's with the book?"

"Oh yeah." I tried to collect my thoughts and summarize how this book spoke to me.

I explained my disenchantment with *the movement*. "You know, I thought our generation was going to end the war. It's still going on. The civil rights movement is all screwed up since King got killed, and now there's the Panthers. Nixon's fucking up the war on poverty.

"This guy Reich, a law professor at Yale, thinks our generation will lead a new kind of revolution. I like the way he explains why the generations don't get each other. We grew up with different experiences. My father was raised during the Depression and fought in World War II. I grew up with TV, technology, drugs, and music. It makes sense."

Bobby thumbed through some pages.

"Anyway, you'd have to read it to appreciate his ideas. It sort of gave me new hope."

***

My apartment started to replace the Makiki house as the place to hang out. Several of the musicians who joined Augie Ray's band would stop by and jam with us. If I was going to be the leader of the Electric Flesh,

I'd have to work on my musical chops. Bobby showed me some stuff on the trumpet. I had played it for a while in school before switching to the unwieldy sousaphone. I could read music, but needed to strengthen my lips and practice the fingering.

I was becoming more aware of how music could change the mood and vibe of a room, and with my growing collection of tapes, I became the house DJ. I chose music to enhance the ambiance I wanted to create at this non-stop party. Depending on my audience, I'd pontificate about my vision for the future, and supplement it by orchestrating jam sessions.

Bobby hibernated for a couple of days after I gave him *The Greening of America* to read. He eventually emerged and we discussed concepts and passages that intrigued him.

"So your old man's conservative."

"Yeah. His thing is, 'We need to stop communism at all costs.' And 'Everyone should pull themselves up by their bootstraps.' But after a year-and-a-half at Palolo housing, I know that's easier said than done."

"I dig it."

I began to think that in fact, the slackers at the Makiki house weren't that much different from the Palolo paint sniffers. They were either talented like McCrillis or educated like Alan Johnson, but for whatever reason, they were alienated from the system and usually unemployed. The kids in Palolo couldn't function in school or get jobs because they didn't know how, or chose not to. It was the same thing at the house. What if I could play the same role for the Makiki residents as I did with the kids in Palolo? It would be cool to figure out a way to help these adult dropouts get back into the system. Maybe I could serve as their talent agent and cut through the bullshit they didn't want to have to deal with?

21

DUKE, AN ACQUAINTANCE OF MCCRILLIS, STARTED SHOWING UP AT my apartment. He'd hang out, schmooze, drink our wine, and smoke our weed. He was soft-spoken with a very mellow, low-key personality. I liked having him around. He was enthusiastic about Captain Energy and the Electric Flesh and my nascent idea of starting a corporation to help employ talented dropouts. Unlike McCrillis and Bobby, he always seemed to be on a steady keel, very optimistic, upbeat, and dependable. McCrillis and Bobby were predictably moody. Some days, they were enthusiastic and engaging, and sometimes they preferred to keep to themselves. Bobby moved into the apartment with me, and McCrillis ended up living with an attractive local Chinese girl he was dating.

"Let's take a ride and see my friend George in Waikiki," Duke suggested.

He drove an old station wagon with an India Import bed sheet over the mattress in back. George was a black graphic artist who lived in a small bohemian enclave at the Diamond Head end of Waikiki known as the Jungle. It was a low-rent area of one- and two-story cottages and apartments that were inhabited by an assortment of locals and transients from the mainland.

"Me and George met when I worked at a tobacco shop in the Ala Moana shopping center," Duke explained. "He'd come in to buy pipe tobacco and we just connected. He'll like your corporation idea. He's an artist and can work on a logo. He also plays congas and can help us with the band. Anyway, he'd come in the shop and I'd know which tobacco he wanted and he'd tell me about some project he was working on. Sometimes I'd go over to his place after work and we'd smoke dope and listen to some music. People were always dropping by with a lid or a six-pack. We'd get the scoop about the latest club bands in Waikiki, or the new chicks who just moved in down the street."

Duke and I started hanging out all the time. He'd stop by my apartment and we'd drive around in his station wagon, usually to Waikiki or Ala Moana, and I'd spin my plans for the band or the corporation. For every idea or scheme I would come up with, Duke had a friend with connections or he had done something like that or was willing to give it a try. He wasn't pretentious or boastful, but he'd been around. He grew up in Los Angeles an only child of divorced parents. His mother ran a dress shop to support the two of them. He had dropped out of college, served some time for dealing marijuana, and traveled extensively around the country with his camera.

One day, he walked into my apartment with a gorgeous young local girl. She had long black hair that swayed when she walked, and she wore a macramé top and hot pants.

"Energy, I want you to meet my girlfriend, Carol." She smiled shyly at me and I fumbled for words as the three of us chatted in the kitchen.

"Let's go for a ride. I need to take Carol back to school."

After we dropped her off, I just looked at him.

"You letch...she's still in high school and you're what, twenty-seven?"

"I know, but she's mature for her age. Plus, did you get a look at her?"

"How did you pull that off?"

"Met her throwing a Frisbee. We've been dating for the last six months."

Carol joined us on many of our adventures. She was smart and funny, and on several occasions displayed her artistic talent by doing sketches of Duke and me and whoever was around. I learned she came from a respected local family of successful entrepreneurs.

Duke was a real schmoozer who could get along with anybody. It seemed as if he knew every sales person and store manager at Ala Moana, and they'd greet him enthusiastically. He was four years older than me and, though he didn't have a college education, he struck me as being worldly and experienced. He'd done a lot of things, knew a lot of people, and had a great upbeat, optimistic personality.

He always had weed on him and we were constantly stoned. When I was high, my mind was always spinning with ideas about what I could accomplish, what the possibilities were. I shared with him my thoughts about managing and promoting the talented and creative dropouts we were hanging around with. They were either unemployed or underemployed and I could envision more productive and lucrative ways to harness their skills.

"Energy, I think that's a great idea. In fact, I've been thinking about doing something like that myself."

"Really, you wanted to promote and manage these people?"

"Well...I would have if you hadn't thought of it first."

I laughed. "I guess we're on the same wave length."

"Well, I want to be on your wavelength. What should we call it?"

"It's got to be international and something that relates to our clients."

"How about International Stoners?"

"Stoners? Dude, we've got to mainstream this. How about International Head Consultants?"

"Perfect."

22

DUKE BROUGHT ME OVER TO HIS KAPAHULU HOUSE WHERE HE lived with a couple of roommates.

"Steve, this is Captain Energy."

"Captain Energy?" he snorted, as our hands fumbled for the right handshake. My brotherhood shake was being rejected, as he kept his grip rigid.

"Steve's my landlord. He rents the house from our neighbor and sublets the other two rooms to me and John."

Tall, with broad shoulders and a Marine's buzz cut, Steve's pale eyes watched me warily.

When we got to Duke's room, he explained that Steve was cool. He was an ex-Marine and had just been released from a tour of duty in Vietnam. When we returned to the living room, a guitar was on the coffee table.

"I'm selling my guitar if you guys are interested."

"How much?" I asked.

"It's in good shape. I'm only selling it because I want to buy a twelve-string I've had my eye on."

"How much?" I asked again.

"Fifty bucks," he offered.

I pulled out my checkbook, wrote the check, and slapped it on the coffee table for effect.

"Is this check any good?"

I looked at him and then at Duke, who was watching from the other side of the room.

"It's good," Duke assured him

I picked up the guitar and strummed the one chord I knew.

"Come on, Energy, let's go. We've got things to do, places to be, and people to see."

"Thanks, Steve, great guitar," I said as I bounded out the door. He sat on the couch staring at my check.

"Do you know any chords?" I asked Duke once I got in the car.

"Yeah, I know a couple."

I sat in the passenger seat strumming away, moving my left fingers up and down the neck of the guitar, listening to the different sounds I was creating.

When we returned to my apartment, the landlord met us at the elevator.

"Bruce, I need to speak to you." He pulled me aside while Duke waited.

"The tenants on your floor are starting to complain about the traffic going in and out of your place. My son just moved in the apartment next to yours and he's mentioned to me that you should play your music softer, especially late at night."

"Mr. Adams, I'm so sorry. I'll definitely be more considerate. I'd like you to meet my friend Duke."

"Nice to meet you, Mr. Adams." Duke greeted my landlord with a friendly smile and a handshake. Adams muttered something and walked away.

"I guess my neighbors aren't appreciating all the visitors."

"Well, it's been a pretty good party."

The traffic had been non-stop since I moved in, probably due to the variety of intoxicants on hand 24/7. The residents over at the Makiki house started hanging around too, along with their friends. Bobby was also a draw, as the established experienced musician.

When we walked into the apartment, McCrillis was singing and strumming his guitar, with Bobby accompanying him on his synthesizer. McCrillis's girlfriend Brenda was singing harmony.

"That sounds pretty good," I commented when they'd finished.

We passed around a joint and Duke put his arm around my shoulder. "Meet the President of International Head Consultants."

"Cool name," Bobby commented.

"What's that?" Brenda asked.

"Energy is going to start a corporation and make a bunch of money," McCrillis explained.

"He's going to get everybody jobs," Duke chimed in.

"Ok, President of International Head Consultants, what are you going to do for me?" McCrillis drawled cynically.

"What do you want?"

"I want a gig, man!"

I sat back on the couch and took a long drag on the joint that was being passed around.

"How would you like to be on TV?"

McCrillis glanced over at Brenda with a smirk. "You're gonna get me a gig on TV? What show?"

"How about the Don Robbs Show?"

"That's pretty popular," Brenda commented.

Don Robbs was a local media celebrity who had, over the course of his career, been a newscaster and a sports announcer. His daytime talk show was quite popular, and in addition to his lineup of guests, he would invite local and sometimes nationally recognized musical guests to perform.

"Cool, but how're you going to manage that, Energy?"

"Excuse me, you're speaking to the President of International Head Consultants." I grabbed the phone book, found KOAT-TV and dialed.

"May I speak to Vivian Harmon, please?"

"Vivian, hi, this is Bruce Leonard. I don't know if you remember me, but I was on Don's show about a year ago. I was the VISTA volunteer working in Palolo Valley?

"I'm flattered you remembered. Well, I'm currently involved in music and I'm also promoting some talent. I was wondering if the show was in need of any musical guests."

"Really? His name is Mike McCrillis. He's a talented singer and guitar player and he's performed in a few Waikiki clubs. That's great. Sure, I can hold." I grinned as my audience watched, transfixed.

"March 28th? Hold on, let me check Mike's calendar." McCrillis looked at me, his joint frozen in midair. Brenda leaped up, mouthing, "Yes, yes!" and Mike finally nodded. "Vivian, that sounds perfect. Thanks so much, give my best to Don."

McCrillis sat back, shaking his head.

"Can't believe you did that, man, how'd you get me on?"

"I was a guest two years ago. Luckily his producer remembered me. Well, McCrillis, you're on your way, man. You get on that show, thousands of people will see you and the phone will start ringing."

He shook his head. "Far out, man."

A few weeks passed and I would run into Mike hanging out in Waikiki or at Ala Moana where Brenda worked. A week before his appearance, Duke and I saw him at Hula's night club.

"Mike, one week to go before your big debut. You're listed in this week's TV guide. You ready, man?"

He looked at his feet. "Yeah, about that..."

"Well you better be ready. This is your big chance."

"I hear you."

Duke and I took off in his station wagon.

"Is McCrillis going to bag me?"

"I wouldn't put it past him." Duke explained that Mike was definitely talented, but the reason he hadn't made it so far was because he lacked confidence and he wasn't reliable.

"But I thought he was stoked about this."

"Yeah, me too." Duke shrugged.

23

MCCRILLIS WAS TO APPEAR ON THE DON ROBBS SHOW THAT DAY. I called him at his house.

"Well dude, today's the big day, your premier on prime time TV."

"Yeah, I'm not going on, Energy."

"You're kidding."

"I'm not ready."

"You're kidding."

"I'm not, Energy, sorry."

"You're freakin' kidding me? You are not going to blow this opportunity. You're always complaining you never get any breaks and now you do this?"

"Sorry, man."

"You asshole!" I yelled as I slammed down the phone.

"I knew he'd get stage fright," Duke said, shaking his head.

"I can't believe this."

"What are you going to do?"

"Let me think."

I sat on the living room couch, taking deep drags on a joint Duke passed me and strummed the new chord I had just learned on Steve's guitar. I picked up the phone and dialed the producer.

"Hi Vivian, this is Bruce Leonard, how are you?"

"Hello Bruce, we're looking forward to meeting Mike and seeing you again. Everything set?"

"Well, that's why I'm calling, Vivian. Unfortunately, something's come up. Mike's not coming on."

"That's a going to be a problem, Bruce," she said, her voice rising. "You realize this is a live show!"

After a long, muffled pause, Vivian returned.

"Bruce, didn't you say you were involved with music? Could maybe you perform?"

"No problem!" I said.

"Great, we'll see you here at 1:00."

"Right on! See you then."

Duke was looking concerned. "What's going on, Energy?"

"I'm going to make my musical debut on the Don Robbs Show."

"You only know three chords."

"Is that too many?"

He handed me another joint. "Here, you're going to need this."

"Do you want to come on with me?" I asked.

"I think I'll pass. This is your show, but I'll be there, buddy. I wouldn't miss this for the world," he snickered.

Bobby walked into the kitchen and grabbed a beer.

"Bruce is going on the Don Robbs show today. McCrillis backed out."

"All right, Energy! This should be good," he chuckled.

Duke drove me to the KOA-TV studio on Ala Moana Boulevard.

"Hey Vivian, good to see you again."

"Nice to see you, Bruce."

"This is my partner, Richard Duke."

"Nice to meet you, Richard. Bruce, you may remember how this goes. Don's co-host this week is Martin Denny. They will visit for the first portion of the show. You'll be the second guest. Oh good, I see you've brought your guitar. I thought you and Don could talk for a couple of minutes, then we'd break for a commercial, and you could perform to close out the show."

"Sounds great."

"Good, well guys, make yourselves comfortable over here, help yourself to the refreshments, and I'll signal you just before Don introduces you. Here's an index card. Why don't you write down a couple of notes about yourself and the title of your song?"

The set was brightly lit and decorated with a desk that Don and his co-host sat behind, a fake palm tree, a couple of chairs for the guests and the colorful KOA-TV logo on the wall. Martin Denny was a popular Hawaii bandleader who had recorded songs popular in the forties and fifties featuring exotic percussion and occasional bird calls. He still had a following and was appearing nightly at a Waikiki club.

Don chatted a while with Martin about local events and the lovely weather, and announced that Martin Denny and his band would be continuing their successful appearance for the next several weeks at the Ilikai Hotel. Don's first guest was a middle-aged woman in a florid muumuu and flaming red hair. She talked about the Honolulu Chamber of Commerce and plugged their upcoming fundraising auction that Don would MC that weekend.

Don and Martin concluded their chat with the Chamber of Commerce lady and broke for a commercial. Vivian asked for the card I had written my bio notes on and told me to follow her over to the side of the set. She handed the card to Don and I stood alongside one of the cameramen and watched the TV monitor as a commercial for Meadow Gold milk appeared. The stagehand looked over at Don, pointed to one of the cameras, and silently counted down five fingers.

"Our next guest is Bruce Leonard. The last time we had Bruce on the show was a couple of years ago and he was involved in a very innovative project working with troubled youth in Palolo Valley.

"Hi Bruce, nice to see you again. Boy, it seems you've completely changed directions since we saw you last. My notes say you're now president of International Head Consultants and playing music with Captain Energy and the Electric Flesh." Martin Denny was leaning forward in his chair as Don read from his card. He squirmed a bit in his seat and shot an anxious look over at Don.

"Well Don, in some ways things are different and in some ways they are exactly the same."

Don looked at me blankly.

"What I mean is, when I was helping kids in Palolo, I was working for change and, though my current clientele is a little different, I'm still working toward change. It's all part of the revolution."

Martin Denny coughed or maybe choked and Don's face went pale. "Now wait a minute, we're not going to..."

"A peaceful revolution, Don, don't get excited. Did you happen to read *The Greening of America*?"

"No, but we're not here to discuss revolution. Peaceful or otherwise."

"*The Greening of America* speaks of the different levels of consciousness that a lot of us work from. This revolution is about changing attitudes and values, about peace and love. Our generation relates to music and since I'm into social change, it seems to be the most effective vehicle to reach an audience peacefully."

"Well, we all enjoy music," Don said, nodding at Martin.

"Yes, music is important to every generation," added Denny. They seemed to relax a bit.

"Maybe I can explain this better by singing my song."

"That's a great idea, Bruce. Why don't we take a break and we'll return with Bruce Leonard, or is it Captain Energy and the…"

"Whatever."

The stagehand signaled for me to move over to a stool that was a couple of feet from the set. Duke handed me my guitar and patted me on the back. "Juice, you're doing great."

I sat on the stool and strummed the three guitar chords I knew. My head was racing, I was perspiring profusely and, never actually having sung my song before, I balanced the sheet of lyrics on my knee.

I had written it at the kitchen table in Makiki. It involved a variety of images I had in mind, namely my college girlfriend Lenna, metaphors about sitting at a kitchen table considering the here and now, and concerns about the troubled world we lived in. It was a very personal abstract piece that might be too personal or abstract to be appreciated, but according to the *Greening of America,* my generation should get it. I hoped that everyone else who heard it would get my message once they reached a higher level of consciousness.

I stared at the camera with the little red light for a few seconds. Then, hoping to make everything clearer and better understood, I decided to take a minute to introduce the song first.

"Music is a powerful medium for our generation. It delivers intellectual and poetic messages of change and revolution, but is received emotionally, and sensually." I was on a roll. I strummed a chord.

"Whereas political rhetoric may not be successful in moving society to harmonious action, music can make you tap your feet, clap your hands, and move your body and mind to the same rhythm. Music is the language of our generation. It transcends consciousness and communicates on a deep and spiritual level." I strummed another chord.

I looked up to see Don Robbs standing next to the stage manager, who was holding up ten fingers. I paused my introductory monologue and asked, "How much time do I have left?"

Don waved his hand over his head and then across his neck, indicating none. I could see the red light go off, and they cut to a commercial. Duke gave me the thumbs up sign, his face flush with excitement.

Don was back on the air, engaged in an animated conversation with his co-host.

"Well thanks for joining us today for one of our more…interesting shows. Martin Denny will be back with us again when we'll welcome our special guest Hilo Hattie. Until tomorrow - Aloha."

Don pushed away from his desk and marched over to where I was getting off the stool. "You've got some nerve coming on this show, spouting your revolutionary gobbledygook! What the hell are you on anyway?" He stared at my bloodshot eyes.

"I've got nerve? What about you? You have the platform to educate people about what's really going on and you abuse that power by airing a bunch of meaningless shit."

"My job here is to provide entertainment."

"Well, I suspect this was one of your more entertaining shows."

He glared and sputtered as I grabbed my guitar case, flashed a peace sign, and headed toward the exit.

"Come on, Duke. Have a good one, Don. Thanks for having me on."

We climbed into the station wagon and drove back to the apartment.

I lit up the joint I had stashed in my guitar case, took a deep drag, and tilted my head back and exhaled.

"Juice, that was a pisser, you freakin' blew their minds!"

"He didn't seem to be buying the program."

"The hell with him, you were great."

My head was spinning, I was excited and agitated, defensive and indignant. I was disappointed that Don didn't get it.

When we entered the apartment, Bobby was in the living room sitting over a wooden bowl and rolling a fat joint.

"Energy, killer interview, man! That was television history in the making." He passed me the joint and we sat around listening to music and laughing.

I went to the bathroom and looked at my face in the mirror, stared at the specks of green, yellow, and brown that surrounded my pupils. My blondish brown beard was thick around my chin and mouth but thinned out as it crept up my cheeks. I took a razor and scraped the whiskers off my cheekbones and carefully attempted to even the right and left sides. My tongue was in its usual position when I was concentrating—sticking out, pressed against the corner of my mouth. As I shaved and compared each side, I lost more and more of my beard. And then I started working on my hair, trying to even it out. When I emerged from the bathroom, I not only had no beard left, but barely any hair.

"What happened to you?"

"Got a little carried away. But it's time for a change."

I sat down and Grand Funk Railroad was playing—"I'm Your Captain."

"That's your theme song, Energy," Bobby exclaimed.

I sat back and took another deep drag from the joint he handed me. My stomach was rumbling and I was starting to get agitated. I didn't know what to do with this nervous energy. "We need an adventure," I proclaimed. "Let's go to Maui."

I was having trouble sleeping at night. Getting stoned all the time made me more and more manic and I was constantly organizing my few possessions or drawing schematics of the corporate structure of International Head Consultants.

One of the ways I managed to calm down was to take a hot bath and listen to music. It was one of those sleepless nights, and I was in the tub with the radio on, trying to unwind. When Chicago came on, I jumped out to grab my trumpet so I could play along. I had recently taught myself to mimic the trumpet part in several Chicago songs, and I was pleased with my progress. I usually played with the mute on so I wouldn't bother anyone, but this time I forgot and started blaring away, oblivious to the volume. Just as Peter Cetera sang, "Does anyone really know what time it is?" someone started pounding on our front door. Bobby went to see who it was, and the landlord's son screamed, "Does anyone know what time it is? It's four in the morning and somebody is playing a damn trumpet! Shut up so we can all sleep!"

The landlord's call later that morning giving me twenty-four hours to vacate the apartment sealed my resolve to pursue our adventure in Maui.

Captain Energy welcoming guests to his Makiki apartment.

Contemplating life in Makiki

Captain Energy with Greening of America

Bobby Graham, reading Greening of America

Explaining International Head Consultants

Captain Energy and McCrillis discussing appearance on the Don Robbs Show

Energy with Brenda, McCrillis's girlfriend

Captain Energy attaining wisdom

Captain Energy with newly purchased guitar on his way to a Sandy Beach Theater of Madness

Members of the Electric Flesh.
Kimo, Mike McCrillis and Billy Kim.

Bobby Graham, Captain Energy, and Kimo

Promoting the future with Marshall McLuhan

Captain Energy sharing his vision of the future

PART 6

—

FLASHBACK

—

JUNE 1968 – DECEMBER 1969 VISTA

24

*"HI, MRS. HENDRICKSON. THIS IS BRUCE LEONARD. I WAS DYKE'S COL-*lege roommate last year."

"Of course, Bruce, how are you?"

"I'm great, how are you and Mr. Hendrickson?"

"We're just fine."

"I understand that Dyke is a VISTA volunteer. I was wondering if you could give me his address so I could get in touch with him. It's my senior year and I'm considering applying to VISTA."

"Of course, hold on, Bruce, let me get his address and I also have his phone number. You know, he was sent by VISTA to Hawaii."

I paused. "I'm sorry, did you say Hawaii?"

"Yes, can you believe it? Dyke was fully expecting to be sent to Appalachia or an inner-city ghetto, but they thought that with his tennis experience he might be more suited to working with the Hawaiian youth. Okay, do you have a pen? Here's his address and phone number."

I got off the phone, shaking my head in disbelief, and paused briefly before making a long distance call to Hawaii, realizing there was a six-hour time difference.

"Hello."

"Hello, Dook..." My nickname for Dyke

"Showman, what a pleasant surprise."

"Dook, you're in Hawaii?"

"Yes, Shows, it's true, I'm a VISTA volunteer in Hawaii."

"You are fighting poverty and saving the world in fucking Hawaii, are you shitting me?"

"There are shows to be had in Hawaii."

"Dook...get me there, I'm sitting here with my application and I don't want to go to Harlem or some holler in Kentucky. I want to go to Hawaii and get a tan while I'm saving the world."

"A man after my own heart, Showman, I'll see what I can do."

***

I graduated from Franklin and Marshall College (F&M), Lancaster, Pennsylvania in June of 1968. Within two weeks, I was on my way to San Francisco State University, where I would attend VISTA training for ten days and if selected, would be sent to Hawaii.

VISTA (Volunteers in Service to America) was an anti-poverty program created by Lyndon Johnson's Economic Opportunity Act of 1964 as the domestic version of the Peace Corps. Volunteers were sent to serve in impoverished communities all over the U.S. to help empower them to address their respective issues and to enrich their educational and vocational opportunities. I decided to arrive a week early to visit Enzo, my best friend from high school and college, who was a VISTA volunteer in Oakland, CA. Enzo had been there for six months. I figured it would be great to have him share his VISTA experience and introduce me to the Bay Area.

This was 1968 in Oakland. Robert Kennedy had just been assassinated after having won the California presidential primary. Training would be held at San Francisco State University, the site of a school-wide shut down led by the Black Panthers and the SDS. They demanded the creation of a Black Studies curriculum, an ultimatum opposed by the school's colorful president, S. I. Hayakawa. Neighboring Haight-Ashbury was ground zero for the flower children of the sixties and the alternative lifestyle movement.

Enzo picked me up at the airport and took me over to the house that he and his three VISTA roommates were renting. It was located in a predominantly black, low-income neighborhood in Oakland, near the storefront office of the Peter Maurin House, the sponsoring agency for Enzo's VISTA project, and three blocks from the National Headquarters of the Black Panthers. He shared the house with three roommates, Ed from Washington State, Vernon from Virginia, and Bill, a Japanese-American guy from Kailua, Hawaii.

We were excited to visit Haight-Ashbury, which was teeming with exotically dressed hippies. Young women with flowers in their hair, braless in embroidered peasant blouses and long batik-print skirts, walked hand-in-hand with long-haired guys, love beads around their necks, in drawstring pants and sandals. Our timing was good. Apparently there was a free concert scheduled for that afternoon at Golden Gate Park featuring Janis Joplin and her band, Big Brother and the Holding Company. A year after the 1967 Summer of Love, the profusion of flower children in the Bay Area was still an amazing sight. I was self-consciously walking around gawking, with my Dippity Do-controlled hair and my preppy button-down shirt, sleeves pushed up just so, khaki pants, and Bass Weejun loafers. Loud electric rock was emanating from somewhere as we ambled wide-eyed through the park, surrounded by hundreds of smiling, friendly hippies handing out flowers and marijuana joints.

I had never smoked pot, and had rejected several opportunities to do so in college. This time, I was ready. The students who had been stoners when I was at F&M were beatniks who listened to folk music and participated in anti-war and civil rights protests, generally a group I didn't relate to. I was in the beer-drinking, jock cohort, and to me the pot smokers were just plain weird. However, during the second semester of my senior year, several of my fraternity brothers, including Enzo, started to smoke weed, and some progressed to psychedelic drugs. They didn't act crazy; they just tended to sit around giggling and listening to music. I can remember Stu Magee and John Hurlbut, who lived across from me at our fraternity house, sitting in a thick marijuana cloud in their darkened suite, listening to Jimmy Hendrix's "Purple Haze," a black light illuminating the day-glo posters on the walls.

Both my parents were heavy cigarette smokers as I grew up and I wound up hating smoking. I had a difficult time with the mechanics of sucking on a joint, inhaling the hot smoke, and drawing it into my lungs. I'd cough and gag and found the whole process repulsive. I kept waiting for the uncontrollable giggling, the munchies, the exaggerated perceptions of color and music. I smoked with Enzo twice during my visit and never felt anything.

When we arrived at the park, a series of rock groups were performing, warm-up acts for Janis Joplin and Big Brother and the Holding Company. The area in front of the large stage was crowded with young people sprawled on India Import blankets, doing their thing. Enzo and I shared a bottle of wine and spent the afternoon engaged in some of the most entertaining people-watching I had ever experienced. Finally, I spotted Janis Joplin, with her wavy reddish-brown hair, layers of love beads around her neck, bangles on her wrists, and a long, velvet skirt.

Swigging from a bottle of Southern Comfort, she and her band electrified the crowd and brought us to our feet with "Piece of My Heart" and "Ball and Chain." Enzo nudged me and pointed to a guy on a tree branch twenty-five feet in the air. We looked at each other in amazement. The kid, obviously stoned out of his mind, was gyrating in synch with the music, the branch bouncing under his weight. Enzo and I watched with trepidation, but the crowd seemed to accept the tree dancer as just a blissful dude with the best seat in the house.

25

AFTER OUR VISIT, ENZO DROPPED ME OFF AT SAN FRANCISCO STATE where I registered for my training and met my roommate. Jim was a good-looking guy with a quick smile. He shook my hand, a cigarette dangling from his lips. He was from New Jersey and had graduated from a two-year community college.

The training would consist of an overview of the agencies that would supervise the VISTA projects, a brief presentation about community organization, and psychological interviews to assess the candidate's fitness for assignment. The two agencies that would supervise the VISTA volunteers in Hawaii were the Honolulu Community Action Program (HCAP) and Queen Liliuokalani Children's Trust (LT). HCAP was one of several agencies created through President Johnson's War on Poverty. Queen Liliuokalani Children Trust (LT) was one of the large estate trusts that were established to protect land and provide social and educational services for Native Hawaiians.

Among the training staff were John Hayakawa from the University of Hawaii School Of Public Health; Larry Koseki, the director of HCAP; Hideo Tanaka, the director of LT; some of the previous year's VISTA volunteers; a small group of psychologists; and Harry McKnight, from the VISTA national office. Buzz Gilbert and Bill Sutkus were the VISTA leaders who heeded Dyke Hendrickson's recommendation and facilitated my assignment to Hawaii.

Of the forty candidates who attended the training, thirty of us were going to be selected to go to Hawaii. We were from all over the country, mostly recent graduates from community colleges or universities. There were two married couples and the rest of us were single. Many of the guys were like me and had joined VISTA to avoid getting drafted.

After a couple days of orientation, we were informed that we would not be allowed to stay in our dorms for the next two nights. We had to demonstrate our resourcefulness by finding a place to stay in one of the impoverished San Francisco communities. My roommate and I set off for the Mission District, where many of the residents were of Mexican descent. Jim was confident we could maneuver in the neighborhood with his high school Spanish. We had no plans other than to hang out at the bars and see if we could pick up some women.

As we were sipping our Dos Equis, trying to figure out what we were going to do next, Jim decided to play some pool. Before I knew it, we were no longer paying for beers, and Jim was challenging all comers.

"You never told me you were a pool hustler."

"How do you think I paid for college?"

"You're full of surprises."

We didn't pay for another beer for the rest of the afternoon, and we performed our own version of community organization by dominating the pool table for several hours. Jim's Spanglish and exceptional pool skills allowed us not only to bond with the affable bar patrons, but the bartender/owner also let us crash at his apartment above the bar. As I spent more time with Jim, I found out that he had also been a high school wrestler, was homesick for his girlfriend, and was ambivalent about becoming a VISTA volunteer.

After our two-day adventure in the Mission District, we rejoined the rest of the trainees. Apparently the majority of them had wound up sleeping at a church shelter in the Tenderloin District.

The staff posted their list of the thirty volunteers selected to serve in Hawaii. While several candidates had been un-selected, some of them, including Jim, decided they didn't want to be volunteers. He ended up joining the Marines. Those of us who made the cut were assigned a partner and a community project.

26

WE MILLED AROUND THE LUGGAGE CAROUSEL AT THE HONOLULU airport, waiting for our suitcases. I got some cynical looks from some of the volunteers and staff when I grabbed the golf bag and clubs I had brought with me.

Dick Brown and I had been paired up to work together in Palolo Valley, which was located near Kaimuki, adjacent to Manoa Valley. Palolo Housing, a federal low-income housing project, consisted of several identical two-story concrete apartment buildings. Our vague assignment was to help this community address and resolve any of their issues. The residents were primarily single mothers on welfare with households full of kids. The population encompassed a mixture of races and ethnicities, primarily Hawaiians, Portuguese, Pacific Islanders, Asians, and a few whites, referred to as haoles. The indigenous Hawaiian population was dwindling as a result of intermarriage with other ethnic groups. Palolo was one of three of the HCAP projects located in Honolulu, along with Mayor Wright Housing in Palama and Kuhio Park Terrace in Kalihi.

My roommate, Dick, was a skinny, shy, freckled kid with an associate's degree from Thief River Falls, Minnesota. He wore thick black glasses, came from a family of seven kids, had never been away from home, and was a self-described nerd. He thought VISTA would be a good experience and a nice break before he returned to college to obtain a teaching degree. We temporarily stayed in an apartment rented by an HCAP employee who was away on a mainland vacation. The following week, we moved into the apartment of Wendell Sparks, the previous year's volunteer who, after a week-long overlap with us, would return to his home in Kentucky.

We sat in the makeshift office facing our new boss, Clancy Bunyon, Director of the Palolo Community Action Program (PCAP).

"You guys are going to have some big shoes to fill. Wendell was popular and very effective at relating to the community. His youth group spent last spring doing yard work and earned enough money to take a trip to Kauai. You will be living in a fishbowl. The whole community will be watching you with high expectations. Val Valasco, our Community Social Worker, will work with you. I'm available for any additional assistance. Good luck. This will be a life-changing experience."

Our VISTA duties were ambiguous and we struggled to find something meaningful to do. It soon became apparent that Wendell was going to keep us at arm's length and made little effort to help us get to know his kids or help us take over where he left off. Apparently, he decided that since he struggled for a year to be accepted by the community, we should also have to struggle. He spent his remaining week saying goodbye to friends he'd made in the neighborhood. We went to his going away party and judging by the number in attendance, it was obvious he had made an impact.

As we continued to flounder after his departure, we became increasingly frustrated that Wendell hadn't provided us more assistance. Our immediate supervisor, Val Valasco, a mixed-Hawaiian woman in her mid-thirties with a master's degree in social work from the University of Hawaii, was visually impaired. She always wore a brightly patterned muumuu and was engaging, articulate, and knew the community well. During our first couple of weeks, we would dutifully give Val a ride to and from the office, where she assigned us some meaningless bureaucratic office tasks.

Dick and I enjoyed talking to Val. She sympathized with our difficulty in sorting out our role in the community, especially considering we were following in the wake of the venerated Wendell. She loved to gossip, knew everything about everyone, and had a great sense of humor. After several weeks of hanging out at the office, shooting the breeze with Val, Dick and I realized we were just going to have to get out into the community and find something to do.

Dick liked little kids and was comfortable with the 9-to-5 structure of the Head Start Program. Part of Johnson's War on Poverty, Head Start was a comprehensive early-childhood program for low-income preschool-age children and their families.

When the fall academic year began, I was invited to participate in a task force, comprised of counselors from the Palolo area schools, community clergy, and other social service personnel, who were trying to develop strategies to address the school drop-out rates, drug abuse, and delinquency.

I became involved coordinating a program that recruited college students to serve as tutors for elementary, middle school, and high school students. This required pairing tutors with kids, coordinating transportation, obtaining school supplies, and identifying places to meet. This program produced modest results.

Since I had been a college wrestler, I decided to introduce wrestling to the middle school. Working with the vice principal, I got permission to borrow the school bus to drive six middle school kids to the high school twice a week to teach them to wrestle. After securing permission from the coach, we practiced in the wrestling room. The program lasted only a couple of weeks as participation and interest slowly fizzled.

Being a VISTA volunteer in Hawaii was an eye-opener for me. Growing up middle class in the suburbs of New York, I had little exposure to other lifestyles. Both my parents worked, so I was raised by black maids. They were like members of our family, and when my parents were not at home, they were the ones who raised my brother and me. The perception in town was that my high school was completely integrated, having eleven African-American students in my graduating class of two hundred and nineteen students. I had a few black friends, one of whom was Gene Carruthers. He was not only one of the co-captains of the football team, but also vice president of the Student Council my senior year. However, the reality was that most of the black families lived in the low-income apartments down by the river. The same was true at F&M, where only 5% of the student body was African-American. They were relegated to about three of the twelve fraternities on campus. Our fraternity had no black members and had only allowed Jewish students in the previous couple of years I was in college. So I found myself for the first time in my life in the minority and experiencing subtle hostility in the land of Aloha. It didn't help matters that I couldn't understand the pidgin English that was spoken there.

My exposure to poverty was sobering. After moving out of converted Army barrack housing when I was six, my family always lived comfortably in upper-middle class neighborhoods. My Palolo neighbors were primarily single mothers on welfare with a house full of kids and a boyfriend who may or may not show up on weekends. Unfortunately, when one did drop by, it wasn't unusual for there to be some excessive drinking, often leading to loud brawls. Though nearly every family could somehow afford a television, the apartments were sparsely furnished, and most had to depend on the bus system for transportation.

Dick and I each bought motorcycles to get around. Whenever we were bored, frustrated, or depressed, we could be in Waikiki or at the campus of the University of Hawaii within fifteen minutes. A lot of the VISTA volunteers experienced frustration and boredom and spent many evenings sitting around, drinking, debating politics, whining, and contemplating our futures. Many of us had joined VISTA to avoid the draft, so much of our conversation revolved around the war and the historical events occurring around us, including the civil rights movement and the war on poverty.

Reading was a constant pastime of mine. I had arrived in Hawaii having read James Michener's *Hawaii*, which proved to be a very useful primer to understanding the history and culture of the islands. I later read Michener's *The Source* about the creation of Israel. As the months progressed, my reading moved from fiction to non-fiction, mostly pertaining to Vietnam, civil rights, psychology, and a range of other subjects that were relevant to the times and my circumstances. In addition to reading, we spent time watching television, playing card games, and working jigsaw puzzles. We wrote letters to friends and relatives, and a barometer of our respective moods was whether or not we received mail.

College had been the happiest and best social experience of my life. I was surrounded by a large group of great friends. My dream of being a popular "big man on campus" had finally been attained. I had been co-captain of my college wrestling team and vice president of my fraternity. Wrestling was the most prestigious and popular sport at the school since, as a small school, it was the only sport where we competed at a Division I level. Living in the fraternity house was heaven, surrounded by twenty-five fellow hedonists I felt completely compatible with.

After serial dating in college, I had finally fallen in love during my senior year. Lenna was a senior at Skidmore College in upstate New York and we started dating the second semester of my senior year. There was instant chemistry between us. She was gorgeous, funny, and smart, and fortunately, we liked each other's friends. I felt blessed to have a girlfriend to share my senior year with. When I left for VISTA, she applied to be a stewardess, and our hope was that she might be assigned to a Honolulu route. As time passed, that plan didn't materialize and she eventually got a job as a stockbroker and moved to New York City. We corresponded by mail and exchanged occasional phone calls. Long-distance relationships being inherently difficult, it was understood that we would date others and just see if the relationship would survive.

My first several months in VISTA, I maintained a cordial but superficial relationship with the other volunteers. I missed the close friendships with my fraternity brothers and I spent a lot of time thinking about Lenna. The lack of structure and direction pretty much meant we did what we wanted. Emotionally I was a mess. Though my primary motivation to be a VISTA volunteer was to avoid the draft, I was also hoping it might help me sort out what I wanted to do with my life. I considered myself a caring and compassionate person, but I had no burning desire to save the world. On one hand, I felt an obligation to fulfill my VISTA responsibilities and find something meaningful to do. On the other, I was a twenty-one-year-old red-blooded hedonist living in Hawaii.

Interestingly, I was plagued with the same guilt-ridden dilemma that I faced in college: have fun or study. If I headed to the beach or threw my golf bag on my back, there was always that voice in the back of my head: "You have an obligation to fulfill your duties as a VISTA volunteer." Most of us in VISTA were in the same situation, but unlike in college, where there was always someone looking to have fun and not study, the volunteers were reasonably responsible individuals, and I had not made any close friends. Consequently, I would often sleep until noon and wake up bored, depressed, and feeling guilty.

27

OUR NEXT-DOOR NEIGHBORS IN PALOLO WERE THE CUTZINGERS, A single mother bringing up three boys and two girls. They were part Hawaiian, Portuguese, and haole. Wally was the youngest boy. He would race over as soon as he saw that Dick and I were home. He was in first grade and very precocious, funny, smart, and engaging. We loved having Wally over and let him watch television with us and we'd occasionally help him with his homework. His older brother Randy was eleven and in the sixth grade. He hated school, had difficulty making friends, and was depressed and troubled.

Randy's mother asked if I would make sure he got to school and see that he completed his homework. Several days a week, I would walk him to school and often stay in class with him. As time went on, it became more and more difficult to even get him out of bed, much less get him to school. Most of the teachers were haole or non-Hawaiian locals, and none spoke Pidgin English, the dialect of his community. There was a subtle disdain for kids who lived in the project. Textbook illustrations were limited to white kids in suburban environments. None of the books depicted kids who looked like him, or scenes from the islands. The teachers and much of the curriculum were foreign to him.

I reflected on how dull and uninspiring my own academic experience had been and how I wished I could be retaking those courses now, armed with my newfound curiosity and quest for answers. I was motivated to read about and discuss poverty, discrimination and the war. I remembered how I'd procrastinate and drag myself to the library to struggle through my reading assignments and how bored I'd be in class. This was in such contrast to my compulsive motivation to read and discuss things now.

It struck me that education could be meaningful and enjoyable if it coincided with one's interests. At the age of twenty-one, the impracticality of that notion hadn't occurred to me, but it was a novel concept and I went with it. I knew I wasn't blessed with superior intelligence, but if my classes weren't so boring, I was sure I could have achieved a higher GPA. There was the additional disappointment of never having had a meaningful relationship with any of the faculty. It annoyed me that my motivation to study and immerse myself in intellectual pursuit might have gotten a kick start if I'd only had a mentor or a faculty member who showed any interest in me.

So I could relate to Randy's sense of alienation. He was smart, but he just wasn't motivated. And I worried about Wally, who was so bright and engaged now. Would he eventually become embittered and start to hate school like his older brother?

***

Dyke Hendrickson, the college roommate who had been responsible for my Hawaii assignment, was in his second year as a VISTA volunteer in Hawaii. He was assigned to the Halawa housing project, about a forty-minute drive from Honolulu. He had established a close relationship with two of the VISTA leaders, Buzz Gilbert and Bill Sutkus, and my roommate Dick and I eventually became good friends with them. We would all go drinking at watering holes near the University or at night clubs in Waikiki. Buzz and I occasionally played golf together, and Bill consistently kicked my ass at handball at the local YMCA.

Another close relationship we developed was with Larry Harrington, a VISTA volunteer from Massachusetts who had graduated from Fairfield University in Connecticut. He had initially been assigned to Job Corps, another program conceived as part of Johnson's War on Poverty. Job Corps was located about a half hour from Palolo and Larry would come over to our apartment and we'd watch television or go for a beer. He reminded me of my fraternity brothers, whose interactions were typically laced with sarcastic teasing and self-deprecating humor. He was eventually transferred to a project on the Big Island of Hawaii.

***

On December 4, all the Hawaii volunteers attended a VISTA conference on Maui. One of the speakers, a University of Hawaii psychology professor, Scott McDonald, got me interested in his program for high school and middle school dropouts living on the leeward side of the island in Nanakuli. McDonald used surfing to create an educational curriculum for those kids. They read books, wrote stories, learned math and science using surfing as the unifying theme.

This approach made so much sense to me and stimulated my own interest in reading about learning theory, which included *Summerhill*, about a British boarding school founded in 1921. The school's philosophy was that learning should be directed by the student, who decides what they want to learn and how they want to learn it. At the age of twenty-one, the impracticality of this notion hadn't occurred to me, but it was a new and exciting concept that I hoped to put into practice.

I made several valuable contacts at the conference, including John Sharpe and Ray Kimura. John was an imposing African-American guy who used to play college football on the mainland. He was a youth outreach worker at Palama Settlement, a social services center for the low-income neighborhood of Palama. Ray worked as a youth outreach worker for the Kalihi YMCA. They both had extensive experience dealing with troubled juveniles. John invited me to visit him in Palama to observe the different programs and activities available to the kids he worked with.

When the conference ended, Larry, Dick and I decided to rent motorcycles and explore the island. Maui is basically two volcanoes joined by an isthmus. We planned to ride from Lahaina, near the smaller volcano, to Haleakala, the larger one. Somehow we were under the impression that the entire road around Haleakala was paved.

By the time we picked up the motorcycles, it was six in the evening and getting dark, so we spent the night in borrowed sleeping bags on the beach in Wailea on the Haleakala side. We woke early and awakened to a typically hot, clear day. Our plan was to take a leisurely four-hour ride to Hana, have some lunch, and then ride for another couple of hours to Lahaina. After about a two-hour ride along smooth, barely traveled paved road, we reached Kaupo and there the paved road ended. We were faced with miles of washed out rutted dirt paths, often requiring us to walk our bikes. What we assumed would be a two-hour ride from Kaupo to Hana turned out to be a seven-hour grueling stop and start slog. Our bikes fell several times as we attempted to push them over rough terrain and through stretches of sharp, treacherous lava rock.

The ordeal left little time to enjoy the beautiful view of the ocean or banter with the hippies we met who were hiking out of Haleakala or camping along this rural stretch of the island. We were totally wasted by the time we reached Hana. Now we had to get our bikes back to the motorcycle rental shop in Lahaina before six, but we faced the winding, precarious 52-mile ride along Hana Hwy and thirty additional miles to Lahaina. We made it back to the rental place with five minutes to spare, exhausted and very much relieved. Once we turned in our bikes, Larry looked at us, pulled out his American Express card and grinned.

"Let's get a room at the Banyan Tree Inn, take a hot shower, and get something to eat and drink. And then get some more to drink—my treat!" I wanted to kiss him on the lips, but settled for a wet one on his cheek.

28

*ENZO CALLED AND SAID HE WAS GOING TO VISIT ME IN HAWAII BE-*fore he returned to New York after his year in VISTA ended. He showed up in Honolulu on January 8, 1969 bearing gifts. He had purchased Beatles, Cream, Doors and Sergio Mendes albums at the famous Tower Record store in San Francisco. He also brought along a lid of grass. It was the first we'd seen each other since I saw him in Oakland during my VISTA training. We compared notes on our respective VISTA experiences, and reflected on how we had changed since leaving home and college. Our conversations covered the gamut from Vietnam and inner-city poverty, to a host of social issues that we had been grappling with. And, of course, we updated each other on the status of mutual friends. It was great to have my best friend with me to share this experience.

Bill Oshiro, one of Enzo's VISTA roommates from Hawaii, informed his family that Enzo was visiting and they invited us over for dinner. Bill's father was a cigar-smoking avid golfer and quite a character. He showed us a newspaper clipping of himself up in a tree, watching the Hawaiian Open professional golf tournament. We also met Bill's sister Mary, who was an attractive junior at UH.

I introduced Enzo to my VISTA friends, Buzz, and Bill, and we saw Dyke, who Enzo knew from our fraternity at F&M. I took him for lunch at the swanky Outrigger Canoe Club on Waikiki Beach, which I had access to through a reciprocal relationship with my dad's membership at the New York Athletic Club.

On January 11, Enzo and I flew to the Big Island to visit Larry Harrington and his roommate Art, or A.T. As I walked off the plane, Larry sprinted across the tarmac and jumped into my arms, his legs wrapped around my waist. He was happy to see me. Larry and A.T. rented an old house located in the shadow of Mauna Loa Volcano with a porch offering an amazing view of the ocean. A.T., whom we affectionately referred to as the Japanese House Boy, made us dinner and later we sat around listening to music and smoking some of Enzo's grass.

The next day was the AFL/NFL football championship game. It was going to be televised at eight in the morning in Hawaii due to a six-hour time difference. In preparation, we had purchased three cases of Primo, a popular locally brewed beer. We all rooted for the New York Jets and their flamboyant quarterback, Joe "Willie" Namath. The Baltimore Colts were the heavy favorites and had been rated the best NFL team the previous ten years. This was the third championship game between the two football leagues and with the Jets providing the first AFL win of the series, this annual competition became known as the Super Bowl. Our consumption of Primo continued throughout the morning and by the end of the Jets' 16-7 upset, we were deliriously happy and completely inebriated. After the game, we took pictures of ourselves celebrating, then staggered down to the beach and spent the rest of the day swimming. Enzo and I flew back to Honolulu the next day, after a great weekend and a Super Bowl game that cemented my friendship with Larry.

29

AFTER OUR DINNER AT THE OSHIRO'S, I INVITED BILL'S SISTER MARY to meet Enzo and me for lunch at the University of Hawaii's East West Center. The place was designed by my father's architectural firm, I.M. Pei and Partners, and accommodated an education and research organization established to strengthen relations and understanding among the Asian-Pacific nations and the United States. We had a nice lunch and walked around campus a bit before Mary left to go to class. After Enzo went back to New York, I asked her out to the movies.

The following weekend, I rode my motorcycle through the Pali tunnel to her home on the other side of the island. Her parents lent us their Toyota sedan so Mary wouldn't have to ride my motorcycle. We went to a W. C. Fields movie on campus. Fortunately, she shared my appreciation for old comedy. After the movie, we went to my favorite University hang out, the Gingerman, shared a pitcher of beer, and got to know each other. She was a junior at UH majoring in sociology. We shared our backgrounds, my work as a VISTA, and our political views.

The next weekend, she drove to my Palolo apartment, and we rode on my motorcycle to Haunama Bay for sunbathing and snorkeling. Back at my apartment, we sat on the bedroom floor, listening to the albums that Enzo had brought over from San Francisco, and smoked his pot. I put on the *Sgt. Pepper* album and we slowly explored each other's palms and fingers as we held hands.

For the first time, I was truly stoned. I had smoked with Enzo a half a dozen times and experienced a slight buzz, but this time was different. I was experiencing marijuana as an aphrodisiac. Our erotic movements were in synch with the music, and I could hear every instrument and distinguish every musical nuance.

After a while, I lifted my head to look at Mary and, in my altered state, saw that I was with an Asian woman for the first time, and I started to laugh. She began to laugh, not really knowing why I was laughing, but the laughter was contagious and uncontrollable as we cracked each other up. Suddenly, I was overcome by hunger. We raced to the refrigerator and scavenged for whatever was available. I unscrewed a jar of chunky Peter Pan, scooped out a spoonful, and it was if I was discovering peanut butter for the first time. I marveled at the texture, chewing each chunk of peanut and thoroughly savoring its sweet, creamy, oily flavor. My mind was reeling.

"You know, this is the first time I've ever gotten stoned. Music sounds different and I got the munchies for the first time. And I can't remember ever laughing so hard or being so horny."

She giggled and planted an approving kiss.

Mary and I continued to date through the spring. We appreciated each other's company and shared a common interest in discussing contemporary social issues. We hung out at the Gingerman bar and went to the beach and the movies with my VISTA friends. Though I enjoyed our relationship, I was still not over Lenna.

30

JUVENILE DELINQUENCY WAS A SERIOUS PROBLEM IN THE PALOLO housing project. Many of the kids were dropouts and drug users and were often involved in vandalism and petty theft. The preferred high was inhaling vapors from glue, gasoline, or spray paint. They would pour or spray the substance onto a cloth and inhale the noxious vapor. The effects ranged from an alcohol-like intoxication to intense euphoria and vivid hallucinations, depending on the substance and dose. When high, sniffers often engage in dangerous and violent behavior. Brain damage occurs in chronic, long-term users.

John Lynch was a notorious neighborhood paint sniffer and at the age of twenty-one (my age), he was an unusually old sniffer. He was homeless and either crashed with friends or slept under bushes. Wendell hadn't given us much advice before he left, but he warned us about John Lynch. He recommended we steer clear of him. About six months after we moved into the project, John started showing up at our apartment. He was wary at first, but as he got to know us, he let his guard down. He was never hostile or aggressive around us, and we would invite him in to watch TV and have a bite to eat, as long as he hadn't been sniffing, which was easy to smell.

We reported our interactions with Johnny Lynch to our supervisor.

"Hey Val, John Lynch has started hanging around our apartment."

She raised her eyebrows and called over to CAP director, Clancy

Bunyon. "Clancy, did you know these guys have made contact with John Lynch?"

"That's interesting. How's he been behaving?" he asked.

"He's been pretty pleasant and friendly around us. We invite him in to watch TV and we'll feed him, as long as he hasn't been sniffing," I replied.

"Well, be careful, he's one of the oldest sniffers in the neighborhood and he has a following," Clancy warned.

"If you could develop a trusting relationship with him, this could be significant. Paint sniffing is probably one of the toughest problems in this community," Val said. "Be careful, but keep us posted. This could have possibilities."

As time went on, Dick and I decided to work with John and we invited him to live with us. We told him he could stay if he looked for a job and quit sniffing. He was the gateway to interacting with the Palolo sniffer community, and with his amiable personality, he was a role model of sorts. A lot of the younger kids looked up to him because he had been living on his own for years and seemed to be happy. He had been arrested multiple times for a variety of petty crimes. Though we didn't know all the details, we figured out he was from a part-Hawaiian family, his father was not in the picture, and he had multiple siblings, several of whom had dropped out of school, abused drugs, and were familiar with the criminal justice system. Slowly but surely, more and more sniffers started hanging around the house.

John had a following of young kids that he would indoctrinate. The process involved buying or stealing a can of spray paint, soaking a washcloth with the paint (preferably clear, silver, or gold), rolling the cloth into a tube and inhaling the vapor by mouth. Paint sniffing is often a group activity and the paint saturated cloth is passed from one sniffer to the next. They not only reek of paint, but their speech and motor skills are severely impaired. They slur their words, stagger around, and often pass out. When they try to describe their graphic hallucinations, they seem to be in a state of stupefied euphoria.

In order to introduce some structure into John's life, we allowed him to sleep on our living room couch as long as he wasn't high on paint, and we'd feed him as long as he cleaned the dishes. After a few weeks of successfully following the rules, we took him to job training opportunities. It was a very slow and difficult process. Sometimes he'd show up at the house loaded, and we'd tell him he couldn't stay. We'd set up an appointment for him with job training and sometimes he wouldn't show up.

***

In February of 1969, I attended a conference on behavior modification, conducted by the psychology department of the University of Hawaii. I listened in on presentations about using token economies to reinforce behavior in a variety of settings, including schools, hospitals, and therapeutic settings. This really excited me, because it gave me a new approach to dealing with John and the other sniffers we were working with. It got me thinking about a future career, as I contemplated graduate school in psychology. I had hoped when I joined VISTA that I might be able to figure out what I wanted to do with my life, and now here it was.

31

MY POLITICAL AND INTELLECTUAL GROWTH DURING MY YEAR IN VISTA was intense. I had had a very close relationship with my father in college, especially after my mother died my sophomore year. He was a staunch Republican and had been a supporter of Eisenhower, and subsequently of Nixon. Together we observed and commented on the social upheaval that was occurring during my college years. We shared a disdain for the long-haired protesters, and were troubled by the growing prevalence of drug use. America's involvement in the war was crucial in halting the communism we feared would spread throughout Southeast Asia and beyond. But we were also concerned about how the war was being conducted, and my father supported my reluctance to enlist. He felt VISTA would be a worthwhile experience.

During my senior year, Lenna and I presented a united front, defending capitalism and conservatism in heated discussions with our more liberal college friends. In November, I was old enough to vote in the 1968 election and unlike most of my VISTA friends, I voted for Nixon.

As the year progressed, I engaged in extended discussions with a variety of people, including my fellow VISTA's, about Vietnam, poverty, racism, and a range of social issues. These discussions were supplemented with considerable reading and attendance at numerous lectures that were offered at the University of Hawaii. *Warfare State* was a book suggested by Dyke that challenged my political view. Author Fred Cook addressed the "military industrial complex," outlining how our economy's growth was dependent on the production of weaponry. This term gained popularity after its use in President Dwight Eisenhower's farewell address in 1961. Other books that solidified my opposition to Vietnam included: *Vietnam: Crisis of Conscience*, by Robert Brown, Abraham Heschel, and Michael Novak; *War Crimes of Vietnam*, by Bertrand Russell; and *Dr. Spock on Vietnam*, written by Dr. Benjamin Spock, the doctor who provided child rearing advice to a generation of baby boomer parents.

Spock's book elaborated on the colonial history of Vietnam, which included its successive occupation by the Chinese, Dutch, Japanese, and French. This framed the war as a struggle for their independence from colonial rule, not unlike our own Revolutionary War. The conflict between North and South Vietnam was more of a civil war and our interference and involvement was not only inappropriate but immoral. It became apparent that the spread of communism or the "domino theory" was flawed. Communism wasn't a monolithic system. The form of communism in the Soviet Union was different from that of China, which was in turn different from the form of communism in North Korea and in Cuba. In some cases, there was as much animosity among those countries as there was between them and us.

My examination of Vietnam also led to a comparison of economic systems. Supporting democracy was a given, but I went through a period of comparing the pros and cons of capitalism and socialism. I read Ayn Rand's books, *The Fountain Head, Atlas Shrugged*, and *The Virtue of Selfishness*, which supported capitalism. But living in a low-income housing project, I began to appreciate the barriers that the families in Palolo faced, and I became more critical of the concept of capitalism.

This was reinforced when I read Eric Fromme's *Man for Himself* and *The Sane Society*, which started an exploration of the nature of capitalism. Fromme argued for a humanistic and democratic socialism and described a variety of social pathologies related to our preoccupation with materialism.

The inequities I felt were inherent in a capitalist system appeared to be compounded by racial discrimination. Hawaii had, in fact, been colonized just as Vietnam had been, and the poverty suffered by the Hawaiian population echoed that experience. I read the *Autobiography of Malcolm X, Soul on Ice, Manchild in the Promised Land*, and a number of books addressing the Black Power movement. They provided me with explanations for why these kids were dropping out and turning to inhalants. I began to understand why they weren't performing well in school and had difficulty developing the skills to get jobs. Substance abuse was almost understandable, considering the obstacles these kids faced every day.

At the University, I attended a number of lectures by distinguished speakers such as Saul Alinsky, who demonstrated the power of community organization by highlighting projects conducted in inner-city communities in Chicago, New York City, Michigan, and California. I heard Seymour Hersh, a Pulitzer Prize-winning journalist, who reported on the My Lai massacre and reinforced my opposition to the Vietnam War.

My head was spinning and as the year progressed, my views and values changed. I had left college and New York strongly and emotionally attached to my father and striving for his approval. I wanted to be able to articulate my new world view with compelling facts, and not just a bunch of radical clichés. I knew that I was going to have to explain to him how a conservative supporter of Nixon had evolved into a critic of capitalism and our government, and knew I better have my shit together. Because my father would not be able to accept that my conversion happened just because I had spent a year "saving the world" in Hawaii.

32

I TOOK A TRIP BACK HOME IN MARCH AND SCHEDULED IT SO THAT I could attend the Intra-Fraternity Weekend at F&M. I suspected my relationship with Lenna was on the rocks when she told me she had other plans for that weekend. Instead, I invited Kathy Smith, who both Enzo and I had dated while we were in college.

My father made dinner reservations at the New York Athletic Club, where I arranged to meet Lenna. After exchanging greetings and ordering our dinner, I abruptly announced that my political views had evolved and that "capitalism stinks." Lenna gasped and my father took a long swig of his vodka martini. That blunt announcement sabotaged any chance for a meaningful discussion and resulted in a barrage of defensive and useless exchanges that spoiled the dinner and created a tension that took the rest of my visit to diffuse. I had gained confidence in expressing my views when I was in Hawaii among my peers, but I became tongue-tied trying to convince the people I loved.

I went into culture shock at the F&M fraternity weekend. After having spent a year living in a Hawaiian housing project, immersed in a multi-cultural, multi-ethnic environment, and preoccupied with my newly acquired liberal views, my system was shell-shocked by this sudden immersion into mindless hedonism. This fraternity romp was like being in a post-adolescent Disneyland of beer drinking, infantile insults, flirting with girls, and dancing. My resentment toward F&M for my dismal grades still festered. I blamed "the system" for my not having been stimulated and motivated enough to do better academically.

All I really cared about in college were women, wrestling, avoiding studying, and hanging out with my fraternity brothers. After my disastrous attempts to discuss my new political positions with my father and Lenna, I found myself ill at ease at school. There was no way I could begin to describe to anyone except Enzo what my year had been like. I couldn't tell anyone that what they were into was just frivolous escapism. We were on different planets.

I went to one of the team's wrestling practices and initially managed to take down John Stevenson, one of their freshmen studs at 190. But then he proceeded to totally dominate me. Things turned even weirder when Enzo and I ended up with each other's dates. He spent more time with Kathy Smith, a girl he had dated at F&M, and I ended up with his date, Gail Cutler, whom I dated my junior year. Being with Enzo was one of the few comforts I experienced that weekend. He was a masterful storyteller and mimic, and we spent hours at his apartment making each other laugh.

One of the highlights of the weekend was dinner at Dean Lacy's home. The Dean of Students, O. W. Lacy, who we called the Owl, taught Abnormal Psychology, which I took my senior year. He had been the only professor who ever cared that I was a varsity wrestler and he would often congratulate me after matches. When I spotted him on campus, we talked for a while. I mentioned I had served nine months as a VISTA volunteer, and he seemed intrigued. He generously invited me over to his place for dinner, something which never happened when I had been an undergraduate student. After having worn his hair in a crew-cut his entire tenure at F&M, he now sported shoulder-length hair, which was a little shocking.

He and his wife were the first people with whom I had a meaningful conversation since I returned from Hawaii. It was almost like a therapy session. They never challenged or refuted any of my opinions, especially my tirade about my lack of academic achievement at F&M. I acknowledged my own immaturity and preoccupation with hedonism and admitted I wasn't as disciplined and responsible a student as I could have been. But I faulted the faculty for what I felt was indifference toward their student's success. Dean Lacy was interested in my experience with paint sniffers and we had an interesting and open discussion about drugs in general. I felt comfortable enough to go into detail about my experience smoking pot.

I returned home after my weekend at school and tried to resume my conversation with my father. Neither of us enjoyed confrontations and he patiently listened as I attempted once again to articulate my new set of values. I didn't change his mind, but I think he understood where I was coming from and the tension eased. Lenna and I went out to dinner that evening and she made it clear that she didn't see a future in our relationship. It wasn't a complete surprise, but it still hurt. After this difficult visit home, I looked forward to my return to Hawaii.

33

ONCE I RECONCILED MYSELF WITH THE REALITY THAT LENNA AND I were no longer a couple, my relationship with Mary resumed with renewed ardor. We continued to see each other but, with my VISTA termination date approaching and my future uncertain, we both sort of allowed the relationship to run its course.

Peter Goo, the Kaimuki High School wrestling coach who had provided me access to his facility for my junior high school wrestling program, introduced me to the Hawaii wrestling community. Several Olympic Style wrestling tournaments were scheduled for the spring, after the high school wrestling season concluded. I wanted to compete in them, so Pete put me in touch with a number of workout partners, including his assistant coach Matt Kline, who was the defending AAU 149-pound champion. Matt was a pre-med student at UH and had been a high school wrestler in Oklahoma, one of the strongest wrestling states in the country. We soon began to work out at the high school and at the Nuuanu YMCA. Over time, I ended up meeting more wrestlers and got to work out on a regular basis.

The high school wrestling season begins in November and ends in March. I supplemented my meager $100 a month VISTA salary by working as a high school referee, giving me better access to the Hawaii wrestling scene.

The University of Hawaii didn't have an official wrestling team, but it did sponsor an informal wrestling club. Each branch of the Armed Services, including the Army, Navy, Marines, and Coast Guard, had their own teams. Drawing from those teams, as well as some outstanding high school and post-college wrestlers, the Hawaii spring wrestling tournaments were highly competitive. Folkstyle or Scholastic wrestling is a form of amateur wrestling practiced mostly in high schools and colleges. It consists mainly of mat wrestling, and rewards control. The two styles sanctioned by the Olympics, Freestyle and Greco-Roman, are practiced throughout the world and were the styles sanctioned by the Hawaii spring tournaments.

Both Freestyle and Greco-Roman emphasize back exposure. Greco-Roman is restricted to upper body moves, and doesn't allow any attacks to the legs. I entered and won both the Freestyle and Greco-Roman tournaments in my 163-pound weight class that spring of 1969.

34

DURING MY WRESTLING WORKOUTS AT THE YMCA, I MET A FEW GUYS who played basketball on the court adjacent to our wrestling mats. Jim Treadway was a mechanical engineer who worked at Pearl Harbor. After we'd spent some time getting to know each other, he invited my roommate Dick and me to sail to Maui with him to attend the Lahaina Whaling Spree, a popular spring festival that included music, crafts, and boating contests. Neither Dick nor I had any sailing experience, but Jim assured us he had sailed to Maui before and that his 35-foot sailboat comfortably slept three. We would have to navigate between the islands of Molokai and Lanai to reach Maui. Sailing against the current, he estimated it would take about twelve hours to get there, and suggested that the best sailing conditions would be at night.

We set off for Maui at six in the evening, and Jim estimated we'd arrive in Lahaina around 6:00 a.m. He suggested we nap in the afternoon because we probably wouldn't get much sleep at night. He also urged us not to eat after lunch in order to keep from getting seasick.

He gave us an orientation of the workings of his sailboat and how we would share the responsibilities of steering the tiller and following compass directions. Initially, the ocean was fairly calm, but Jim warned us that within a couple of hours, we'd face rougher waters as we entered the channel between Molokai and Lanai. Around 8:30 p.m. we encountered a strong head wind, and Jim constantly tacked the sails to maintain the boat in the right direction. There was a spectacular sunset that evening. It gradually faded to reveal a dazzling sky filled with stars that shined even brighter as we sailed further from Honolulu's city lights.

All of a sudden, the swells began to surge and the boat pounded against a procession of waves. Jim explained that we would be tossed and slapped by these waves most of the night until we got past Lanai. I saw Dick slowly turn green, and I went downstairs to try to get some sleep. Once I closed my eyes, I was overwhelmed with nausea, raced back up, hung over the side, and proceeded to unload. When Dick saw me vomiting, he got sick too, and both of us were nauseous for the rest of the night. Mercifully, as the sun crept slowly above the horizon, the ocean calmed and we spotted the Maui coast. As predicted, we arrived around 6:00 a.m., docked, and then slept on the boat for a couple of hours.

The Lahaina Whaling Spree was unlike anything I'd ever experienced. It seemed as if every one of the flower children I'd seen in Haight-Ashbury had flown over for the festival. I even thought I spotted the space cowboy who had been up in the tree, dancing to Janis Joplin. A never-ending cavalcade of long-haired, braless hippies paraded down Front Street.

Dick and I met up with Buzz and Larry for lunch. They had flown to Lahaina for the weekend. Larry and I started to laugh as soon as we saw each other. He knew I could tell by that distinctive grin on his face that he was stoned. His blood-shot eyes were dancing as he announced, "Shows...I'm wrecked."

"We can see that."

After lunch, we took Larry and Buzz back to the boat and we all got wasted and stayed that way for the remainder of the day. My marijuana use had been limited to occasional weekends, but there in Lahaina, we got stoned as soon as we woke up in the morning and remained in that blissful state until we passed out at night. The bandstand was set up adjacent to a field bordered by a large banyan tree that provided welcome shade from the ever-present sunshine. The Steve Miller Band was scheduled to play that Saturday night.

The marina was occupied not only by boat owners from Maui and Oahu, but several from California, as well as some international adventurers who either came from or were on their way to other Pacific Islands. Among the many friendly and intoxicated people we met was John, a guy who sparked my imagination with his declaration that Hawaii had been his first stop on his plan to travel around the world. He had hired on as a seaman with a freighter to get to Hawaii from his Canadian home. He found jobs cleaning pools to earn money for the next leg of his trip, which he announced would be Australia. After we returned to Honolulu, we would often get together for a drink at the Gingerman.

Jim invited Larry to join us on our sailing voyage back to Oahu. He assured us that since we'd be travelling with the current, our return to Honolulu would be calmer. Jim and Larry pledged to remain sober in order to get us back safely. Dick and I remained wasted, stoked at the novelty of sailing while stoned. Jim captained the boat while Dick and I giggled, looking for whales and marveling at how the land masses kept changing in size as we navigated across the channel.

About an hour into the voyage, I glanced over at Jim. I was puzzled by the look on his face, and then I noticed our sailboat was slowly traveling in circles.

"Hey man, what's happening?"

"Our fucking rudder just broke off," Jim replied evenly, trying to remain calm.

"Far out," Dick giggled in his own little world.

"It's not good," Jim said grimly.

Once the seriousness of the situation set in, our exuberant high devolved into a state of terrifying paranoia.

"Without a rudder, we can't steer, and if we can't steer we're just going to keep spinning. If we miss any of these islands we'll end up in open waters, on our way to Tahiti," Jim announced with a sick look on his face.

"Let me see if this motor helps. I've only used it to maneuver into a slip once I arrive at a marina. It's not actually strong enough to power us in the open ocean."

The motor managed to slow the rotations enough so that, after seventeen long and tense hours, we were able to navigate the boat toward Molokai. We docked and scrambled out on wobbly legs, filled with enormous relief. We spent that night on the boat, and flew back to Honolulu the following day. Jim got the rudder repaired and eventually sailed his boat back to Oahu.

35

AMONG MY VISTA FRIENDS IN HONOLULU WERE JACK CURREN, WHO went to Holy Cross in Boston, and Paul Petrie from upstate New York. They lived in Kuhio Park Terrace, a low-income housing project consisting of two high-rise towers in Kalihi. Their summer project was to take some Kalihi kids to the outer Island of Molokai for a couple of weeks. They had received $250 in funding from a local church and invited me to recruit some kids from Palolo to join them. Jack wasn't able to participate, as he had to return to Boston after getting sick. Paul put me in touch with Bob Dye, who worked in the Mayor's office. Dye had been involved with a similar project taking troubled kids to Molokai the previous summer. His contacts at the University and in Molokai were extremely helpful in formulating strategies and suggesting additional funding sources. My enthusiasm for the project increased as I received a lot of encouragement and increased our funding by $1,000 from five additional sources.

Soon I was totally obsessed with the project and could think of nothing else. The prospect of a young VISTA volunteer attempting to address the intractable problem of paint sniffing was very appealing to the growing number of contacts I was making. VISTA as an organization had considerable credibility and facilitated my ability to promote my project. I eventually spoke to Governor John Burns and U.S. Senator Patsy Mink about it. It was intoxicating to have so many important people supporting me. Many of them suggested I start thinking about what to do when the kids returned from Molokai. I started exploring job training programs and possible alternatives to the school system.

I floated the prospect of the Molokai trip to gang leader John Lynch and he began recruiting participants. In addition to him, there were several kids at Palolo Housing who had either run away or had been discarded by their families. Pic had long wavy black hair, was part-Hawaiian and twenty-years old. He was missing several teeth and was difficult to understand. Lawrence "Termite" Gillarde was also part-Hawaiian but primarily Filipino. He was thirteen, small for his age, and his family had kicked him out of the house. John suggested we include his younger brother William, an angry sixteen-year-old. Gary Corpus was one of the few who came from a family with both a mother and father at home. He was fifteen, with curly hair and a quick smile. I also invited our next-door neighbor, eleven-year-old Randy.

The nine boys from Palolo were between the ages of eleven and twenty-one. Five of them were high school dropouts. None of them had jobs. Seven of the nine reported to probation officers and had spent time in either the Koolau Boys Home, the Honolulu Detention Center, and/or the Salvation Army Home for Boys. Seven were chronic sniffers. The boys Paul Petrie brought from Kalihi were a more stable, better-behaved group between the ages of fourteen and sixteen. They were all close friends and none of them had dropped out of school or sniffed paint.

Mark Merlin was a doctoral student in geography whom I had met at the University of Hawaii. He was leading a research project conducted by the anthropology department to unearth a community on Molokai that had been destroyed by a tidal wave in the early 1900's. I agreed to pay the boys to work with him on the project. This would be such a great opportunity to give them not only some work experience but exposure to their Hawaiian heritage.

Fred Bicoy, the Director of the Molokai Community Action Program (MCAP), was an indispensable resource for this project. We needed to drive through the privately owned Murphy Ranch in order to reach our campsite in Halawa Valley. He made introductions and obtained the necessary permits from Fred De Mello, the ranch foreman. Bicoy promoted our project to the community and was able to solicit $50 worth of groceries from local merchants.

Molokai is the fifth largest of the eight Hawaiian Islands. It was one of the least developed of the islands, with only one hotel and a high unemployment rate. Father Damien's Kalaupapa Leper Colony was located on the east side of the island. It was rural and populated primarily by pure Hawaiians.

We flew to Molokai on Friday, June 27, and were driven the twenty-six miles into Halawa valley in pickup trucks provided by the MCAP office. Paul and I set up separate camps for our respective groups. In order to generate cooperation and camaraderie, the boys in each camp elected their own leaders and were required to ration and cook their own food. In spite of John Lynch being the oldest, the Palolo boys surprised me by selecting fifteen-year-old Gary as their leader. They had enough food to last them for five days, but in case they ran out, Halawa Valley had an abundance of trees loaded with mangoes, coconuts, bananas, passion fruit, and mountain apples. Equipped with snorkels, fins, fishing lines and nets, we were prepared to catch the abundant fish, crab, and shrimp we saw in the cove.

I anticipated a rough week. The boys would find it difficult adjusting to camping in an isolated valley. Kaunakakai, with a population of less than 2,000 was the only large town in Molokai and was twenty-six miles from the valley. It would be challenging for them to plan, cooperate, and ration their food so that it would last for the five days. However, each boy had fishing equipment and access to all of the available fruit.

Along with letting them lead and organize themselves, they were warned that if they sniffed paint they'd be sent home. They could each earn $5 a day working with the anthropology project and were told that they could fly home when they wanted, once they had earned the $15 airfare.

I was a hands-off kind of camp counselor, and provided little guidance or supervision, hoping my Palolo kids would somehow learn to do everything on their own. One thing they didn't know how to do was ration their food and they started stealing from the Kalihi boys. They had also smuggled spray paint from Honolulu and were sniffing behind my back. When they ran out of paint, two of the boys hitched a ride out to Kaunakakai and stole some cans from a hardware store. They fought with each other and proceeded to make everyone miserable. On Tuesday July 1, after only five days, Paul arranged for six of his eight boys to fly back to Kalihi. Separating the remaining Palolo boys into two groups, I monitored the three youngest boys and let the six older ones camp together. Even though sniffing continued among the older boys, there was improvement in their behavior and they began to manage their food better. They began to take an interest in the anthropology project and earned some money and learned about the early Molokai settlement that had existed in the valley.

On July 3rd it rained heavily and the anthropology dig was called off for the day. Several of the boys began sniffing out of boredom. William, very high on paint, grabbed a thick branch and started hitting John and Daniel. Hearing the commotion, I ran over, tackled William and wrapped my legs around him, restraining him with a full nelson. His furious screaming and flailing finally subsided when he realized he couldn't escape from the hold. Once I let him go, he caught his breath and stomped off in a rage. As I was tending to John and Daniel, Randy yelled, and I looked up in time to narrowly avoid being hit by a large rock that William had hurled at my head.

The situation was spiraling out of control. Five of the boys insisted on going home. I reiterated that they could return to Honolulu once they'd earned $15 for their plane ticket by working on the anthropology dig. They ignored me and called Gary's mother who paid for the five of them to return to Honolulu on July 4th. I sent the two youngest boys back to Honolulu on July 5th. We now had two boys from Palolo and two boys from Kalihi remaining, and on July 9th the kids from Kalihi returned to Honolulu. I spent the week of July 6—12 with John Lynch, his arm broken by William, and Daniel Manako, with a broken finger. We returned to Honolulu on July 13th, with both Daniel and John paying for their own tickets, having each worked to earn the $15 fare.

The summer didn't turn out as I'd hoped. My unrealistic dream of radically changing the behaviors of this group of hardcore sniffers was not even remotely realized. None of them quit sniffing, and five out of the nine boys, with the assistance of one of their mothers, had pulled a mutiny and left. Their departure was devastating to me because, though I knew it would be difficult, I naively hoped that in such an isolated place there would be no access to spray paint and that if they weren't high all the time, maybe they could learn how to enjoy themselves sober. I hoped they would have some fun camping and fishing.

Despite the chaos and the mutiny, I loved camping in Halawa Valley. Fred DeMello, the ranch foreman, brought us venison, goat, and wild pig meat that had been hunted by his crew. I drew on my Eagle

Scout skills to show the kids how to fish, gather fruit, build a fire, cook, and construct a lean-to for sleeping. There were a number of hippies in the valley who had set up camp nearby and were living off the land. I enjoyed spending evenings over at their tents, discussing their pursuit of a more spiritual, non-materialistic lifestyle.

Those discussions sparked my own journey toward clarifying my values. I began seriously considering applying for a Conscientious Objector (CO) exemption to the draft. My resolve deepened when I learned that several other VISTA volunteers were considering applying as CO's, as was my college roommate, Jimmy Clair. This would require an examination of my personal convictions and spiritual beliefs.

Traditionally, a conscientious objector status was only awarded to someone who had been raised in a pacifist religious tradition such as the Quakers or the Mennonites. I had been brought up an Episcopalian. Due to my mother's insistence, I had been a faithful church attendee from fourth grade through high school. I had gone through confirmation and ultimately became head Crucifer, which involved leading the processional of the chorus and the minister into the church at the start of services, assisting with communion, and sitting at the altar during services.

Reverend Henry was a frequent visitor at our home during the four years of my mother's unsuccessful struggle with breast cancer. I carried the cross, lit the candles, passed the wine, and assisted with communion. I recited the prayers and made a conscious effort to listen attentively and follow the sermon, only to drift into daydreams of my girlfriend Christine's swelling breasts as the droning sermon lulled me into a stupor. My attendance and devotion to church were totally dictated by maternal pressure and I stopped going to church as soon as I left home and entered college.

As my opposition to the Vietnam War grew during my year in VISTA, I studied the philosophy of pacifism. I read *The World's Religions* by Huston Smith, the writings of Paul Tillich, the life and work of Gandhi, and of Martin Luther King, Jr. Additionally, I was drawn to the literature of Nobel Laureate Herman Hesse including *Siddhartha, Journey to the East, Narcissus and Goldmund,* and *Steppenwolf.* It seemed that one of the underlying themes of all religions, including Christianity, was forgiveness. Christ taught us to *love thy neighbor as thyself, and turn the other cheek.* War seemed to me to be the antithesis of that sentiment. It became apparent I had to choose, either to support and participate in the war, or reject and oppose it. As an Episcopalian, I wasn't raised in a pacifist tradition, so I needed to be able to articulate my religious convictions in order to justify an exemption from military service.

36

*WHEN I RETURNED TO HONOLULU, I WROTE A REPORT OF MY SUM*mer on Molokai with the Palolo kids. I called it the Molokai Youth Project. My report was read by Larry Koseki, Director of the Honolulu CAP, and he approved my request to extend my year-long obligation by three months, through October. This was an attempt to ensure some continuity for my program, which I referred to as the Palolo Youth Project. I needed those extra months to make sure the transition went smoothly for the VISTA volunteers that would replace me, unlike my experience following Wendell Sparks.

***

One evening, after returning to Honolulu, I was spending time at my favorite watering hole and ran across my friend John, whom I had met at the Whaling Spree in Maui, the one who had dazzled me with his plans to travel around the world.

"Hey John, how you doing?"

"Hey Bruce, meet Leo Dubois."

"Hey Leo."

"Leo's in the Coast Guard and he's very short."

I eyed Leo. "Short?"

"Yeah, I get out in a couple of weeks."

"Oh okay, are you happy about that?"

"Big time."

"Bruce is a VISTA volunteer in Palolo."

"What's that?" Leo asked.

"VISTA is like the domestic Peace Corps. Volunteers get year-long assignments to work in impoverished communities in the U.S. I've spent the year living in Palolo Housing," I explained.

"Bruce is involved in a pretty interesting project. He works with some rough Hawaiian kids that have dropped out of school, and a lot of them sniff paint."

"You know I've seen some of them down near our Coast Guard base. Those kids get pretty screwed up. What's with paint?"

"It's the poor man's drug. They'd be smoking pot or taking pills if they had the dough, but paint is cheap and really intense," I explained.

"I hear you can get brain damage and sometimes OD and die."

"Yeah, that's true," I confirmed.

"So what do you do?" Leo asked.

"Tell him about your trip to Molokai," John suggested.

After hearing about the Molokai summer project, Leo asked if he could come to Palolo sometime and check out the scene.

"I think what you're doing is pretty cool. Now that I'm short with the Coast Guard, I have a lot of spare time. I could take some pictures if you'd like to document the activities."

***

As the summer progressed, I was able to enlist additional help for the project. In July, Ted Hyde and Mark Bauer were assigned as the new Palolo VISTA volunteers who would replace Dick and me. Though they weren't required to live in the housing as I had been, they soon got involved in the Palolo Youth Project. Leo, over time, became a regular companion. He developed a genuine rapport with the kids and he could speak the local pidgin. Not only was he an accomplished photographer, but he was very artistic and before long was encouraging the kids to draw. We found many of the sniffers were quite talented artists.

John Lynch, who hadn't demonstrated the leadership I'd hoped to see in Molokai, unexpectedly turned into a supporter after we returned to Honolulu. He convinced the community that I genuinely cared about the boys and was trying to help. The kids eventually trickled back to the apartment and I was able to continue to work with them. Dick finished his year and returned to Minnesota and I had the apartment to myself. John, Pic, and Termite stayed in Dick's room, and more and more of the neighborhood sniffers started hanging around the house. Many of the parents and community members started to support me, especially Gary's mother, Rose Corpus, who had earlier paid for the five boys to fly home from Molokai.

Once the kids started living in the house, a surprising and gratifying transformation took place. They spontaneously set up their own rules. They divided up cleaning and cooking responsibilities, and forbade paint sniffing. They managed to scavenge additional furniture from neighbors and took ownership and pride in living in the apartment.

There was considerable effort to document the Molokai Youth Project and its transition into the Palolo Youth Project. I had a cassette recorder I kept with me and would often capture thoughts and events that were occurring, or sometimes tape my interaction with the kids. One of the pivotal events that gave the project its momentum was when John Lynch got hold of the tape recorder and recorded his own testament to what was going on.

"I ain't ashamed to say who I am. My name is John Lynch and I'm a sniffer. But what I'm trying to tell you guys is, you shouldn't be ashamed of what you are, but you gotta try to be something better.

"Sniffing is only for someone who's got no sense. If you sniff, people will hate you. You want people to look up to you. You want to walk down the street and have people say, 'There goes a man', not 'There goes a sniffer.'

"Boy, if you sniff because you want to be someone, let me tell you, that's not how to be someone, it's how to be no one.

"Let me tell you something else," the voice continued. "You guys think Bruce Leonard is a fink. Listen to me and get wise. He ain't no fink. He's okay, man, and he's trying to help you. He helped me. And I ain't gonna sniff no more. Cause that don't make you a man. You think it makes you big, man, but you ain't big..."

Leo took lots of pictures and we put together a slide presentation, using John's testimony as a sound track. We began accepting invitations to speak at community meetings and University classes.

37

*BEFORE I LEFT FOR MOLOKAI, MARY LEFT TO SPEND TIME IN CALI-*fornia with her brother Bill, one of Enzo's VISTA roommates. We wrote to each other not knowing where I'd be in a couple of months and whether we'd ever see each other again. After she left, I would take my bike down to Waikiki and check out the nightclubs.

One night I spotted a cute blond and asked her to dance. Judy Bush was from Southern California and worked as a hairstylist at Hino's Beauty Salon at Ala Moana Shopping Center. Over the next several weeks I'd visit her for lunch and we started dating. She was attentive and supportive as I shared my activities in Palolo. We found similarities in our attempts to relate to our respective fathers and had similar political views.

One night we went out with Warren and Linda, a married couple who were also hair stylists at Hino's. They took us to a gay bar, where I learned that Warren was bi-sexual. Several men approached him while he was sitting with his wife. This was definitely a new scene for me. As hair stylists, this group was very conscious of their appearance, their outfits and their make-up. I showed up in a raggedy golf shirt and my pants were ripped at the knee, which they thought was cute.

By the time Mary returned, I had been granted the three-month extension and would be with VISTA until October. We started dating again, but I was still seeing Judy. I didn't want to deceive Mary, but I didn't want to give up Judy. I cared for them both, and didn't want to lose either of them. Judy was aware of my relationship with Mary and didn't put any pressure on me to make a choice. I continued to see them both, and finally admitted to Mary the truth. She didn't take it well, but she didn't give me an ultimatum.

***

I eventually wrote a paper describing the Palolo Youth Project, hoping to generate community support and obtain technical assistance and possible funding. I structured the paper to include a background, objectives, results, and future goals.

The background listed my theories of the underlying causes of delinquency and drug abuse. Lack of male role models, alienation from both the educational and employment "systems", scarcity of recreational activities and dysfunctional home environments were among the causes I identified. As objectives, I proposed programs that would address those underlying causes. The document was updated three times and by the time I left, the following progress had been made:

1. The University Volunteer Tutoring Program assigned a graduate student to serve as a Palolo coordinator; this student paired a dozen Palolo students with university and local high school tutors. Mentors were also identified from the University and community to provide art and music lessons.
2. The New Kind of School, an experimental school modeled after the principles of Summerhill, was created at the Church

of the Cross Roads. As a member of its Board of Directors, I made arrangements with Palolo Elementary School, Jarrett Intermediate School, and the Honolulu Department of Education to send ten students to the "New Kind of School." Mark Bauer coordinated this part of the project.

3. Ted Hyde coordinated job training and placement opportunities. Four of the boys completed a City Manpower Job Orientation program and six boys were placed in jobs through the State Employment Opportunity Center.
4. A football team and several basketball teams were formed with volunteer coaches and donated uniforms.
5. My VISTA apartment was turned into a halfway house where some boys had a place to stay and others a place to gather.

I worked on this paper diligently, often waking at 4:00 in the morning, compulsively writing, my mind filled with ideas. I shared my paper, which filled an entire legal pad, with Bill Sutkus, one of the VISTA leaders. He in turn shared it with Masaru Oshiro, his boss. I was invited to Masaru's home for a Sunday afternoon visit and his wife graciously typed out my paper as I dictated it to her for over five hours. There were no copiers back then. In those days, you had to place a carbon sheet between the original and a second sheet of paper in order to type copies. The Oshiros' support confirmed to me that my report and my ideas were credible and worth disseminating. I made multiple copies of the forty-page report and developed a distribution plan.

I was a member of the Palolo Community Council (PCC), which included representatives from community social service agencies such as HCAP, the Palolo Housing Authority, school officials, clergy, elected city and state officials and community residents. Over the summer

I had reported to the PCC the results of the Molokai Youth Project and now I was able to present documentation and a plan for the Palolo Youth Project. It was gratifying to receive overwhelming support from the council, with several members expressing that there had never been a more effective effort implemented to address the intractable "sniffing problem." It was suggested that a funding proposal be submitted on behalf of the council, which I enthusiastically wrote and gave to them to review and approve.

As I continued to accommodate requests to speak at the University, the Palolo project began to attract media attention. A community meeting held at my apartment, which by then had been turned into a halfway house, was covered by a reporter from the Honolulu Advertiser and appeared as a full-page spread in the Monday paper. I was interviewed on a variety of local radio shows. One of the council members facilitated my first appearance on the Don Robbs Show, a daytime TV variety program. After my on-air appearance, Robbs said, "This young man is changing the system from within, as opposed to the hippies that complained and protested but didn't provide any solutions." He seemed also impressed that I was administering this project with minimal resources, while attending classes as a graduate student. It was pretty intoxicating to be so publicly lauded.

38

*I BECAME COMPLETELY OBSESSED WITH THE PALOLO PROJECT. AF-*ter months of spinning my wheels as a directionless VISTA volunteer, I felt that I was finally involved with a worthwhile endeavor. Having Leo as a devoted partner in the project boosted my confidence and resolve. He believed so much in the project and in me that he volunteered his time and talents with no compensation. It's hard to express how much that meant to me.

It was not only satisfying to feel I was accomplishing something, but I finally had a direction for my future. After the disappointment of graduating from college with a dismal GPA and no idea what I wanted to do with my life, I found that I might have a career in helping people. My decision to take a couple of graduate courses in psychology was kick started by the presentation made at our December VISTA conference by UH psychology professor Scott McDonald, who spoke about his innovative surfing-based school curriculum. I later heard him speak at the University Behavior Modification conference.

Attending school while trying to manage the Palolo Youth Project made for a very busy life. It wouldn't have been so bad if my experience at the university had been more positive. My attempts to develop relationships with instructors and curry favor by sharing my Molokai and Palolo experiences which by the way utilized their behavioral principles were met with indifferent, patronizing smiles. I hoped that at least one of them would show more than a passing interest and take me under his or her wing as I pursued my psychology studies.

Once again I found it difficult to focus as I sat through the boring, uninspiring, mandatory introductory courses. I hoped this academic encounter wouldn't be a repeat of my underwhelming undergraduate experience. Though some of the theories made sense, the lack of support and the indifference I felt from the faculty, and the fact that I was still working on the project full time, slowly eroded my enthusiasm. Unable to focus or memorize the material in my textbooks, I eventually dropped two of the four courses I had signed up for.

It became apparent that remaining in the apartment was not going to be tenable, now that I was a part-time student. I eventually rented a room in an apartment several miles away, occupied by an engineer who worked on a military base. Joe Beste was a couple of years older than me and had played football at Long Beach State. I turned my Palolo apartment into a halfway house and spent time there every day trying to assist the boys with productive vocational, educational, or leisure activities. Joe Beste recruited some of the Palolo kids and formed a football team. He solicited donations for their uniforms and equipment.

My VISTA extension ended October 1. I applied for a $20,000 grant to create a demonstration project and requested a three-month extension for my Palolo apartment so it could continue to be used as a halfway house. My father told me he would be stopping in Honolulu for a brief visit on his way to Japan on a business trip. I was excited to showcase my project and hopefully make him proud of me. I was starting to feel like I was burning the candle at both ends, trying to keep this project viable and attending graduate school at the same time. Adding to the stress was my involvement with both Mary and Judy, as well as with one of the teachers at the New Kind of School.

Leo and Judy were fervent supporters and reinforced my delusions of grandeur. There were times I could imagine that the Palolo Youth Project was historic and groundbreaking, and that what I had accomplished was amazing. But Mary, the new VISTA volunteers, and my father were less enthusiastic. Though they supported my efforts, they would play devil's advocate and weren't about to put me on a pedestal. I bounced from swelling with confidence and self-esteem to being riddled with self-doubt.

Suddenly all of the balls I had been juggling started falling to the ground. I didn't get the $20,000 grant. My request for an extension on the apartment was denied. I dropped two of the four graduate courses and was losing interest in the other two. Though I encouraged Mary to date other people, when it finally happened, it tore me up. The community meeting I invited my father to was a disaster. Though I had many community supporters, there was considerable animosity towards the paint sniffers. Many Palolo residents felt that the media attention my project was receiving drew unwanted attention to Palolo's paint sniffing problem. At the meeting, they turned on me and even accused me of enabling the sniffers. Not only did my father have to witness that, but both Mary and Judy showed up and met each other for the first time.

I was losing it. On December 1, 1969, my 23rd birthday, Nixon instituted the Selective Service Draft lottery. This eliminated all deferments. When my birth date December 1st was picked as number 129, I got my reprieve from the chaos in Hawaii. I would return to New York and face my draft board.

Newly arrived Hawaii VISTA volunteers,
Bruce Leonard and roommate Dick Brown June 1968

Bruce Leonard with best friend Enzo DiMaio, during his visit January 1969 at Outrigger Canoe Club.

John Lynch, Palolo paint sniffer

Pic, a Palolo paint sniffer who completed Job Training.

Camping in Halawa Valley Molokai June 1969

Palolo Youth Job Training Graduates

Palolo youth, John Lynch, Termite, and Pic sniffing paint

PART 7

—

APRIL — AUGUST 1971
MAUI — HONOLULU — MAINLAND

39

THE APPEARANCE ON THE DON ROBBS SHOW WAS MEMORABLE, AS was the eviction from the Makiki apartment. It was time for an adventure, and both Bobby and Duke wanted to go to Maui. Bobby had lived there previously and claimed to have a group of friends we could hang out with. We arrived in Wailuku with our packs and sleeping bags and camped at a local beach park inhabited by a motley group of itinerant hippies. We shared some pakalolo with some local surfers who gave us a ride to Lahaina in their pickup truck. When we got there, we headed for the Banyan Tree Park adjacent to the boat marina, which served as a local gathering place.

Bobby spotted an old friend getting out of a van.

"Eh, howzit, Bobby!"

"Kimo, howzit."

"Where you been, brah?"

"In Honolulu hanging out. Dis is Captain Energy and Duke."

"Captain Energy... heavy, man."

"Yeah, he's heavy all right. What's going on?"

"Still livin' in Paia, just came to see my sistah."

"Who? Linda?"

"Yeah, she stay at a friend's sailboat. Come over, she like see you. You guys too," he pointed at us.

"Cool," answered Bobby as he glanced at Duke and me and shrugged.

"Kimo, could we leave our stuff in your van so we don't have to carry it around?" Duke asked.

"No problem, brah."

"Yeah I was just walking ovah dere. You remember my sistah's old man, Calvin da plumbah? He did work for da guy dat owns da boat. He t'rowing a party before he go da Big Island. Les' go!"

Kimo walked us over to the marina and pointed to a 30-foot sailboat with a growing number of young people gathered around it. We were introduced to the boat owner, and then Kimo proceeded to tell stories about Bobby.

"Yeah, Bobby heah is heavy, brah. When he was in Paia last year, he wen' jam with anyone in town. Trumpet, sax, flute, piano—da buggah play everyt'ing."

"Yeah, we know," Duke nodded, pulling on a doobie. "We're part of Bobby's group, Captain Energy and the Electric Flesh."

"So dat's why you Captain Energy. You da leadah?"

I shook my head. "I'm Captain Energy, but Bobby's the leader. He's the musician, I'm the energy."

"Cool," Kimo nodded. "You guys like go Paia wit' me tomorrow? Da Rippers like see you, Bobby."

Bobby flashed the shaka sign. "All right, man."

With "Purple Haze" on the boat stereo system, someone handed me a hash pipe which I inhaled and passed on to Bobby. I smiled contentedly over at Duke. The adventure was unfolding.

We spent the night mixing with the party guests, enjoying the music, and continuing to partake of the assorted circulating intoxicants. Duke and I jumped in the water after having dispensed with my shorts under the deck table. I loved the exhilarating sensation of swimming while stoned. We spent most of the evening drinking and smoking on an inflatable raft that one of the party guests provided and occasionally floated back to the boat when the Doors and Jefferson Airplane were playing. Somebody pointed out an impressive yacht several slips over that was supposedly owned by David Crosby.

At the end of the night, Kimo invited us to crash at his sister Linda's. We staggered into Kimo's van and headed to her place.

When we woke the next morning, our post-party heads gradually focused and I realized I had left my shorts with a pocketful of cash on the boat. We packed into Kimo's van and swung by the marina, only to discover the sailboat had left the dock and was on its way to the Big Island.

"Shit, I had all my cash in my shorts!" I muttered with exasperation.

"What're you gonna do?" Duke asked.

"Fuck it, who needs cash," I retorted after a brief deliberation. "This'll be a chance for me to detoxify—I'm going on a fast for a couple days," I announced. "And we'll sleep on the beach."

"Good idea, I'm in," announced Bobby.

"Me too," Duke chimed in.

Excellent! The three of us would take a spiritual trip on the beach, commune with nature, and cleanse our bodies. Maybe I could convince them to practice some yoga and meditation. We needed to bond on a deeper level in order to become the music group I envisioned. Losing the money had been a blessing, and once again I was convinced that we were being guided by destiny.

When we arrived in Paia, an old sugar mill town on Maui's north shore, we set up camp at Ho'okipa Beach Park, which would become a world famous wind surfer location ten years later. No sooner had we arrived than a group of local teenagers Bobby called the Paia Rippers descended on our campsite. Bobby was welcomed like a rock star and he reveled in the attention.

Our self-imposed fast did not preclude partaking of the local Maui Wowie. In addition to fasting I decided that I would include a daily jog on the beach and after, a yoga ritual of postures, chanting, and meditation. The Rippers hung around our beach campsite and watched our "spiritual activities" as if we were from another planet.

After a day of fasting, Duke and Bobby succumbed to one of the Rippers' offer of a plate lunch of meat loaf and gravy, rice, and macaroni salad. I continued with the fast and incorporated a vow of silence to further deepen my immersion into myself. I would often find a group of Rippers staring at me following a prolonged period of meditation in the lotus position. After twenty-four hours, I no longer felt hungry. My flexibility and balance improved as I practiced my yoga postures. The state of euphoria and peace I experienced through the combination of yoga, meditation, fasting, and occasional marijuana smoking was indescribable. I was having what I thought was a deeply spiritual experience and was disappointed that Bobby and Duke were being distracted hanging out with the Rippers and not joining me.

"How come Captain Energy make li' dat?" they'd ask Bobby.

"He's a trip," Bobby would respond.

After five days, Bobby and Duke started to get restless.

"Energy I want to get back to Honolulu, I've had enough fun watching your quest for enlightenment," Duke admitted.

"Ok, I'm good," I replied. "Let's go."

"Hey, it's been a blast, but I think I'm gonna stick around. Kimo offered me a job on this construction site up in the valley. I need to make some bread," Bobby said.

Disappointed that we not only had not spiritually bonded but we were splitting up, I proposed to Duke that we hitch to Hana, stay with my high-school friend John Stone, and then fly back to Honolulu.

When we arrived in Hana after catching a ride in the bed of an old rusted out Chevy pickup truck, it was pouring rain. We ran over to John's cottage, our backpacks soaked, and found the place locked and no one home.

After checking every door and window, I discovered a slightly open louvered window. Squeezing my hand through a slat, I reached over and unlocked a door. The cottage was empty. I deliberated for a second about going in, considering John and Jean, and Doug and Linda weren't home and this would technically be breaking and entering. But the alternative would've been spending the night in the pouring rain, so we walked into the kitchen and made ourselves some peanut butter sandwiches and then ate some of the random fruit and crackers we found.

John had visited me the previous month at my Makiki apartment with his college buddy Tom Mason. I remembered his name because my mother's maiden name was Mason, and Tom's telephone number was next to the phone on the kitchen counter. I dialed it.

"Tom, hey it's Bruce Leonard, John's friend you visited in Makiki?"

"Yeah, Bruce, how you doing?"

"Good, as a matter of fact I'm here in Hana at John's house and since he isn't here, I figured he might be in Honolulu staying with you."

"Good guess, yes as a matter of fact, he's right here."

"Bruce, how you doing? Doug and I are on spring break visiting Tom. What are you up to?"

"Well actually Duke and I are in your house in Hana."

"How'd you get in?"

"I stuck my hand through the louver window and unlocked your door. It was pouring rain. We'll be catching a plane back to Honolulu first thing in the morning."

Suddenly a loud voice came on the line. "Hey, this is Doug! I want you two shitheads out of our house now! I'm freakin' calling the police. Get out! Now!!" And he slammed the phone in my ear. I looked at the phone for a while, stunned.

"Shit, guess we gotta get out of here."

"What's the matter?" Duke inquired.

"John's roommate Doug isn't one of my biggest fans. He's calling the cops."

We decided to call his bluff and stick around until our flight the next day. We crept around the house, keeping our heads down, trying to conceal our presence until the next morning, when we hopped on the first plane back to Honolulu.

40

*DUKE AND I RETURNED TO THE HOUSE HE SHARED WITH ROOM-*mates Steve and John. It was several streets over from Kapahulu Avenue, a thoroughfare that dead ended in Waikiki.

During my Christmas visit to New York City, I updated my wardrobe with some of the latest psychedelic form-fitting, long-collared shirts and polyester bellbottom pants. Though our normal apparel in Hawaii usually consisted of shorts, T-shirts, and flip flops, or slippahs as they're called in Hawaii, Duke and I would get decked out in the evenings and hit the Waikiki nightclub scene. During my month's stay in Makiki, trying to inspire musical creativity with the loosely forming rock group, I had also bought, with some money borrowed from my father, a stereo cassette player and a collection of tapes of all the latest music.

After I got evicted from the Makiki Apartment, I had stashed all my possessions in Duke's bedroom at the Kapahulu house before we headed to Maui. When we walked into the living room, I found Steve wearing my clothes, my stereo was sitting on a shelf in the living room, and my cassettes were strewn all over the floor. Duke saw the enraged look on my face and before I exploded he grabbed me and ushered me into his bedroom.

"Bruce, let me handle this. We can't piss him off or we're both going to be out on the street."

I stayed in the room while Duke, in his smooth voice, calmly negotiated with Steve. Soon my clothes, my stereo set, and the cassettes were moved back into Duke's room.

I slept on the couch that night, and the tension between Steve and me simmered. He was a Vietnam veteran dealing with a slew of unresolved issues, and he barely tolerated what he perceived to be our anti-establishment hippie lifestyle. His fury simmered just below the surface, and Duke and I did our best to avoid him. He ended up spending most of his time at his girlfriend's place and stopped by the house just to change clothes.

One day he returned while I was sitting on the couch eating cereal and he flew out of the kitchen in a rage. "Damn it Energy, that's the last straw, get the fuck outta here!"

"What's your problem?" I asked as Duke emerged from his room, ready to arbitrate.

"You drank up all the milk I bought. I'm tired of you mooching off of us and sleeping in the living room."

Duke walked over. "Steve, easy man. I'll buy you some more milk."

"Fuck the milk… I want him out."

"Juice, let's go," Duke said as he escorted me to his car.

"That guy's a psychopath, man."

"I know. He's wound pretty tight. Just try to steer clear of him. He's rarely around, so for the time being, why don't you sleep in my station wagon?"

"Sounds like a plan."

We lit up a joint and drove to Ala Moana Shopping Center for lunch before heading for a day at the beach.

That night we returned to the Kapahulu house. After patrolling the street to make sure Steve's car wasn't around, we snuck into Duke's room, changed, and went to Waikiki for a night on the town.

There were several nightclubs that we frequented and we'd bounce from one to the other, socializing with some of the regulars, scoping out the crop of ladies, and assessing the quality of the music.

One of our favorites was Hula's Surfer Bar which was adjacent to the International Market Place. The six-member band, Nightlife, had a skilled conga player and a talented guy on the horns, and their set consisted of contemporary cover songs ranging from Santana to Chicago. During a break, Duke sidled up to their lead guitarist and singer and started his sweet-talking pitch.

"Man, you guys are great. Where you from?"

"Mostly from southern California. I'm from Venice Beach."

"Really, I used to have an apartment in Santa Monica! I'm Duke and this is Captain Energy."

"I'm Randall Coates. Captain Energy, huh?"

"Yeah he's the lead guy of our group, Captain Energy and the Electric Flesh."

"What kind of stuff you play?"

"Very similar to you... we like Santana, Grand Funk. Our horn player is over in Maui, but he plays trumpet, and sax."

"So what does the Captain play?" he asked as he looked at me.

"Mostly percussion," I answered.

"Well let's see what you got. Want to sit in with us?"

"Lay it on me, man." I answered enthusiastically.

Nightlife returned to the stage and played Santana's "Black Magic Woman" and Chicago's "Color My World", and then the lead guitarist, Randall, announced the next song, Grand Funk Railroad's "I'm Your Captain," with Captain Energy from Captain Energy and the Electric Flesh sitting in on drums.

I was having the time of my life banging away with abandon, in the groove. The band kept glancing over at me, so they must have been digging it. I was having a little trouble maintaining the beat with the foot-operated bass, but the band was loud and the audience didn't seem to notice. At the conclusion of the song, Randall grabbed my drumsticks and unceremoniously ushered me off the stage.

Duke was on the dance floor laughing and hooting.

"You were great, Energy," he assured me.

"Randall didn't seem impressed."

"Well you're a little rusty, but you showed enthusiasm. That's the important thing. Anyway, this is Ellen and she thought you were great." He introduced me to a smiling young local woman with long black hair, a caramel complexion, and very bloodshot, spaced-out eyes.

"That was far out, man," Ellen slurred, feeling no pain and impressed that one of the performers was dancing with her.

Smoking grass not only inflated my confidence as a musician, but it enhanced my dancing coordination. I sensed a synchronistic connection between my feet and the drumbeat, my hips and the bass, my shoulders and the melody. Ellen and I were both lost in the music. We finished the set and Duke suggested that we hit more clubs. I nodded to Randall as we left. We danced at several of the local night spots until about 2:00 am, then drove back to Duke's house in Kapahulu. Ellen and I spent the rest of the night rolling around in the back of Duke's station wagon.

Ellen woke before me and asked to use the bathroom. We both snuck into the house after a quick scan of the street for Steve's car. She peed, then we filled the tub and hopped in. The bathroom could be accessed from both the living room and Duke's room. He greeted us, smirking as he relieved himself in the adjacent toilet. While Ellen continued to soak, I got out and plopped on the toilet to take a dump.

Suddenly the front screen door slammed open and we heard Steve enter the living room. Duke and I exchanged glances.

"What the fuck are you doing here?" he bellowed as he opened the bathroom door.

"I'm taking a shit, what does it look like?"

"Energy, I want you out of here NOW!"

"Cool it Steve, I'll leave when I'm finished. Be nice and say hello to Ellen." She discreetly covered her breasts with her arms and Steve grunted and retreated to the living room.

Duke slipped into the tub to comfort Ellen.

"Oh my God, Bruce. Don't go out there," she said.

"No worries," I assured her.

Steve was pacing the living room like a caged animal.

"Come on, Energy, I want you out!"

Ellen kept whimpering as Duke sat behind her, cuddling and cooing. "Don't worry, Bruce can handle this."

"Cool your jets, Steve. You can't rush a healthy bowel movement."

While Steve paced the living room and snarled, Ellen moaned, Duke cooed, and I grunted contently.

Finally I got up, pulled on my pants, and entered the living room.

"You know, Steve, you're really an asshole."

"What the hell you called me?" he yelled as he lunged across the room, his fist glancing off the side of my head. I dropped to my knees, tackled him, and threw him against the couch as a lamp fell off the adjacent table.

Ellen's cries alternated between concern for me ("Oh, Bruce!") and moans of pleasure ("Oh, Duke!") while my partner did his best to console her.

As I pulled him from the couch onto the floor, Steve raged. "You fucker I'll kill you!" I calmly applied an instinctual wrestling move and pulled him onto my lap, trapping his right forearm with both my hands and lacing my legs around his. All he could do was buck and flail impotently. We rolled from side to side, but he eventually stopped resisting when he realized he was helpless and flat out exhausted.

Once the struggle subsided, the only sounds to be heard were Steve's heaving gasps and Ellen's purrs of pleasure.

41

I RAN ACROSS LEO AT THE YMCA BEFORE ONE OF MY WRESTLING workouts with Alan Johnson.

"Hey howzit, Leo."

"Juicie, long time no see, you look like you're staying in shape. I'm pumping a little iron myself."

"Good for you. How's school?" I asked.

"Keepin' on. I've been wondering what happened to you since I saw you at the Makiki apartment."

I shared my adventures with Duke and Bobby, my TV appearance, and our trip to Maui.

"I saw Ann the other day. She's worried about you, man."

"Why?"

"She says you got arrested for indecent exposure and lost your job."

I chuckled. "Yeah, that's sort of a long story. But I've been having a blast, hanging around with some musicians, trying to form a rock group and start up a job placement company. Serve as kind of an agent to get work for some of the guys I'm hanging out with."

"What?" he asked.

"You know, nobody wants to work for The Man, so I would serve as the middle man so they don't have to deal with all the bullshit. It's called International Head Consultants."

"How do you make money?" Leo asked.

"I'm still working out the details."

"Where you living?"

"I'm looking for a place. I was living with Duke, but it's not working out. How about you?"

"I'm in a house up on Prospect. I think there's a room available for rent." He wrote a number on a piece of paper. "Call Darlene, she's knows the landlady."

"Mahalo, I'll be in touch."

Alan showed up and we flopped down on the wrestling mat and began our workout.

***

During periods of self-reflection when I wasn't stoned, which wasn't often, a voice would gnaw at me with questions like, "What the hell are you doing?" Captain Energy and the Flesh just wasn't happening. Though I appreciated the confidence Bobby had instilled in me, he was useless in terms of the crucial details of mobilizing musicians and getting everyone up to speed and organized. We had just sat around the Makiki apartment listening to music and entertaining the non-stop stream of guests who wandered in, looking to get stoned and hang out with us. Billy Kim came by, but he and Mark, the drummer, had joined Augie Ray's band. McCrillis was useless. Duke was enthusiastic but had no musical experience. After my stint in Maui, Bobby had bailed out. Now it was just Duke and me.

He didn't seem too concerned and was cool with just chilling, going to the beach, getting stoned, hitting the clubs, and fabricating an endless stream of get-rich-quick schemes we'd conjure up in our cannabis-addled brains. He was surviving comfortably on his weekly unemployment checks, but the money I had borrowed from my father was dwindling quickly. I was sharing my impatience with our lack of a viable money-making project, and Duke, as usual, had advice.

"Come on, Juice, we need to visit my friend John Patton. He works for the American Heart Association and he can help get International Head Consultants off the ground."

John had an apartment in the Waikiki Jungle, near Duke's friend George. The Jungle was a bohemian enclave at the Diamond Head end of Waikiki. In marked contrast to the manicured shops and hotels further to the west, it was a low-rent area of one and two-story studio cottages, small hotels, and old homes converted into rooming houses and apartments. Its denizens were a constantly shifting group of mostly young men and women from the mainland, here temporarily, as though on hiatus from another life.

"John's going out with Leigh, who is best friends with Carol." I found this situation hard to comprehend. John and Duke were in their late twenties, about five years older than me, and dating foxy high school girls. Only in Hawaii. The relationships had been going on for several months, though Duke and John were not beyond occasional wandering. Carol and Leigh attended the most exclusive private school on the island and came from solid upper-middle-class families.

"So John, dig it...we've got this idea of forming International Head Consultants," Duke began. He then turned it over to me to describe our vision for bridging the gap between talented dropouts and employers, finding them jobs in the mainstream. John handed us a joint he pulled from a shoe box half full of marijuana leaves and put a *Doors* album on his stereo.

John's bloodshot eyes gleamed and he proceeded to brainstorm with me, listing decisions that needed to be made. I picked up the shoebox and started cleaning his marijuana.

"Cool idea, but you need to figure out if this is going to be for-profit or non-profit for tax purposes." He took a deep drag on our joint and passed it back to me.

"Then we need to recruit a board of directors. I know some influential people who might be interested and an attorney friend who could help us."

John and Duke walked into the kitchen to get us some beers and I remained in the living room fastidiously cleaning the pakalolo. I sat with my legs crossed, tilted the box to let the seeds slide to the bottom, picked out the stems and branches and ground the marijuana leaves in my fingers for joint rolling.

Suddenly I heard a knock on the screen door. I looked up and found myself face-to-face with a cop. He opened the door, walked over to me, looked inside the shoebox, and announced that I was under arrest for possession. John and Duke emerged from the kitchen. The cop explained that he had been summoned to the apartment on a neighbor's complaint that we were playing our music too loud. John was instructed to turn the music down and I was escorted out of the apartment with my hands in cuffs.

After sitting in a jail cell for a couple of hours with the evening's crew of miscreants, Duke and John showed up to bail me out.

"You have the worst luck, man. Cop shows up on a noise complaint and you get busted with John's dope," Duke snickered.

"Dig it, man."

42

DUKE AND I WERE CHATTING OVER A COUPLE OF BEERS AND I RE-flected on all the crap that had gone down lately, all the dumb decisions I had been making. This was now my third arrest in a couple of months. I had been evicted from my apartment, lost a really good job, and would probably be killed if I showed up at the Kapahulu house where Duke's psycho roommate still lived. Captain Energy and the Electric Flesh wasn't happening. Bobby was in Maui, and neither Duke nor I were musicians. This whole thing was going nowhere fast.

Duke managed to lift my spirits when he introduced me to the members of The Theater of Madness. They were an innovative rock group that integrated theater, sound, lighting, movies, and audience interaction and were often compared to Frank Zappa and the Mothers of Invention, Alice Cooper, and the Fireside Theater. The group was composed of Cosmo Ohms on guitar, bass and sitar; Captain Metronome on percussion; Dosa Tooner, keyboard and vocals; Gail Greenberg, flute and vocals and Mr. Prism, manager and head of production. They were a well-established local group who often opened for mainland bands such as Steppenwolf, Credence Clearwater, and Jefferson Airplane.

We would watch them rehearse and were eventually hired on as part of their crew, helping them set up at various venues. On weekends they often played free concerts at Sandy Beach where they had an enthusiastic following. They stored and transported their equipment for their multi-media presentations in a colorfully decorated van. I was finally getting to observe how a band operated.

Every now and then, I returned to Palolo to check on the boys I had worked with as a VISTA volunteer. Most of them had moved away by then, so I would visit with my old neighbors the Cutzingers to catch up on the neighborhood gossip. I convinced the Theater of Madness to put on a free concert at the Palolo neighborhood pavilion.

That June, the Theater of Madness was cast to star in "Fast Quack," a science-fiction film produced and directed by a University of Hawaii film student, Bruce Osborn. Duke and I would travel around the island with the crew, carrying equipment and appearing as extras in a few scenes. I remember a 4:00 am filming session conducted at the Honolulu airport.

***

Besides Steve, Duke's other roommate was a guy named John. He was a graduate student in music at the University of Hawaii. He sported a droopy sandy-blond walrus mustache, and was usually holed up in his bedroom playing or writing music. When Steve wasn't around, Duke and I would sit at the piano with John, singing and sharing with him our vision of Captain Energy and the Electric Flesh. We were stoned most of the time, which was probably one of the reasons we didn't make much progress coalescing the group. We were having a great time but just couldn't get ourselves to focus on a plan. In the meantime, Bobby had returned from Maui and would occasionally join us at the Kapahulu house for a jam session.

In addition to attending school, John played with the Honolulu Symphony Orchestra. They were performing in a local production of "Jesus Christ Superstar."

One afternoon John had some amazing news.

"Energy, you aren't going to believe what smooth talking Duke just pulled off."

"What now?"

"Last night after the show, Duke and I and some of the Superstar cast members were at a bar, celebrating the symphony's invitation to perform at the Crater Festival next month. Well, among the cast members was a guy named Ken Rosene, the Crater Festival organizer. We were trying to figure out how we could spice up the production and Duke convinced Rosene that Captain Energy and the Electric Flesh could collaborate with the symphony to jazz things up. And Rosene went for it."

"Wait. We're going to perform at the Crater Festival?"

"You stoked?"

Finally! The culmination of a six-month odyssey, triggered by the Maui peyote trip. Witnessing Santana perform at the Crater Festival the previous December had been the catalyst for my long-held fantasy of performing at a rock festival. Just as I was losing faith in my music career, Duke came through once again.

John and I began brainstorming about possible scenarios. He showed me a list of the songs that the symphony would perform at their Jesus Christ Superstar festival gig. I wanted to come up with a way to make our performance relevant by adding a topical spin to the lyrics. When John mentioned that one of the songs was the powerful and moving "Judas' Death", I perked up. In the song, Judas plaintively tries to rationalize his betrayal of Jesus. I decided the new lyrics would pertain to Vice President Spiro Agnew's betrayal of Nixon, having lied to him about the war. Both John and Duke thought the idea was brilliant. We quickly brainstormed and scribbled down our lyrics. We pulled in Bobby and Billy Kim to work with John to put it all together.

Our presentation was inspired by the Theater of Madness, so this would be a skit where we would interrupt the *Jesus Christ Superstar* production by leaping onto the stage and announcing that Judas' betrayal could be reinterpreted today with Agnew's betrayal of Nixon. And then we'd launch into our version of the song. We were pleased with our idea and psyched about this momentous gig.

In addition to Bobby and Billy Kim, we recruited part-Hawaiian brothers Kimo and Roger to join us. We were beyond excited about performing at the Diamond Head Crater Festival with the Honolulu Symphony. Not a lot of attention was paid to quality control, though. I figured if we just got on stage and managed to get through the entire skit unscathed, we would be discovered as the innovative, socially relevant rock stars we were, and our inevitable musical careers would take off.

The festival was spread out over the expansive grassy field in the crater of Diamond Head volcano. An estimated 25,000 scantily clad long-haired hippies were in attendance that sun-drenched Hawaiian day. Three stages surrounded a village of makeshift booths manned by artisans touting their artwork, water pipes, roach clips, and bamboo flutes. Others sold avocado sandwiches, apple juice and brownies to ravenous stoners with the munchies. One of the prominent headliners was San Francisco's It's a Beautiful Day, whose hit song was "White Bird."

In the middle of the Honolulu Symphony's performance of "Judas Death", Duke and I jumped up on stage. I wore an American flag tied around my shoulders and when I grabbed the mic, the music came to an abrupt halt. I exclaimed that the singer had it all wrong—yes, Judas had betrayed Jesus, but we were here to announce that Spiro Agnew was the betrayer of Nixon and he in fact was going to end the war in Vietnam and reveal Nixon's treacherous duplicity. The audience was shocked at the interruption and it took a while for them to figure out that this was part of the act. With mic in hand, surrounded by Duke, Kimo, Roger, Bobby playing the flute, Billy Kim on guitar and John on piano, we fervently belted out our song.

The performance received a smattering of applause, and a couple of stoners yelled "Right on, man!" After a few awkward seconds, the symphony started back up and finished performing the rest of their music.

Adrenaline coursed through my veins as I leapt off the stage. We had just blown some minds. Our future as a rock band was assured. The performance may not have been polished, but it was original. We hoped someone would notice and direct us to our next creative gig.

43

DUKE AND I CONTINUED TO HANG OUT AT THE KAPAHULU HOUSE, jamming with whoever was around, working with the Theater of Madness and getting stoned. After a couple of weeks, we got impatient when nothing appeared to be happening and no one contacted us for any more gigs. In the meantime, trying to keep the band together was like herding cats. Billy returned to the Augie Ray Band and Bobby announced that he was going back to visit his former musical community in Miami.

With no prospects on the horizon, Duke decided maybe Hawaii wasn't ready for Captain Energy and we'd find better luck on the mainland. He was pretty sure his southern California contacts would love the idea of Captain Energy. I continued to believe that there was some role in it for me, and that I just needed to put myself in the right position or associate myself with the right people.

Duke and I found out about some discounted round trip airline tickets to Los Angeles. We began to tout this trip to California as the second coming of Ken Kesey and the Merry Pranksters. (In the early sixties, Ken Kesey, a graduate student in creative writing at Stanford University and a former college wrestler and author of the critically acclaimed novel *One Flew Over the Cuckoo's Nest*, volunteered to take part in what turned out to be a CIA-financed project to study the effects of psychoactive drugs such as LSD, psilocybin, and mescaline.

He subsequently took a group of friends dubbed the Merry Pranksters on a cross-country trip in a psychedelically decorated school bus nicknamed Further. The journey was documented in Tom Wolfe's best seller *The Electric Kool-Aid Acid Test*.)

I stored my possessions in my room at the house Leo had turned me on to, and I paid my rent for an additional month.

We began our mainland trip with a stop at Duke's mother's house. Doris owned and operated a dress shop in Los Angeles and lived alone with her yippy miniature poodle in an immaculate, white-carpeted apartment with pastel-colored furniture. She was pleasant enough, but she wasn't overly impressed when Duke introduced me as Captain Energy, the leader of his rock band The Electric Flesh. She was even less impressed when we revealed our plans to hang out indefinitely in L.A. and explore gigs for our band. There was only the two of us, we had no instruments, and she knew her son had no musical talent. She loved Duke, but he was pushing thirty, and she was anxious to see him settle down and start an actual career.

Duke explained that I was the creative force responsible for our triumphant performance at the Crater Festival, and that Captain Energy was actually a college graduate from an upper middle-class family from New York, whose father was a famous architect. This presentation gave me some credibility initially but didn't completely ease her misgivings, especially since Duke kept borrowing money from her. Her continued scrutiny of our plans became more and more probing. Duke never seemed to let his mother's nagging get to him, but she clearly wasn't buying his plans and barely tolerated me. I stayed in the background as the mother/son tension grew.

It soon became apparent that Duke's hype about his southern California contacts had been exaggerated. His friend Dominic, a dude he thought would be a potential band recruit, turned out to be a piano-playing hairdresser. We hung out with him for a couple of days, sat around his pool checking out the chicks, sang songs at the piano, told stories, and smoked weed. Though we had an enjoyable visit, it was obvious Dominic had no intention of abandoning his career as a hairdresser to join the Flesh.

Duke had also claimed that his cousin Charlie worked in the movie business and maybe could hook us up. Charlie was a lowly accountant with MGM studios with minimal influence or contacts in the industry. I could tell Charlie saw Duke as a smooth-talking ne'er-do-well college dropout with little to show for his bluster and get-rich-quick fantasies. Though Duke continued to introduce me with exaggerated fanfare, I felt like a fraud.

We were doing nothing but mooch off his relatives, and my enthusiasm for this visit was waning fast. I tagged along for lack of anything better to do and the longer we stayed, the more discouraged and disillusioned I became. Duke was looked at by his family as a Peter Pan-like character, always up for an adventure but not ready for prime time. They wondered when he would finally grow up. I was starting to see Duke the way his relatives saw him.

It surprised me that their criticism didn't seem to deflate him. We would debrief after these uncomfortable encounters, and he'd reassure me that his relatives were lovable, but just didn't get it. He framed it in the context of *The Greening of America*. They were just at a different level of consciousness. Somehow his optimism kept the last remnants of my fading hope alive.

When it became apparent that we had exhausted Duke's network of contacts in L.A., we told his mother we planned to hitchhike to the east coast to visit my friends and family. Uncomfortable with the prospect of her son hitchhiking across the country, Doris let us borrow her pink Eldorado Cadillac. She also suggested that we stop in New Mexico to visit her brother and work on his ranch in Santa Fe to earn some money. And so we began our strange journey in Doris's 1959 pink Eldorado Cadillac with its massive tailfins. It wasn't Ken Kesey's psychedelically-painted school bus, but we were off on another adventure.

44

THE RECEPTION WE GOT IN SANTA FE WAS CONSIDERABLY WORSE than the one we'd received at Duke's mother's house. His uncle Marvin was a redneck rancher with no tolerance for the foolish antics of his nephew and his useless friend. As far as he was concerned, we were just a couple of long-haired commie hippies, and he was only letting us stay as a favor to his sister. He needed some cheap labor to complete some ranch work that didn't require any skill, so he put us to work.

Duke explained that his uncle was at an even lower level of consciousness than the one his mother was on, and we needed to suck it up, make some money, and soon we'd be back on the road. I skulked around the house, keeping my distance, while Duke joked and bullshitted with his uncle, diffusing some of the tension. We spent our days in the hot dry heat of the high desert, digging holes for fence posts, hauling barbed wire in a beat-up pickup truck, and checking to see that the cattle had enough water and hay.

In the evenings we'd go bar hopping at some of the local taverns and take in the colorful Santa Fe multi-ethnic culture. Among U.S. states, New Mexico has the highest percentage of Hispanics, including descendants of Spanish colonists who have lived in the area for more than 400 years. It also has a high percentage of Native Americans from the Navajo, Pueblo, and Apache tribes. We remained at the ranch for about another week, then headed northeast to Chicago to see my college friend, Rick Mesard.

Since our depressing visit with Duke's extended family, I had been losing energy and my mood was spiraling downward. Duke's optimism and mood, on the other hand, was on the rise. He gave me pep talks to keep my spirits up, assuring me that my friends and family would be impressed once they saw his slide show documenting our adventures and culminating in our performance at the Diamond Head Crater Festival. En route to Chicago, we saved our money and slept in Doris' Eldorado.

***

Rick and I had been close friends in college. He was the president of our fraternity, Chi Phi, and I was vice president. We were both economics majors and we both joined VISTA to avoid the draft. As a volunteer in Minnesota, he worked with migrant farm laborers and was selected as a VISTA leader the following year. At the time of my visit he was working for the project-sponsoring agency.

Rick had a spare bachelor's pad, furnished with a second-hand sofa, three beers, and an expired jar of mayonnaise in his refrigerator. After he returned from work, the three of us went down to his favorite neighborhood tavern and caught up on our respective lives. Rick seemed entertained as I recounted the tumultuous adventures of Captain Energy over the previous eight months. As Duke related some of my hapless misadventures, I noticed an imperceptible shift in his attitude towards me. Usually complimentary and supportive, Duke seemed to be edging off the bandwagon and his condescending tone started to make me uncomfortable. I hadn't recognized this aspect of his personality before. When he got up to go to the bathroom, Rick looked me in the eyes. "Lenny, what the fuck are you up to? And who is this clown?"

"Oh, don't worry, Duke's a good guy. We've been having a great time these last several months," I sputtered.

"Okay. But where is all this leading?"

During the remainder of our brief visit with Rick, I found myself seriously reassessing my situation. Where *was* this leading? I had surrounded myself with an entourage who I thought shared my dream of combining music with social change. There had been slivers of success. I got myself on the Don Robbs Show and we performed in front of thousands at the Diamond Head Crater Festival. On the other hand, neither of these events had led to any opportunities. Bobby Graham initially gave me the confidence and moral support to pursue my dream of performing music, but we never managed to create a stable, functioning rock group. Duke was an enthusiastic huckster with great interpersonal skills, but The Electric Flesh was still a pipe dream. Our dissimilar temperaments had initially made our relationship work, but they were now creating a fissure that would eventually lead to a chasm between us.

Whereas Duke seemed content to live in the moment, I was brought up to set goals and I based my self-worth on my accomplishments. Duke was a fun-loving, socially adept cheerleader, but he was looking more and more like the Wizard of Oz. Now we were headed to New York to visit my parents and see if I could make something happen.

45

AFTER PARKING THE BIG FINNED PINK CADDY, WE STRODE INTO THE opulent high-ceilinged lobby of my parents' Park Avenue apartment.

We were greeted by the uniformed doorman. "May I help you gentlemen?"

"I'm here to see Eason Leonard."

"Of course, you must be Bruce and I assume this is your friend Richard, welcome to New York."

Duke shot me a wink and a thumbs up as we were escorted into the elevator to my parents' eighth-floor apartment.

My stepmother Jeanne graciously entertained us while we waited for my father to get home from work. Once he arrived, we all sat in the tastefully furnished living room with our cocktails, and they listened politely as we related our trip across the country in Duke's mother's pink Cadillac. Jeanne was from Dallas and had a big, Texas-sized personality. She and Duke hit it off immediately. They watched my father's reaction as I struggled to put a credible spin on my previous nine-month odyssey.

My father had just been through a couple of significant life changes. He had recently married Jeanne and they moved to the city to fully commit to his demanding career as the managing partner in a prominent architectural firm. No longer required to commute to work, living in the city would allow him the opportunity to socialize with clients, which hadn't been possible back in Tarrytown, during my mother's four-year struggle with cancer.

The only part of his life that wasn't settled was the status of his two sons. His new wife's three children seemed to be on productive and stable paths. My dad had been preoccupied with my high-maintenance brother for years. Craig had been kicked out of numerous private schools, and after my mother's death, had returned to attend our local high school, only to be expelled for a marijuana possession arrest. Once he obtained his GED with the assistance of an expensive tutor, his enrollment at Miami Dade College in Florida was derailed by his escalating drug use and the heroin bust. He was currently enlisted in the Navy and my dad could finally breathe a sigh of relief.

So it must have been crushing for my father to witness his oldest, straight-arrow son heading in a bewildering and self-destructive direction. Not only had I abandoned our shared conservative values and joined the ranks of my left-leaning generation, but I was on an alarmingly delusional path, searching for relevance as a socially-conscious rock star. It seemed I had become a living metaphor for the fracturing of the country's social fabric.

Duke pulled out the slides of Captain Energy and the Electric Flesh, the man who had single-handedly mobilized this band of creative musicians and snagged a gig to perform in front of thousands of enthusiastic fans at a star-studded rock festival. Jeanne and Eason refilled their drinks as they watched the slide show. When it was over, Jeanne said, "Well, that was interesting," and chuckled about the American flag cape. My father was visibly disappointed.

After a couple of days, Duke and I were summoned by Bobby to join him in Miami. When we left, I saw my exhausted father's shoulders slump as he bid us goodbye.

46

ONCE AGAIN WE HIT THE ROAD. I WAS DEFLATED AND EMBARRASSED after the visit with my parents. This Miami rendezvous with Bobby would be my last shred of hope for salvaging any possibility of realizing the Captain Energy dream. Maybe Bobby, with his Miami musical cohorts, could finally make something happen. To save money, we drove by day and slept in the Caddy at night.

We drove to Miami by way of Georgia. As we pulled out of Valdosta, I noticed a police car tailing us. He stayed right on our bumper as I drove with my eyes nervously darting from the road to the speedometer to the rear view mirror and back. Fortunately, we had smoked all the marijuana in the car days ago. Though my hair was still pretty short thanks to my stoned hair-clipping episode several months earlier, Duke was bearded, and his hair was down past his collar. This was the American South in 1971 and there was no tolerance for Negroes, long-haired hippies, or a pink Cadillac with California license plates. After riding on our bumper for at least twenty minutes, the cop's red light started flashing and we heard the whoop of his siren. I'm sure he suspected we were running drugs, and if not, we were probably some white commies on our way to a civil rights demonstration.

The trooper in his drill sergeant hat and sunglasses confiscated my license and registration with no explanation and ordered us to follow him in our car. Duke and I exchanged nervous glances as we were escorted to a room in the back of a drugstore in Valdosta.

"These here hippies were driving all over the road south of town," he informed the pot-bellied justice of the peace, who apparently was also the town pharmacist.

"So what brings you boys to Georgia all the way from California?"

After we explained that we were just driving down to visit a friend in Miami, we were fined $50, which we could barely afford, and instructed to "drive safe, now" and never return.

Relieved to be out of Georgia, we drove the tedious, unending length of Florida with one eye on the rear-view mirror.

***

Any hope that our visit with Bobby was going to salvage this trip was dashed when we met his friend and saw our accommodations. We would be staying with Brad, a kid who was a couple of years out of high school. Overweight and unemployed, he was a stoner who lived with his mother, a night-shift nurse's aide. They shared a sparsely furnished two-bedroom tract house in a bleak, treeless, humid Miami subdivision. Brad's rumpled clothes spilled out of every dresser drawer, his mattress was surrounded by piles of comics and litter, and there was a black-and-white television with a rabbit eared antenna propped on a bare table in the corner. What in the world was Bobby doing hanging out with this useless toad? And where were we supposed to sleep?

We accompanied Bobby to several of his old haunts — small, smoky coffee houses and jazz clubs where he was invited on stage to jam on his sax with some of his old musician buddies. His talent as a jazz saxophonist was obvious, and we were duly impressed. What wasn't obvious was where Duke and I fit in. With the slightest amount of interest or energy, Bobby could have easily slid right back into playing with a band—our band—but he didn't seem to want to. Nor did he have any plans to incorporate Duke or me in his musical activities. We endured a meaningless and painful couple of days in Miami, hanging with his useless friend, hitting the beach, watching TV in that cesspool of a room, getting stoned, and sweating every night, trying to sleep in the car or on the living room couch in the oppressively thick, humid heat of Miami.

My predestined role as a musical change-agent for the Age of Aquarius had just evaporated. I had to face the fact that the past nine months had been nothing but a foolish, crushing waste of time. Bobby announced he wanted to join us on our drive back to the west coast and then fly back to Hawaii. During the 3,000-mile trip back to Los Angeles I realized the music died.

Captain Energy promoting fasting

Lianne Chong, Richard Duke, Carol Ing (Duke's girlfriend later to become Mrs. Bruce Leonard, Cosmo Ohms of Theater of Madness, May 1971

Energy with Richard Duke, partner, member of Flesh, and photographer of Captain Energy at June 1971 Diamond Head Crater Rock Festival.

Captain Energy and Duke, jumping on stage during the Honolulu Symphony's production of Jesus Christ Superstar, June 1971.

Captain Energy performing with Duke room mate John at June 1971 Diamond Head Crater Rock Festival

Richard Duke and Captain Energy performing on stage at Crater Rock Festival June 1971

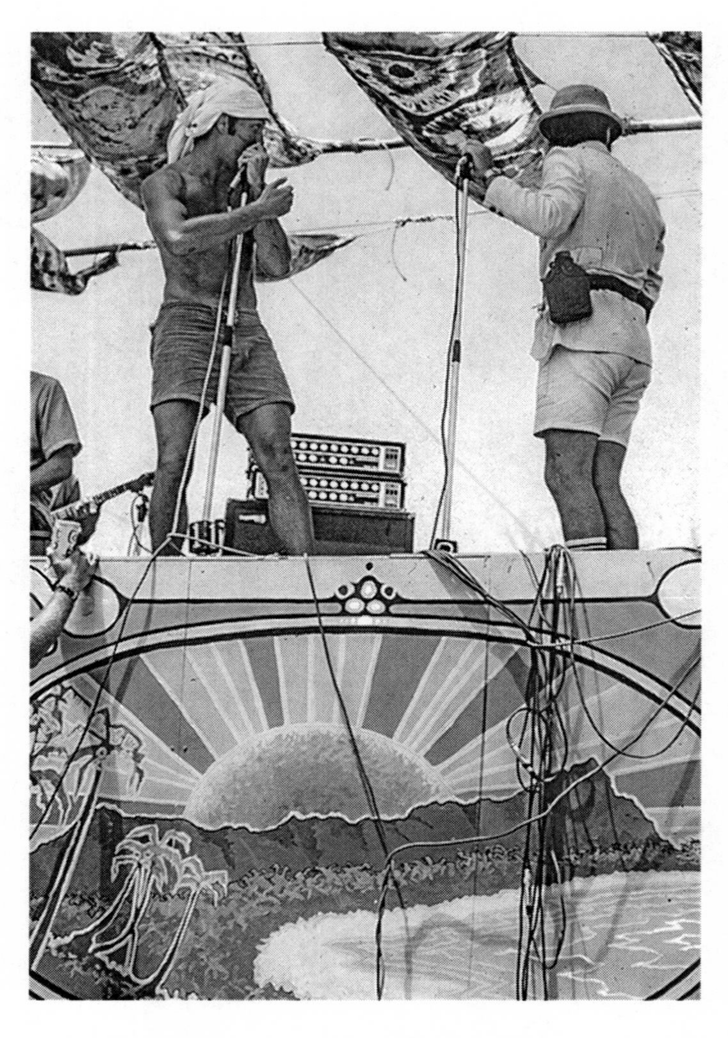

Captain Energy performing on stage at June 1971 Diamond Head Crater Rock Festival with Duke room mate Steve.

Captain Energy and The Electric Flesh performing at June 1971 Crater Rock Festival

PART 8

—

FLASHBACK

—

1946 – 1968

47

*AFTER GRADUATING FROM OKLAHOMA AGRICULTURAL AND ME-*chanical College (now Oklahoma State University) with a degree in architecture, my father served in the U.S. Army Corps of Engineers in southern France during the Second World War. He married my Nyack-born fashion model mother, Jeanne, after his stint ended in 1945.

My parents were living in Tappan, New York on the Hudson River, when I was born in December of 1946, the cusp of the post-World War II baby boomers. We lived in the converted army barracks of Shanks Village, a "Levittown"-like housing project for the surging number of returning Second World War veterans. Each barrack was transformed into three two-bedroom, 900-square-foot apartments. Camp Shanks, spread over 2,040 acres, used to serve as a point of embarkation for troops departing overseas. It was dubbed "Last Stop USA" and housed about 50,000 troops.

Through a friend, my father got a lead for a job overseeing the renovation of the offices of William Zechendorf, a real estate developer at Webb & Knapp who was working with a rising architectural star, I. M. Pei. This opportunity was the beginning of my father's spectacular 40-year career as the managing partner of I. M. Pei and Partners.

My mother eventually left modeling and found a more stable job in public relations. With both parents commuting to New York City, I was shuttled back and forth to my grandparents' house in Spring Valley. My grandfather Joe was a policeman who worked the night shift. For breakfast, my grandmother would make us soft-boiled eggs and toast and while we ate, Joe cultivated fantasies about the two of us hunting for bears when I got older. On weekends I'd run around their property chasing geese and fishing for sunnies at the neighboring pond.

In 1950, my brother Craig was born, and three years later my father was assigned to manage the construction of the 23-story tall Mile High Center in Denver, Colorado. My father placed a plywood plank across the back seat of our 1948 Studebaker and covered it with an Army blanket so that Craig and I could play with our toys and sleep as we drove halfway across the country to our new life in Denver.

I attended second grade in my new school and at the age of seven, got my first bicycle for Christmas. I wasn't anywhere near tall enough to ride the 26-inch bike Santa got me, so my father affixed wooden blocks to the pedals so I could reach them. I often attribute my high speaking voice to the trauma my crotch encountered with the cross bar as I tried to learn how to ride the monstrosity. It was the only bike I owned from second-grade through high school.

We spent many weekends taking road trips to locations around the snow-capped Rocky Mountains. One summer, my parents sent me to an overnight summer camp for several weeks where I learned to swim and ride horses.

We returned to New York in 1954 when a colleague, Leonard Jacobsen, replaced my father in Denver. My father's new position was managing the architectural office of I. M. Pei and Associates in New York City. The number of employees would grow from seven to over a hundred by the end of the fifties. I. M. Pei and Partners was established in 1960 with Pei, my father and Harry Cobb as founding partners.

We moved to Elmsford, N.Y. where I attended the third grade at Pocantico Hill Elementary School. I enjoyed school, made a lot of friends, rode my bike, and performed on a Bongo Board at one of our Cub Scout parent nights. We bought a house in North Tarrytown (now Sleepy Hollow) where I lived from fourth grade until I graduated from college, an area made famous by Washington Irving's 1820 book, "The Legend of Sleepy Hollow." By 1955, I had attended four schools in five years.

My father commuted to New York City by train from Phelps Manor Station for the next 15 years. We lived in one of the new houses in Sleepy Hollow Manor, which was considered an upscale subdivision. I had lots of friends to play with who lived on the circle of houses that skirted Fremont Pond. I had access to several square miles of wooded acreage where I spent many hours exploring, camping, and building forts.

On the other side of the subdivision was an old country club owned by the Benedict family. It had an Olympic-sized pool, a large open field, and a couple of tennis courts. Access to the pool required a personal invitation from the Benedicts, whose son Neil—fortunately for me—was also in the fourth-grade. Neil wasn't in my classroom, but his best friend Billy Erickson was, so I weaseled an invitation and we all ended up best friends, and I was soon swimming in the Benedicts' pool and playing football and baseball in their field.

48

JIMMY WOLITARSKY WAS A CLASSMATE OF MINE IN MRS. THOMAS'S fourth-grade class. He lived in the Van Tassel Apartments, a large apartment complex across from the school. Many of my new friends lived there and most of their fathers worked at the Tarrytown Chevrolet Plant adjacent to the Hudson River. On an early spring day in April, Jimmy invited me to go with him to the YMCA to swim. Winter was receding and mornings were chilly but things warmed up by afternoon. When I got back home from the Y, the neighborhood was frantic. Word was that some boys had fallen off a raft in the pond bordering our subdivision. It was frightening to see the police cars and fire trucks with their flashing lights, parked in front of the houses.

My nine-year-old friends Joey Wolar and Chris Brown had decided to copy some older boys and took a raft ride on Turtle Pond. They had dressed warmly in heavy coats and boots and told their parents they were going hiking in the woods. Apparently the raft tipped over in the deep, icy pond and, hampered by their heavy winter clothes, they both drowned.

When I got home from the Y, I was intercepted by my tearful, red-eyed mother who grabbed my hand and tugged me back to the house as I attempted to run to the pond to find out what had happened. She sat me down in the living room and broke the news that my friends had both drowned. The death of friends at the age of nine was incomprehensible. I heard my mother tell my father that while I was at the YMCA with Jimmy, she had answered a call from Joey inviting me to go "hiking" with him and Chris. I had nightmares for weeks, imagining the horror of flailing underwater, desperately trying to reach the surface for air.

I will never forget the smells, the music, and the raw emotions that I experienced attending their respective wakes. The rooms were unworldly with their back-lit glowing caskets and the overwhelming aroma of lilies and roses. The murmur of sobs mingled with the morbid organ music made my skin crawl.

Joey had been one of my closest friends. As I stood by the door to the viewing room, his father took my hand and we walked over to his casket. We both looked down at Joey's waxy ashen face, his small white yarmulke on his neatly combed hair. His father squeezed my hand and sobbed, "He looks like he's sleeping." I was traumatized for life. Staring at this little boy's lifeless body, I thought I was going to faint. To this day I cannot bear to look into an open casket.

***

My father was my hero. I can remember his picture on my parent's nightstand, handsome in his Army captain's uniform. Ever since the first grade I decided I wanted to be like him and serve in the Army. My military career aspiration was fortified by my resolve to attain admission to West Point, which our popular President and Commander of the Allied Forces, Dwight Eisenhower had graduated from. The U.S. Military Academy at West Point was ninety minutes north of North Tarrytown along the Hudson River. In 1958, Army had a nationally-ranked football team featuring Heisman Trophy recipient Pete Dawkins. Another hero of mine, Dawkins was a three-letter athlete, commander of the Corps, and upon graduation became a Rhodes Scholar at Oxford. Dawkins was on the cover of Life magazine and interviewed by Edward R. Murrow on the TV show "Person to Person."

A four-book series, written by Colonel "Red" Reeder, followed a West Point cadet's progression through the Academy as a plebe, yearling, second-class, and first-class cadet. I read each book several times. "The West Point Story" was a weekly TV show I watched religiously. My father accommodated my pleas and took me several times to West Point to tour the Academy. I wistfully imagined myself marching in their impressive uniforms. For a month I would make my father inspect my room, as I tried to mimic the plebe's requirement to make a bed you could bounce a quarter off of.

Because of my obsession to attend the Academy, I set goals to meet the admission requirements of academic excellence, leadership, and athletics.

***

My father attained the rank of Life as a Boy Scout and four of my cousins became Eagle Scouts. Scouting was a family tradition and I fervently wanted to be an Eagle Scout like my cousins. I figured my scouting experience would be good training for West Point. By learning the requisite information and acquiring proficiency in outdoor skills I would earn progressively higher ranks, develop leadership skills, become self-reliant, and best of all, I'd get to wear a uniform.

After eagerly studying the Boy Scout manual, I passed my Tenderfoot rank test as soon as I was eligible in December, on my birthday. I joined Dick Barker's Coyote patrol with Mark Siderits, Charlie Smith, and other friends. Meetings were held weekly for both the troop and patrols. Under Barker's leadership we won the troop competition for Patrol of the Year. I earned my First Class badge by June, which allowed me to earn merit badges at Boy Scout Camp that summer.

Camp Read was located in the Adirondack Mountains in upstate New York, near Lake George. Typically, a scout attends a two-week session with members of his troop. I wanted to stay longer, and signed up for four weeks, but my mother got the sessions mixed up and brought me to camp two weeks early, so I happily ended up staying for six weeks.

I diligently spent the summer obtaining the merit badges that were required to progress to the next rank. I needed five badges for Star, ten for Life, and twenty-one for the coveted rank of Eagle.

The Pioneering merit badge required the mastery of a variety of knots, the ability to lash poles together, and being able to splice ropes together into useful configurations.

My inability to float on my back delayed earning my swimming badge. Being so skinny, my feet would sink while I tried to keep water from trickling into my nose. I practiced for weeks, inflating my chest with air, arching my back and drawing shallow breaths to avoid another plunge to the bottom of the muddy lake.

A five-mile wilderness hike and camping trip was the culminating event of each two-week session. To most of us, this was a daunting rite of passage. We had to learn to pack our knapsacks with sufficient provisions and ensure that things were distributed properly so our mess kits wouldn't dig into our backs as we hiked the five miles along rocky trails. Once we got to the camp site, we separated into our own troops, and each patrol had its own campsite. We would pitch our tents around a communal fire where we cooked our meals and kept ourselves warm.

The quality of our experience depended on the leadership ability of the patrol leader and the cooperation of patrol members. Building the fire, scavenging for wood, hauling water from a local stream or pond, preparing meals, and cleanup were shared chores.

Those two-night camping trips were more often than not miserable ordeals. We endured little sleep and clumsily prepared meals of burnt pancakes and raw, dirt-speckled hamburgers. But hiking made me ravenous, and I not only ate those pancakes and hamburgers, I overcame my childhood aversion to oatmeal and corned beef hash. The satisfaction of mastering camping skills, enjoying the sights and smells of the outdoors, all became a precious lifetime experience for me.

By the end of the summer I had earned the rank of Star, having acquired the necessary five merit badges. The next fall, in the seventh grade, I was selected to be a leader of the Apache patrol, due to my rapid advancement to the rank of Star and my commitment and enthusiasm for scouting. But regardless of my rank or my enthusiasm, I needed to earn respect and credibility as a leader. Patrol competitions included inspections at troop meetings, individual rank advancement, patrol flag competitions, and performance at such skill events as first aid rallies and camping trips. As a result of my patrol winning the annual competition and my rank advancement, I was selected Troop Scout of the Year.

The following summer I attended Camp Read for a month and secured additional merit badges toward the rank of Life. In eighth grade I was selected as troop senior patrol leader and assisted our scoutmaster in conducting the weekly troop meetings and supervising the four patrol leaders. I loved scouting and the dedication and discipline it took to learn the skills and accumulate the merit badges necessary for me to reach Eagle Scout. The only disappointment was that none of my close friends remained in scouting.

During the summer of 1960, between eighth grade and high school, I earned enough money to attend the National Boy Scout Jamboree that was going to be held in Colorado Springs on the grounds of the newly established U.S. Air Force Academy. Every four years, scouts from around the country attend the National Jamboree. I traveled to Washington, D.C. with a troop of scouts from Westchester County, NY, joining hundreds of other scouts as we embarked on a three-day train ride across the country to Colorado. It turned out to be an incredible experience, and I got to meet scouts from all over the nation and the world.

I earned my Eagle rank a couple of weeks before I reached the age of 14, a feat that was highlighted in our local paper. I remained a scout during my freshman year in high school and worked as a counselor at Camp Read that summer. My interests later shifted to sports and girls and I stopped participating in scouting near the beginning of my sophomore year. But I cherished the lessons and experiences I gained as a Boy Scout. To this day I remain a proud Eagle Scout.

49

*IN THE FIFTH GRADE, NEIL BENEDICT AND I STARTED PLAYING BASE-*ball with neighborhood kids in the field on his family's property. We both joined the Little League and I was assigned to the fire department-sponsored Columbia Hose team. Having been born in December, I was the youngest and smallest in both my class and on the baseball team. At my first at bat, I scored an unexpected and bewildering homerun, when my hit inexplicably popped over the second baseman's head into right field and the fielder's errant throw careened over the third baseman's head. Expectations of my athletic greatness slowly evaporated as I not only went hitless for the rest of the season, but my bat never even made contact with a ball for a foul. Though I continued to play Little League baseball through grammar school, my mediocre performance was early evidence of an unfortunate lack of hand-eye coordination.

In the fall, I briefly harbored fantasies of becoming a star halfback like my West Point hero, Pete Dawkins. Those dreams faded when my eager, skinny 95-pound self was confronted with the bigger and faster teammates on the junior high team. In one of our two games, I got called in to play when our team had already secured an insurmountable lead. As a wingback, I was tasked to block for our fullback, Bob Mauterstock, who needed me to push through an opening between the guard and the tackle. Faster and 30 pounds heavier, Mauterstock impatiently ran right over me, branding my right triceps with his cleats. With my arm in a sling, I slinked sheepishly down the school hallways for a couple of days, mumbling vaguely about a football injury.

Neil Benedict and I spent many afternoons at neighbor and classmate Billy Patterson's driveway, playing basketball. Billy's brother, Jay, was three years older than us and on the high school team. Saturday mornings we played on a YMCA basketball league coached by Jay. After my dismal showing in baseball and football, I refocused my considerable sports enthusiasm to basketball. Once again size and coordination became a factor. We were all pretty small and at 5 feet tall I played forward. I soon became obsessed with the sport and fantasized about making the high school team. Every day after school, I'd be at the Patterson's playing in pick-up games, and shooting a hundred free throws before dribbling the ball with each hand the half-mile back to my house. The summer after 8th grade I attended basketball camp at Kings College, which was a small school in Briarcliff, NY. Emboldened by the coaching I received from the impressive staff that included Lew Alcindor's (Kareem Abdul Jabbar) high school coach Jack Donohue from the infamous Power Memorial High School and Al McGuire of the NIT championship team Marquette University, I figured I should have a good chance of making the team.

50

I'VE ALWAYS HAD CRUSHES ON GIRLS. WHEN WE MOVED TO SLEEPY Hollow Manor, I had a crush on Reggie Kelly, a cute slim blond who lived across the street. Though she fended off my kisses, I was allowed a couple of hugs. My fantasy girlfriend for two years was redhead Karen Sloane. She was the smartest and cutest girl in my fourth- and fifth-grade classes. I don't remember her talking to me until we were in the sixth grade, when I had already lost interest in her and shifted my affections to the cute blond, Georgia Putnam. She showed more interest and we'd tease each other by passing notes back and forth.

It wasn't until junior high that it was finally socially acceptable to announce an interest in girls and pursue crushes. My first real aching, all-consuming crush was Kathy Fuller. She moved into Philips Manor when we were in the seventh grade. She was thin, with dirty-blond hair, attended all honors classes, and captivated me with her self-assured attitude and the way she walked with head held high.

Many of the kids who lived in either Sleepy Hollow Manor or the adjacent upper-middle-class subdivision, Philips Manor, went to Sleepy Hollow Country Club on Friday nights for dance lessons. Though my family weren't club members, I was sponsored by a wealthier neighbor and got to attend. Boys were required to wear suits and girls wore party dresses with patent leather shoes and white gloves. We learned the fox trot, waltz, Lindy Hop, and the cha cha.

I pursued Kathy in dance class where she would command the

space around her, dancing with arm outstretched, craning her face away. When Neil admitted his interest in her, she became even more appealing to me. We would race walk toward her, maintaining formal country club decorum, trying to beat the other for dances with her. We invited her to a winter party on the icy shore of Fremont Pond and played spin the hockey stick, though I don't think either one of us ever got to kiss her.

On weekends, Neil and I would spend the night at each other's houses watching "77 Sunset Strip" and "The Twilight Zone" and pestering Kathy on the phone. One of us would call her with the other one on the extension line, and in the course of the conversation we'd try to get her to reveal which one of us she liked best. Even though I got her a wrist corsage for our one and only date to a seventh-grade dance, she never reciprocated either of our affections.

Over the summer between seventh and eighth grade we would gather at the pebbly, gray Philips Manor Beach on the Hudson River, occasionally swimming but mostly sitting around in groups checking out how we were progressing through puberty. Jan Morris had been a plain and chubby girl in grade school, with glasses and braces. One day Neil and I were at the beach and he turned to me and asked if I knew who the cute girl was sitting next to Pam Wood. I figured she had probably either just moved in or was someone's relative. "That's Jan Morris!" he chortled.

An ugly duckling turned swan puberty miracle, Jan had redistributed the baby fat, gotten rid of her braces and replaced her glasses with contact lenses, revealing pale green eyes and long dark lashes.

That fall Neil Benedict, Billy Patterson, and I attended Ann Siller's birthday party. We clustered with the other boys on one side of Ann's basement rec room and casually strolled over to grab some Coke and potato chips at the refreshment table. As the night progressed, some of the established couples, or girls, would dance to Del Shannon, Fabian, the Everly Brothers, Bobby Vinton, and Brenda Lee. The three of us summoned up our courage and crossed the demilitarized zone. Neil started dancing with Pam Wood, Billy ended up with Sally Gray, and I slow danced with Jan Morris. As we walked home from the party, the three of us speculated as to whether we now had girlfriends.

On Monday I spotted Jan at school and when she smiled at me, I was relieved to find her still interested. When we talked at her locker at lunch, I knew that we were an item. That night I called her on the phone. Nervous about the conversation, I had prepared a list of topics and questions. The conversation went surprisingly well. On the bus the next morning, I caught a whiff of her shampoo as we sat next to each other and my anxiety at the upcoming math test suddenly disappeared. I spent class visualizing her amused eyes responding to my clever jokes. I longed to talk to her at lunch and see her in the hall on the way to my next class.

A few days later Jan invited us to her house. Her basement den was equipped with a large pool table and a wrap-around couch. A Johnny Mathis album, the make-out sound track for junior high slow dancing, was playing on the record player. Jan and I snuggled on the couch watching Pam and Neil poke balls with their pool cues and listening to Billy and Sally pant and slurp next to us. I fidgeted nervously before making my move. After a silent count down, I took a deep breath, turned and squashed the side of Jan's nose with my mouth. She repositioned her face and our lips awkwardly pushed against each other and our teeth clicked in our first kiss. Neil, Billy, and I walked back home reveling in our first make-out session.

That week Jan and I saw each other in school, sat together on the bus home, and talked on the phone at night. I was deliriously happy.

Friday night at dance class, instead of sitting on opposite sides of the room, we sat next to each other. I pulled what I thought was a smooth move when I handed Jan a cup of punch from the refreshment table and with it, my Boy Scout ID bracelet. She wore it for the rest of the night. She still had it on that Saturday when we met up at the science fair. I loved holding her soft hands with their long elegant fingers.

On Monday's ride to school, Neil, Billy, and I recounted the previous night's TV episode of *Alfred Hitchcock Presents*, while we waited for our girlfriends to board the bus. We'd sit at the back and the girls would sit up front, but they'd wait for us after getting off and we'd walk to our lockers together. Pam and Sally waited for Billy and Neil, but Jan walked ahead without waiting for me. The girls anxiously looked over at me and whispered to Neil and Billy. Pam finally announced that Jan wanted to talk to me at her locker. Jan wouldn't meet my eyes as I trudged towards her. It seemed as if the hall was suddenly filled with curious gawkers as this drama unfolded. My stomach was churning and I knew what was coming, but I couldn't figure out why. I felt like running past her to my class. She lifted her face and averting her eyes, handed back my ID bracelet.

"I'm sorry but I think it's better this way." I took the bracelet and walked to my locker in a state of shock and confusion. "What did that mean—better this way?" I knew there must be some mistake, but I didn't want to interrogate her in front of the hallway audience, so I slinked off to class. I felt sick and numb all day.

When I got home after school, I called her and asked her why. She said I was a great guy but she decided she just wanted to be friends. I spent the next month crying myself to sleep and waking up depressed. Pam broke up with Neil a week later, and Billy and Sally called it off soon after. Thus ended the first of many romances to come.

51

*SHARING INTERESTS IN SPORTS AND GIRLS AS WE DID, NEIL BENE*dict remained my closest friend in elementary and junior high school. In the winter we'd play hockey on Fremont Pond. Neil was a better skater and eventually became the star defenseman on our high school team. We were both Boy Scouts, though Neil didn't stay with scouting very long. We never had classes together but our grades were similar and we were both reasonably conscientious students.

I met Enzo DiMaio through Neil. They were both in Mr. Walker's fifth-grade class. Enzo's father was an anesthesiologist from Italy who had moved to Tarrytown with his wife when Enzo, an only child, was an infant. He and I became closer friends when we shared the same classes in eighth grade. We had very compatible senses of humor and loved entertaining each other and our classmates with our antics. Enzo was an uncanny mimic and much of his humor involved impersonating other students and teachers. Soon we were at each other's homes after school and on weekends. Our attempts to study together invariably degenerated into raucous laughter and teasing, often at the expense of his good-natured mother. But as the only child in his extended family, Enzo was adored and fussed over, including me, his blond American friend.

Enzo's mother was an amazing cook and spent most of her time in the kitchen preparing the family meals. I was eventually "adopted" as a member of the family and was invited over for many wonderful meals.

Though Enzo's father was strict and intimidating, he was nice to me. A dinner at the DiMaio's was a culinary extravaganza. Italian was spoken at the table with Enzo responding in English. We'd constantly be clowning around and Enzo would try his best to make me laugh out loud at the dinner table. His mother would sigh and chide him in her wonderful Italian accent to behave himself and be more like his nice friend Bruce.

One evening I was trying mightily to ignore his antics and maintain his parents' approval. He made a ridiculous face while I was about to swallow a mouthful of minestrone soup. Trying not to laugh, I ended up choking and managed to spray soup all over Dr. DiMaio. He sat there as noodles and carrots dribbled off his face, an outline of his profile splattered on the wall behind him. Enzo rolled on the floor laughing as I sputtered and apologized profusely to Dr. DiMaio. Mrs. DiMaio moaned "Brrrrruce...." with multiple r's rolling off her tongue. After cleaning up, we continued with our meals, and I avoided any more eye contact with Enzo.

Sunday dinners were a tradition at the DiMaios'. Enzo's mother and aunt would begin the prep work on Thursday and spend all Friday and Saturday cooking. Relatives from surrounding towns would descend on the DiMaio home after Mass. His mother and aunt served up seemingly endless platters of salad, seafood, pasta, vegetables, and meats. After the meal, everyone would take a break, either at the table playing cards, in the living room watching TV, or in the guest room napping. Then we'd all reassemble at the dining table a while later for fruit, cheese, pastries, and drinks.

It was a treat to be invited over, but it could be a little anxiety-provoking. Mrs. DiMaio would occasionally serve dishes such as octopus and unusual varieties of vegetables that I had never tasted before.

All eyes would be on me to see just how adventurous Enzo's friend was. The whole mealtime ritual was new and exotic to me, especially with everyone jabbering away in Italian, complete with exaggerated hand gestures.

This feasting was in stark contrast to my family's mealtimes. Since my parents were always at work, we had housekeepers who often lived with us during the work week. Neither of my parents cooked. My mother's specialty was Swanson TV dinners, which were stockpiled in our basement freezer. My father could heat up soup, make a grilled cheese sandwich, and maybe scramble some eggs. We rarely shared family dinners since my brother and I usually ate before my parents came home from work.

Few of my friends loved and appreciated food as much as Enzo did. He savored our maid Rosemary's fried chicken which she stashed in our refrigerator to sustain the family during her weekend absences. And despite the plethora of delicious home cooked meals, Enzo would happily chow down on my mother's stash of frozen TV dinners. We'd spend many weekends up in my room watching TV and gorging on fried chicken and TV dinners. On Sundays my father would go to the Flamingo delicatessen and bring home a large supply of roast beef, rye bread, lox, bagels, and assorted pastries for an informal Sunday brunch which was self-served and either eaten on the floor of the living room while reading the Sunday paper or in the den in front of the TV.

52

*BILLY'S OLDER BROTHER, JAY PATTERSON, POSSESSED ALL THE AT-*tributes I felt would get me admitted to West Point. He was president of the student council, captain of both cross-country and track teams, member of the basketball team, and an honor roll student. I wanted to be just like him.

Having finally come to terms with my limited physical attributes, I abandoned my dream of playing football, and with Jay's encouragement decided to go out for cross-country. With a team of upper classmen and freshmen recruits, he organized August practices to get us in shape for the fall season. We were fortunate to have access to the undeveloped 150-acre John D. Rockefeller family estate known as Rockwood Hall, located in Pocantico Hills adjacent to Tarrytown and North Tarrytown. It overlooked the Hudson River and was an idyllic area to grow up in, with miles of hiking trails, sloping fields for sledding in the winter, and miles of open space for running cross-country. Though I enjoyed the camaraderie and was encouraged that my running time was improving, distance running was painful. But this was what was required to get in shape to make the basketball team and earn Jay's respect. As the summer progressed, our training included long runs, wind sprints, hill climbing, and time trials.

As the season approached, I had the best times for any freshman. At our first meet against three other teams I was the only freshman selected to run junior varsity. Our best junior varsity runner was sophomore Dick Barker, my former Boy Scout patrol leader. In anticipation of the inevitable pain and exhaustion, I was usually nauseous before competition.

As the starting gun went off, I took a comfortable position at the back of the pack. The course wound for 2.5 miles through the woods. With each turn I could see the runners ahead of me. After about a mile into the race, I felt strong and sped up to pass one runner at a time in front of me. The sound of the cheering crowd at the finish line grew louder. With less than a quarter mile left, we emerged onto the football field where the lead pack of runners was visible. Dick Barker was two runners ahead of me and I sprinted the last hundred yards, finishing behind him and in 6th place. I was greeted with cheers and congratulations by the coach and my teammates. It was exhilarating and gratifying to have placed so well. My parents were proud of me and once again I was launched into fantasies of athletic stardom.

The week after my triumphant junior varsity performance, I competed in the freshman meet against our rival Ossining High School. Included on our freshman team were Billy Patterson, Jimmy Wolitarsky, Steve Smith, Eric Frandsen, and Jimmy Jacobsen. Since I was expected to win, I was more nervous than I had been before the junior varsity meet. As usual I began at the back of the pack, trying to remain relaxed. My strategy seemed to be working as I began to pass runners, feeling stronger as the race progressed. With a half- mile to go I was in the lead pack and comfortably accelerating. With a hundred yards to go, matching strides with teammate Steve Smith, my lungs were burning, and I lunged forward as Steve's chest broke the tape first. Totally spent, I collapsed on the ground and needed assistance to get up and recover. Initially I rationalized that this was only one loss, but the sickening pattern continued.

The next meet I not only was beaten by Steve, but by Wolitarsky, and the following meet by those two and Jacobsen. By the end of the season, instead of being the fastest freshman, I ended up slowest. Though my times didn't worsen as the season progressed, I realized that I had peaked and plateaued early, while everyone else continued to improve. I was disappointed but consoled myself that my real goal was to achieve adulation as a high school basketball star. Who watched or cared about cross-country?

***

In addition to running cross-country that fall, I continued to spend lots of time at the Patterson's neighborhood basketball court shooting free throws, jump shots from every perimeter position, drilling right and left-handed layups. I thought of nothing but making the high school team.

Traditionally, Sleepy Hollow High School had excellent basketball teams and we were always contenders in the Westchester County Sectional Competition. Joe Sager was the head coach and would select twelve out of the fifty freshmen who competed for the coveted positions. Sager was already familiar with those who played on the junior high team, such as Butch Remmel, Gene Clark, Brad Taylor, and Tommy Wilmott.

With all the attention the junior high team players had been getting, it was obvious Sager had his team preselected. Though I was confident of my basketball skills, it was apparent I hadn't impressed Sager because my name wasn't on the list posted on his office door the next day.

Though disappointed, I wasn't discouraged and was doubly committed to eventually earning a spot on the team. With Jay Patterson's encouragement, I volunteered to be the team manager. I figured the best way to make the team was to get Sager's attention. By attending practice every day, fetching basketballs, supplying towels and water, he would eventually get to know me and maybe let me practice with the team now and then. Once he recognized my ability, enthusiasm, and commitment, he'd have no choice but to let me on the team the following year. After a full month of dutifully fulfilling my managerial responsibilities and patiently sitting on the bench, not only did Sager not know my name, but when I tried to practice with the team, he told me to sit down and stay out the way. My strategy didn't work.

***

With encouragement from friends and the coach, I went out for the wrestling team. I was taking Earth Science from Mr. Pais who, along with being the junior varsity football coach, was also the varsity wrestling coach. Among my friends on the team were Jimmy Wolitarsky, Billy Patterson, Carl Caivano, Steve Smith, his brother Charlie, and Geof Herguth and his cousin Bill.

Though not very strong, I had good endurance from having run cross-country. It took me several weeks of practice to master some of the wrestling fundamentals. As the season progressed, I could resist being turned onto my back when in a half-nelson by twisting the other way and lifting my head. On the bottom, I could sit out and sometimes escape or reverse my opponent. After several weeks of practice, the freshmen team competed against Ossining High School.

High school wrestling consists of three two-minute periods. At the beginning of the first period, both wrestlers are standing and try to take their opponent to the mat. At the start of the second and third periods, both wrestlers are down on the mat trying to either reverse or escape.

During my match, I was quickly taken to the mat with a double-leg takedown, but I managed to reverse my opponent. I was eventually pinned but, Mr. Pais bolstered my disappointment by observing that I had potential. Encouraged by steady progress, I eventually made first string at my weight class.

At the end of the season my parents and my Jewish godparents, Rose and Herm Davis, attended the freshman county tournament. Herm was a big wrestling fan, having earned a black belt in judo while in the Marines. He hoped I had gained some strength from the weights he had bought me after I broke my arm in the fifth-grade. Unfortunately, my match didn't last long enough for him to make any assessment of my strength. When I retell the story of this match I often joke that I can't remember whether I was pinned before or after we shook hands, but it was the fastest pin in the tournament. My family was sympathetic but I was so humiliated that I vowed to never be pinned again and kept that vow through high school.

Wrestling season ended in the spring, and the fall of my sophomore year, after my disastrous experience running cross-country, and with encouragement from coach Pais and my wrestling friends, I went out for football. Several of the better freshman players such as Butch Remmel,

Gene Clark, Steve Conn, and Gene Carruthers had moved up to varsity which provided opportunities for the rest of us on the junior varsity. Though I only weighed 130 pounds as a sophomore, I started as a tackle on both offense and defense. I enjoyed playing but found practice very boring. With basketball no longer an option as my high profile sport, I figured maybe I'd grow and get some attention playing football instead.

After an encouraging sophomore year where I started and played every game, I spent most of my junior year sitting on the bench with Charlie Smith, wearing a sparkling clean uniform with prime 50-yard line viewing. As second- string ends behind Doug Delsodato and Johnny Blalock, we would occasionally get to play when our team had a sizeable lead. Football practice was boring and tedious with a season that spanned blazing, humid heat in August and frigid cold November when the ground felt like cold concrete covered with grass. We had a winning season junior year and were undefeated senior year with players such as Butch Remmel, Gene Clark, Steve Conn, and Gene Carruthers receiving All-County recognition. Though I rarely played, I enjoyed my identity as a team member sitting in the stands in my uniform at pep rallies, at post-game gatherings at Walton's soda fountain, and at evening parties.

One of the thrilling games that threatened to spoil our undefeated record was against a sectional rival, Pleasantville High School. In the last seconds of the game, Butch Remmel caught a Hail Mary pass from Gene Clark to overcome Pleasantville's four-point lead. The town went crazy and there was front-page newspaper coverage the next morning. Thanks to the generous support of our booster club, we enjoyed a season-ending dinner at exclusive Tappan Restaurant where the team was awarded Sleepy Hollow High School letter jackets. Though my contribution was minimal, it was fun to be on an undefeated football team my senior year.

53

MY ATTRACTIVE MOTHER WAS A FASHION MODEL WHEN MY PARENTS married. She eventually moved on to public relations, but I always suspected she wanted a career in show business. She came close to it when she became the secretary for the McGuire Sisters, a popular singing group who had a couple of hit records and were frequent guests on a variety of shows, including Arthur Godfrey and Ed Sullivan. Her association with the McGuire sisters provided us with occasional exposure to celebs and gave me bragging rights with my friends.

I strived to please my parents. My mother was proud of my accomplishments and would casually slip accounts of my exploits into her conversations with my aunt and uncle. I was pleased to have garnered respect from my relatives for my scouting, athletic, and academic achievements, but I was sometimes embarrassed by my mother's exaggeration of my accomplishments. It wasn't enough that I won a school race, but she would elevate it to a school record. Not only was I an Eagle Scout, but the youngest in the history of New York State.

My mother had unpredictable mood swings and, looking back on her behavior, I think she may have been bi-polar. With her raucous sense of humor, she could be the life of the party and like me, she loved attention. She also had a quick and sometimes irrational temper. My brother and I were always trying to read her moods and tiptoed around her cautiously. Extraverted compared to my father, she was the family social director and arranged get-togethers with friends and family. She disciplined my brother and me by yelling and screaming and on rare occasions, administering spankings.

One evening when I was in the 10th grade, I came downstairs to find my father comforting my mother as she sobbed in their bedroom. He sat me down and revealed that she had just been diagnosed with breast cancer. He assured me it had been detected early enough. She would enter the hospital by the end of the week for radiation treatment and our lives were never the same after that. For the rest of high school and until her death my sophomore year in college, the cancer cloud always hovered over the family. She would never work again and would either spend time in the hospital or at home recovering from treatment. She wasn't always bed ridden, but her health would cycle from cancer treatment to recovery, to brief periods of remission, to metastasis, and finally death in 1965 at the age of forty-three.

54

DURING THE FALL OF MY JUNIOR YEAR, NEIL BENEDICT BRIEFLY dated a very cute girl named Christine Flynn who had transferred from a neighboring high school. She was invited to one of Bella Weiss's parties, and when I realized that Neil was interested in Linda Stabin, I danced with Christine all night. She had shoulder length brown hair, a nice figure, and big brown eyes that scrunched up when she smiled.

I couldn't stop thinking about her the following day when I was playing touch football with Neil, Jimmy Wolitarsky and Charlie Smith in the field behind my house. I wanted to call her Sunday night, but not wanting to come on too strong, decided to wait until Monday to see how she greeted me. Monday I walked confidently into the cafeteria at lunch and spotted her sitting with Cathy Van Steen. She glanced at me and as I sat down, my mind went blank. "Hey…um…hey, did you do your French homework?" She looked at Cathy and they sort of giggled and rolled their eyes. Obviously my weird inquiry swept her off her feet and her eyes crinkled up in that warm smile. We eventually slid into a comfortable exchange. Assured that she was interested, I proceeded to walk her to her next class.

That Saturday I was hanging out at Enzo's house. We were fooling around in his room and I received a call from my mother announcing that my grandmother had arrived and that the family was going to celebrate my 16th birthday. I ran home, crossing the field that separated my neighborhood from Enzo's. I almost fainted in shock when I was greeted by a chorus of "Surprise!" as I entered the house. With Enzo's assistance, my mom had planned the party and invited all my friends, including Christine. I paraded around for the rest of the night with Christine on my arm, thanking everyone for coming. Later I took her home with Jimmy Bates, my only friend with a driver's license. We snuggled in the back seat and had our first kiss. Now that I had a pretty girlfriend, high school life was good.

Christine lived with her grandmother during the week and in Thornwood with her parents on weekends. After her sophomore year she decided she wanted to attend Sleepy Hollow instead of Lakeland High School where her parents lived.

Her mother and grandmother had both been pregnant at the same time and Christine's birth preceded that of her uncle Danny, who was a grade behind us. An only child, Christine was adored by her parents and grandparents. Her mother's parents Fanny and Big Danny lived with her uncle in an old house at the bottom of a hill on Main Street in Tarrytown, a couple of blocks from the railroad station and within view of the Hudson River. Big Danny worked at the Chevrolet plant and Fanny was a cheerful stay-at-home mother.

On days that I didn't have sports practice I would walk Christine home and we would hang out in an upstairs den which served as her bedroom or we'd sit in the living room watching TV with her grandparents.

Her father Carl owned a machine shop in Tarrytown and her mother Dorothy worked part time as the shop's bookkeeper. The three generations of Flynn/Brown women were like sisters. I was warmly embraced into the family, and the four of us would spend time laughing and teasing each other.

I was a member of the popular clique which included the athletes and class leaders, so Christine and I were included in all the class social events. The girls in the clique were the cheerleaders, members of the color guard, twirlers, and girlfriends of the popular boys. Unfortunately, these girls, also known as the Rat Pack, felt threatened by Christine, and would exclude or ignore her. I kind of resented having to side with Christine over these girls with whom I had previously been long-time friends, and this caused tension between Christine and me.

But I was proud to be dating the girl voted cutest in our senior class and who was popular among my male friends. I could easily trigger that crinkly-eyed smile with a funny remark as I often did around her. Several months older than me, she got her driver's license first and chauffeured me to school, movies, school games, and parties.

I vacationed with Christine and her parents in Cape Cod the summer before our senior year after having saved up some money I earned working at her father's machine shop. He found me to be a reliable but uninspired employee. The combination of boring tasks and my utter lack of interest in anything mechanical resulted in my preoccupation with willing the hands of the shop clock to move faster. Christine's father Carl was a no-nonsense, intimidating guy. He stood about 5-foot-9 with a black crew cut, coal-black, piercing eyes, and Popeye-sized forearms. He seemed to harbor a simmering anger so I kept my distance, pretended to laugh at his lame jokes, and basically strived to keep his daughter happy in his presence.

As a Friday night ritual after my wrestling match, Christine would cook dinner for us at her house in Thornwood. We had the place to ourselves while her parents went to their favorite neighborhood tavern to celebrate the end of the workweek. Christine would cook a steak dinner, which I would devour after a week of dieting to make my wrestling weight. We would then retire to her room where we would lay in her queen-sized bed watching TV and making out. When her parents would eventually come home, her inebriated mother would stick her head in Christine's bedroom and sit on the bed, giggling and watch TV with us.

The Rat Pack's cruel treatment of Christine isolated her from the girl-dominated social group and she became more and more clingy. I still had lots of male friends I wanted to spend time with and I began to feel smothered, especially during my senior year when Christine had little interest in spending time with anyone but me.

Enzo remained my closest friend in high school and when I wasn't with Christine, I was either at his house or he was at mine. Enzo eventually confessed he had a crush on Christine, which I found endearing since Christine loved spending time with us both but thought of Enzo as nothing more than a good friend. He served as a sounding board for both of us as we maneuvered through the ups and downs of our high school romance.

During our senior year, Christine's insecurity and clinginess grew, as did my need for freedom. I was torn, because there was no one I was more attracted to, but it was my last year and I wanted the freedom to hang out with my former group of friends.

Karen, an attractive red-headed member of the Rat Pack and my fourth- and fifth-grade love interest, was one of the smartest, prettiest, and most intimidating girls in my class. Though I was always interested, she was never approachable until we were in high school and in the same social group. She usually had one of the leading roles in school theatrical productions. When she started smoking, I lost interest but we still circled around each other. Once I started dating Christine, she was one of the members of the Rat Pack who was the most dismissive and rude to her.

Karen and I were both in Mr. Stokes' American History class and we would occasionally study together. One day in class she invited me over to her house to watch TV. Christine and I had just had a fight the night before over her insistence that we spend the evening together. I protested that I needed to stay home and study. After pacing around the house and venting on the phone to Enzo, I decided to call Karen and follow up on her offer.

I drove over to her house and we sat on a couch in her living room watching TV with her ashtray in front of her as she dragged on her Marlboros. Her parents were out and there was a fair amount of sexual tension in the air, but I resisted the prospect of a foul, cigarette-tasting kiss.

Suddenly the doorbell rang and standing at the door was red-eyed, fuming Christine. Karen stepped aside as I went out to face the raw, indignant onslaught of emotions I was confronted with for my treachery. Christine stomped back to her car ride with Cathy, which had been interrupted when they inadvertently spotted my car parked in front of Karen's house. I sheepishly slinked back in the house, plopped down next to Karen and watched the rest of the Dobie Gillis Show in uncomfortable silence. I eventually went home, wallowing in guilt, but also feeling trapped.

55

CONTINUING TO IMPROVE IN WRESTLING AND WITH ADEQUATE strength, speed, and balance, I eventually beat everyone in my weight class my sophomore year. Selected as junior varsity captain, I won both my 130-pound weight class matches and eventually beat the varsity wrestlers in my weight class to become our 136-pound starter. Though I would earn my varsity letter as a sophomore, I lost all six matches. Undeterred, I was convinced I could improve and became obsessed with wrestling. My junior year, I finally got my first victory with a 3-2 decision over a wrestler from Hastings High School and went on to win seven matches and lose six.

In wrestling, I finally found a sport where there's a correlation between effort and results. I could dribble and shoot a basketball until my fingers bled and I never improved enough to make the team. Unlike in football and basketball, size was not an issue in wrestling where you competed with opponents in your weight class. The best wrestlers weren't necessarily the strongest or quickest. Since I was tall for my weight-class, I could use my reach, leverage, and balance to my advantage. Dedication and hard work earned results. Wrestling is considered a grueling and demanding sport and for whatever reason, I was able to tolerate the pain and I loved the hard workouts and practices. Wrestling did wonders for my self-esteem and body image. I was no longer concerned about being skinny. I was never thick or muscular, but my lean physique was adequate for success as a wrestler.

Disappointingly, most of the spectators at our after-school matches were bored students waiting for the bus to take them home, and they usually disappeared before my match even began, leaving my mother, Christine, and a few other wrestlers' parents to cheer us on.

Jack McCleery, a recent graduate of New England's wrestling power Springfield College, was my third coach in four years. Though he hadn't wrestled, he was knowledgeable, organized, committed, and enthusiastic. We developed a unique coach/wrestler relationship since he was only four years older. Since I had been elected team captain and this was his first job out of college, he depended on my team leadership. Ten of my friends that I had started wrestling with freshman year had all quit, so our team was young and inexperienced.

During a practice session after a preseason scrimmage with Nanuet High School, I learned how to execute the Switch from my opponent, the previous year's Rockland County champion. The Switch is a very effective move to reverse your opponent and consists of you as the bottom wrestler sitting out to the side of your opponent and with your opponent's arm around your waist, reaching between his legs, shifting your weight, putting pressure on his shoulder and moving behind him. The shifting of one's hips with timing, speed, and force is an invaluable fundamental skill for mat wrestling that I was able to master, and it contributed to the success of my senior season.

As the year progressed, I beat Port Chester's Peritz in our first dual meet. My next match against Schaefer from Scarsdale was a confidence booster, since he placed third in the previous year's Sectional championships. I continued to win, beating Olmstead from Hastings, Bliss from Ossining, and was able to keep my undefeated season intact by managing a tie against Kelleher from Hastings. During a three-match week I managed three first-period pins against Dobbs Ferry, Peekskill, and John Jay.

As a result of my dominating week I received some county-wide recognition, earning honorable mention in the week's balloting for the prestigious Con-Ed Sports award for the best county winter athlete, which was selected among basketball, hockey, indoor track, swimming, and wrestling.

After dominating wins against Nanuet and Spring Valley, I went into my last duel season match undefeated. Our final dual meet of the year was against Port Chester and I would meet Peritz for the second time. Peritz's only loss of the season was against me, and our matches were closer each time we wrestled. I managed to take him down in the first period with my reliable double-leg takedown, but he immediately escaped and the score after the first period was 2-1. I rode him most of the second period, but at the last second he escaped and we finished the second period tied 2-2. In the third period, I reversed him to his back for 5 points and a 7-2 lead, but I overcommitted my weight and he reversed me to my back for another five-point move to tie the match 7-7. I finished the dual meet season barely salvaging my undefeated record and needed to prepare for the end-of-season's tournaments.

The good news was that I had been selected as the first seed in the divisional tournament; the bad news was that my first match was against a wrestler from Mount Vernon High School. I needed to place in the top four in the upcoming week's divisional tournament to qualify for the following week's sectional county tournament. With nationally recognized coach Hank Littlefield at the helm, Mount Vernon had one of the strongest teams in the state. Littlefield had wrestled heavyweight at 6-foot-five and 250 pounds, not only for Columbia

University but nationally for the New York Athletic Club as a member of both the national freestyle and Greco-Roman teams.

Mount Vernon had secured five of the top seeds. The reason my opponent, Jesse West from Mount Vernon, wasn't seeded was because he had lost some matches to wrestlers from considerably tougher teams than we competed with, from Long Island and Pennsylvania.

Tossing and turning in bed the night before the tournament, I dreamed of becoming the first ever Sleepy Hollow County wrestling champion.

My pre-tournament anxiety mounted with the entrance of the Mount Vernon team into the gym for pre-tournament stretching and limbering. Their hooded sweatshirts revealed only shadowed faces. The crowd gasped as the team pulled off their warm ups at the same time, revealing shaved heads and glistening, sculpted bodies. The physical and psychological competition had begun.

Matches are sequenced by weight class from lightweight to heavyweight. As team captain, I yelled encouragement to my teammates competing in the lighter weights, and kept looking around the gym for my mother and Christine. We secured a couple of victories, but the majority of our lightweights lost their first matches.

Finally, the public address system announced "Leonard and West report to mat 3." My ears were ringing and my stomach churned. Here it was. Neither my mother or Christine had arrived, but I needed to focus. My team surrounded the mat and my coach gave me some words of encouragement, which registered as white noise. Taking off my warm ups, I remained in a soundless zone and jogged onto the mat in what felt like slow motion. West's long rangy physique was unnerving since his height neutralized my customary reach and leverage advantage.

In the last couple of seconds of the first period, he countered my double- leg tackle with an explosive leg sprawl, and after a head-ripping cross-face, he zipped behind me for a takedown. Momentarily deflated by losing the confidence-boosting first period takedown, I instinctively threw my hips out and switched him for a reversal and a period-ending 2-2 tie.

Second period, I struggled with his size and he escaped with a stand-up, which I could usually prevent with a shorter opponent. He sprawled with those long legs, smacked my head with a cross-face, fending off my repeated attempts to take him down. He was leading after the second period 2-1. From the bottom position I was able to switch after a couple of seconds for two points, but he immediately stood up again and escaped to tie the match. I could sense the frantic cheering of my coach and teammates, but couldn't hear anything. We were tied, there was less than a minute left in the match, and whoever got the takedown would win. He wasn't shooting; I considered a less dependable fireman's carry since I hadn't been able to penetrate his legs. Though I was in good shape, fear of losing was draining my strength. A fireman's carry would require a firm grasp of his upper arm, driving my other arm through his legs, sitting through and forcing him to the mat. I needed a takedown to win. Initiating the takedown, his slippery triceps prevented me from securing my grip for the fireman's carry and I was left with my arms wrapped around his left leg. He sprawled and scooted behind me with my arms wrapped around his leg, which technically prevented his control, but the referee inexplicably gave him two points and the match.

Coach McCleery went ballistic, protesting loudly but to no avail. In disbelief, I dejectedly shook his hand and walked off the mat, greeted with sympathetic pats on the back from my teammates, screams from the jubilant Mount Vernon team, and tears in the eyes of my mother and Christine, who arrived in time to witness my heartbreaking loss.

Inconsolable, I sat in the locker room and overheard a wrestler exclaim to his teammate that "first-seeded Leonard just got knocked off in the first round." I had not only lost the most important match of my high school wrestling career, but I choked.

Coach McCleery found me with my head buried between my knees, gave me a reassuring shoulder squeeze, and reminded me I could still wrestle in the consolations and qualify for the sectionals if West won his next two matches and got into the finals. He instructed me to go out and support the rest of our wrestlers and root for West in his next match.

Struggling to regain my composure, I returned to the gym and supported my teammates. My spirits were buoyed by West winning his next match. Aching for West to win his match the following day, I suffered through another sleepless night. The next day, Shaefer beat West and my high school wrestling career was over. The next weekend I went to White Plains to watch the sectional championships and witness West improve with every match, avenge his loss to Shaefer to reach the finals, and beat Exton from White Plains who I had beaten in a preseason scrimmage. West was the Sectional Champion and during the season I had beaten the wrestlers who placed second, third and fourth in the tournament. I licked my wounds and set my sights on becoming a college wrestler.

After the Sectional Championships, Christine and I double-dated with Coach McCleery and his date from Marymount College and we went to the state championships on Long Island. Coach McCleery and I had more than just a coach/athlete relationship. We remained friends and he came to some of my college matches and I would visit him at Sleepy Hollow on some of my college vacations.

56

BY MY SOPHOMORE YEAR, JAY PATTERSON HAD GRADUATED AND HE was replaced by my next hero, Roc Caivano. Roc's impressive credentials included: president of the Student Council, co-captain of the Sleepy Hollow football team, competitive wrestler, star pole-vaulter and the heart throb of every girl in the school. Roc possessed a mischievous sense of humor and excelled academically and was not quite the goody-two-shoes, clean-cut guy that Jay Patterson had been.

My burning aspiration to be popular enough to be elected to a position of school leadership was still simmering. I had been co-treasurer of my freshman class with Billy Patterson and served as our homeroom student council representative all four years.

During senior year, my unappeased ego was bolstered by my nomination for Class President. My opponent was Larry Walton, another bench-warming companion during football season. We were in the same social clique and Larry had been voted cutest boy in the class.

The morning of the election, I woke with a nervous, queasy stomach. Here was another dream that was tantalizingly within reach. After school my shoulders slumped as I watched Jimmy Wolitarsky, our previous class president, approach me shaking his head. He informed me that I had lost to Larry by a single vote.

"Are you shitting me? One vote shy in a class of more than two hundred students?"

Not again. Another dream dashed. This sucked.

I congratulated my friend Larry and told him that I would have voted for him if I wasn't running. He was gracious and returned the sentiment. Ironically, Christine had been nominated for and elected to the position of Class Secretary, a position she accepted with minimal enthusiasm.

Devastated, I spent the ride home in Christine's car trying to feign ambivalence at my loss. When I congratulated her on her election, she quickly responded that she would relinquish her office in a minute if she could trade it for my selection as President, which was as comforting a comment as I could have hoped for.

57

WHEN I WASN'T WRESTLING, I WAS ATTENDING OTHER SCHOOL matches or regional tournaments. One of the Olympic-style tournaments I attended was at the renowned New York Athletic Club. While there, I met one of the coaches and asked if I could work out at the club. Though you needed to be a member in order to access the facilities, special considerations were made for athletes who wanted to work out. The coach gave me the team's workout schedule and instructed me to use the back entrance so I wouldn't be screened for a membership card. Just in case, he told me to use his name if I was ever stopped.

The New York Athletic Club was housed in an impressive twenty-four story building across from Central Park, and boosted not only state-of-the-art athletic facilities, but a fine dining restaurant and overnight guest rooms. Founded in 1868, the massive structure supported a variety of amateur sports such as wrestling, fencing, judo, water polo, rowing, and track and field. It was also a part of the New York cultural fabric hosting receptions, banquets, and welcoming leaders of business, politics, and the arts. Inside, members had access to a large gym, fitness equipment, an Olympic-size pool with surrounding steam, sauna, whirlpools, and a shared floor for wrestling, boxing, and fencing. The club was not only limited to athletic activities. One floor contained a library and rooms for billiards, chess, and cards. At the time, membership was limited to men only, with strict dress codes requiring a tie and jacket for admittance. It was centrally located within a fifteen-minute walk to Times Square, the theatre district, Fifth Avenue, and the Metropolitan Museum of Art.

During my senior year I attended several national American Athletic Union (AAU) tournaments, where I got to watch some great wrestlers such as Olympians Gray Simons, Greg Ruth, and Rocky Aoki (who eventually founded the Benihana Restaurant franchise). That year, the Tokyo Olympics were to be held, and wrestlers from all over the country trained at the New York Athletic Club in preparation for the trials.

I dragged poor Christine to the Singer Bowl at the 1964 World's Fair and we watched the Olympic trials from dawn to dusk for three straight days, occasionally taking breaks to visit other exhibits. During the trials I proudly wore a sling that supported the separated shoulder I had suffered during an Athletic Club workout the previous week at the hands of Gordon Hassman, a two-time NCAA wrestling champion from Iowa State.

58

BY MY JUNIOR YEAR IN HIGH SCHOOL, MY DESIRE TO GO WEST POINT had waned. I realized that what I had actually fallen in love with was the allure of being an Academy cadet rather than the pursuit of a life-long career in the military. I wasn't even sure that I could get into West Point with my poor vision and middling grades. Neither of my parents seemed disappointed that I was reassessing my college plans. Ironically, my father told me he was relieved to see I was considering other career options. Though he was proud of his military service, he hadn't enjoyed his time in the Army.

Without West Point as a goal, I was lost, but knew I needed to choose a college for the next stage of my life. My mother wanted me to go to one of the prestigious Eastern colleges. I placated her by applying to, and soon received rejection letters from, Princeton, Dartmouth, and Amherst.

Enzo and Jimmy Wolitarsky mentioned their interest in applying to Franklin and Marshall College, referred to as F&M. This exclusive men's school in Pennsylvania boasted a stellar academic reputation and a renowned wrestling program. A promotional brochure published by the college profiled three outstanding seniors. What stood out for me was that one of the seniors was a pre-med wrestler and, along with touting his academic experience, it featured his four-year rivalry with a Lehigh wrestler.

Enzo and I drove down together and stayed at our friend Gary Greenbaum's fraternity house. Gary raved about the school and enthusiastically endorsed his college experience, encouraging us to enroll. The campus was impressive and I thought the wrestling accommodations were amazing. The wrestling room was located in a large heated room with wall-to-wall mats and surrounded by windowed walls which allowed athletes to watch practice as they walked to the locker room.

During our visit we met with the admission's officer and our applications were accepted on the spot. The college appeared to be an ideal choice as I wanted to go to a small men's school with good academic credentials and a reputable wrestling program. On the other hand, I knew it was a disappointment for my mother who wanted to brag that her son was attending a well-known prestigious school. A painful memory was her stinging parting shot in one of our last arguments before her death, "And who's ever heard of Franklin and Marshall College?"

***

My Dad drove me to F&M in our family's Plymouth station wagon. The night before we left, my mother picked a fight with me over something ridiculous and I left the house without saying goodbye to her. I was angry, but relieved to have finally escaped the tense home environment. I knew with some satisfaction that I wasn't to blame. My Dad comforted me and as we departed our neighborhood, I experienced the heady realization that I was finally off to college.

The summer before classes began, we received the addresses of our prospective college roommates. My roommate was Kevin Saunders from Cranston, Rhode Island, who had played football and wrestled in high school. Kevin and I were assigned to live in Buchanan Hall, a long two-story dormitory connected to Marshall Hall.

Enzo and Jimmy Wolitarsky had decided to room together. I liked both of them, but I was reluctant to risk our friendship by living with them. My hesitancy was born out, as they ended up getting different roommates for the second semester.

I quickly made friends with two freshmen roommates who lived across the hall. Jimmy Clair was from Burlington, New Jersey and Rick Jarashow was from Long Island. They were both engaging and appreciative of my sarcastic, self-deprecating humor.

Jimmy and I were in the same wrestling weight class and soon began working out together. Though wresting practice didn't start until early November, the wrestling room was available, and we practiced several days a week as soon as school started. Though we possessed different physiques, Jimmy and I were similar in ability, which made for very competitive workouts.

My courses consisted of World History, English, French, and Math. The entire freshman class took World History together in a large auditorium with all five hundred of us subjected to the same bi-weekly lectures with an optional weekly breakout discussion group. The other three classes met three times a week with about thirty students in each class.

I started school a highly disciplined student, committed to excelling academically. I completed my homework, attended all my classes, and studied anywhere from two to five hours every day. Despite my efforts, when we got our midterm grades I was devastated. I received C's in all my classes, except for Math, which I flunked.

Unlike in high school, where your grades were based on homework and multiple tests, our college grades could be determined by just one exam. Our history mid-term grade was contingent upon a single exam requiring two written essays. I got an A for one of them and a C for the other, but I was ultimately given a C for the exam and for my mid-term grade, which pissed me off.

There seemed to be no relationship between the effort committed to studying and my ensuing grades, so I used this disappointing revelation as an excuse to succumb to the social distractions available at school, and ended up goofing off the rest of the semester. In retrospect, I should have learned to study more efficiently, but I pretty well just gave up.

Though I continued to attend class and complete my work, I had lost my drive and discipline to study. As the semester progressed I made more friends and spent more time socializing than studying.

59

WITH THE ADVENT OF NOVEMBER CAME THE BEGINNING OF WRES-tling practice. There were expectations for a successful varsity season as the previous year's freshman team had only lost to Lehigh. School spirit was buoyed by an undefeated football season. The Eastern Championships had been held at F&M the previous year and had given the sport great exposure, with us competing against such Division I teams as Army, Navy, Syracuse, Penn State, University of Pittsburg, Temple, Lehigh (the Eastern wrestling powerhouse), and the Ivy league schools. The best wrestler on our team was Saul Shimansky who had won third place in the Easterns as a sophomore.

About sixty freshman wrestlers showed up for the first practice. Bob Getchel, a non-wrestling graduate of Springfield College was our strict, hard-driving freshman coach. Our rigorous practices drove the less committed freshman off the team in spite of their successful high school records. We had several strong wrestlers at every weight and the competition was intense to make the starting line-up.

The middleweights were especially strong. Steve Sinatra, from fabled Mepham High School in Long Island was at 147, Jim Kauffman, a prep school champion from Horace Mann High School outside New York City was at 157, and Rick Johnson, a very good wrestler from Maryland, was at 167.

Wrestling with Sinatra at 147 was like being in a street brawl. He was extremely physical, and instead of employing traditional setups from standing, it felt like he just punched you in the face. One practice we were shooting takedowns when he slammed the heel of his hand into my forehead so hard I saw stars. Another time, I picked up his leg and he smashed me in the mouth and ripped the skin flap between my gum and lip, filling my mouth with blood. Not only was he a quick and agile wrestler, he was a wild man.

Kaufman at 157 was strong and had great wrestling instincts. He was a counter wrestler and rarely shot takedowns. His lightning fast sprawl and vise- like grip made it almost impossible to take him down. From bottom he would either sit out and quickly turn for an escape or explode to his feet. He used his strength and grip to control his opponents from the top. He didn't seem to use much extra effort to win, but he seldom lost.

After losing to each of them I finally broke into the lineup by beating the heavier starters at 177 and 191. My elation was short-lived with the realization that I would be wrestling competitors who were at least twenty pounds heavier than me.

Workouts were exhausting, with unending pushups, sit ups, wrestling drills, and scrimmaging in a heated room. Sometimes in order to lose weight a wrestler might wear a spandex rubber suit. After barely being able to crawl off the mat, we were expected to push past exhaustion by running laps in the gym or sprinting up and down the stairs.

Jimmy Clair and I worked out hard and were always in great shape. We would often go to the weight room after practice, run laps around the outside track or torture ourselves climbing ropes, the latter being about the most painful workout possible. You hauled yourself up, hand over hand, rope burning your palms and fingers, your arms and torso straining with exertion and pain. It was among the most grueling workouts we endured. I remember walking back to the locker room after a rope session, forearms throbbing, stomach cramping, and the palms of my hands scorched.

Though there were a lot of outstanding high school wrestlers at F&M, there were few with the desire and commitment that I had. Many of them quit the team, unwilling to endure the pain, sacrifice, and dieting required. They were more committed to putting in the time and effort toward the academic demands at F&M.

Jimmy Clair was one of the most disciplined individuals I've ever known. I could keep up with and enjoyed being his workout partner in wrestling, but I lacked the focus that he applied to his studies. Jimmy and I roomed together in an apartment our sophomore year with Rick Jarashow and Bob Mendel. We were both dieting to make our respective weight divisions. We barely survived by drinking *Nutriment*, a liquid supplement that tasted like thick sour chalky milk, and eating bowls of plain yogurt sprinkled with wheat germ. Jimmy would sit in our apartment living room at his desk, meticulously marking his government textbook with a highlighter, and then he'd underline his highlights and create a corresponding set of index cards. On days when my classes wouldn't start until noon or I just chose to skip class and stay in bed, I would hear our alarm go off at 6 a.m., soon followed by rustling sounds as Jimmy got dressed and marched off to the library to study. I had never before witnessed such a disciplined athlete-scholar. Though I would never have experienced my wrestling success without him as a workout partner, I wish his rigorous study habits had rubbed off on me as well.

One of my fraternity brothers, Bob Sawers, likes to tell the story of how I broke into the freshman lineup.

Bob was sitting on the fraternity couch in the Chi Phi living room and his golf teammate Jim Bunting came in to describe the wrestling meet that he had just witnessed.

"How'd they do?" Bob inquired.

"F&M's freshmen are studs. They killed Columbia."

"Any prospects for the house?"

"Yeah, you know that funny skinny wrestler you've been rushing?"

"You mean Bruce Leonard?"

"Yeah I think that's his name. Ate the guy up, pinned him at 177 in the first period."

"No, it couldn't have been Leonard. He wrestles around 150."

"Yeah that's him. When he went out on the mat the crowd kind of groaned because it looked like such a mismatch. The guy from Columbia was a muscular stud. Much bigger. Leonard goes out, takes him down, puts him in a cradle and pins him."

"No shit! Fucking Leonard?"

60

*FRANKLIN AND MARSHALL IS LOCATED IN RURAL LANCASTER, PENN-*sylvania, about two hours west of Philadelphia in the southern part of the state. The eleven campus fraternity houses provided a much needed social life for a men's school situated in the middle of rural Amish farmland and isolated from any significant girls' schools. Rushing fraternities became a consuming activity the first semester of freshman year, with selection and initiations conducted during the second semester. Along with Enzo, my closest friends were Rick Jarashow and Jim Clair. On certain designated afternoons during the week, we participated in the customary ritual of visiting the row of fraternity houses, interacting with the brothers and determining where we wanted to pledge. Each of the houses had different personalities and reputations.

Garry Greenbaum gave me his assessment of the fraternity scene. "ZBT is the big Jewish fraternity, with some cool guys, but a lot of premed closet cases. Phi Psi is a total animal house with a couple of jocks but a lot of drunks and crazies. The jock houses with most of the football players are Lambda Chi, Phi Sig, and Chi Phi. I personally think Chi Phi is the coolest house on campus. It's the preppy jock house. I think you'd probably fit in one of the jock houses, but I'd try Chi Phi."

Walking into Chi Phi, you were confronted with frat brothers clad in preppy sweaters, brown Weejun penny loafers worn without socks, and either jeans or khakis. The preferred button-down shirts were monogrammed Brooks Brothers.

Clever sarcastic exchanges dominated Chi Phi interactions. It was survival of the fittest requiring the ability to joust verbally, deflect insults, and deliver put downs that ranged from funny to hurtful. Conversations required a quick wit, insightful intelligence, and a honed ability to spar without becoming defensive. The verbal competition served as a natural selection litmus test determining mental and attitudinal compatibility. This receptive audience fulfilled my need for attention and lead to the development of an enduring bond among many of us in the group. There was not another fraternity on campus with the consistent level of coolness and compatibility that was present among the brotherhood of Chi Phi.

I had earned stature and recognition as a first string wrestler on the freshman team, but I was still dealing with a variety of issues. My hair started to thin my senior year in high school and it progressed throughout college. In desperation, I was frequently setting my hair with Dippety Do, a gel which would form a textured shell and would camouflage my baldness with a pitiful comb-over. This was an anxiety provoking ordeal with required frequent visits to bathroom mirrors to monitor scalp coverage. I always felt the pressure to look good, probably self-imposed but it existed. I still didn't think I was quite smart enough. I knew I was a slow reader and took summer school classes to help me speed up. I wanted to be liked and would second guess situations, and if I felt slighted or excluded by someone, I'd wrack my brain, trying to figure out why. My desire to be popular had always been a priority and I equated that with looks, grades, and athletic performance. So my acceptance into the Chi Phi brotherhood greatly boosted my confidence. They were a great group of guys, and I considered it a privilege to be one of them.

61

I WENT WITH CHRISTINE EXCLUSIVELY MY JUNIOR AND SENIOR YEAR in high school. I loved her and this was our first serious relationship, soured only by her possessiveness. Since she hadn't made many meaningful relationships in high school or had many other interests, I felt suffocated. I'm sure part of it was that she entered school as a junior and didn't know anyone, and the treatment she got from the Rat Pack compounded her isolation. I had known many of my classmates since fourth grade, so I had a strong social support system with a lot of friends. I didn't find any of the girls at our high school any more desirable or attractive than Christine, but I still felt trapped. On the other hand, our relationship was a boost to my ego. I knew that a lot of junior and senior guys found her attractive and flirted with her, but she was loyal to me. When I would tease her about them, she would assure me I was the only one.

Our physical relationship consisted mostly of kissing and grinding. There was no birth control other than condoms and we both believed in waiting until marriage to have sex.

Despite the quality of our relationship, I was restless and wanted to explore the possibility of other relationships. To ensure my independence from her, I announced I wanted to apply to a men's school. We agreed that once we each went off to college we could date other people.

It didn't take long before I began to regret my self-imposed separation from Christine. Social life at an isolated men's school like F&M proved to be challenging. At the occasional freshman mixers where coeds were bussed in from women's schools several hours away, my insecurities escalated with my inability to connect with desirable girls. My only consolation was that I rarely came across anyone as attractive as Christine.

As my lack of dating success continued my first semester, I grew increasingly eager to see her. I invited her to F&M's homecoming, which included a football game, a Peter, Paul and Mary concert and a campus party. She got along with my new friends and I was proud to have such a great-looking date. We spent time together during our Thanksgiving and Christmas vacations.

I had left for college emboldened that Christine would never dump me, and that confidence was reinforced for most of our first semester. She told me about going to fraternity parties where she turned down guys all the time. She made a lot friends at her all-girls school, and they would set her up with guys they knew. She went out on several dates with Jeff, a varsity soccer player and an officer in his fraternity, and she claimed that he paled in comparison to me. She said she would deflect any of his hopes for a relationship by spending their dates talking about me. Her words reassured me as my social life was going nowhere.

During our Thanksgiving break she announced, "I'm so happy that we have this open relationship and that we can date others."

"Oh really?" I replied a little startled.

"You don't have anything to worry about, it's just that I think it's nice that we can date other people and have sort of a casual social life while we're separated. I mean we only get to see each other a couple of times a semester, and you know it gets boring and lonely."

"Yeah, I know, so what's his name?"

"What do you mean?"

"You wouldn't be so excited about your social life if you hadn't met someone you enjoyed being with."

"Bruuce. You have nothing to worry about. As I told you, I've gone out with lots of guys and none of them compare to you."

"Yeah, I know. So what's his name?" I persisted.

"Well last month, Karen introduced me to this guy Kenny. Now he's not as good-looking or as funny, but he's—you know—good company, and he's Karen's boyfriend's best friend, so we have a good time when we double-date. But don't worry, you're the only one for me. It's just nice to be able to go out and have a good time instead of staying alone in my room on weekends dreaming of you, you gorgeous hunk. Come here and give me a kiss."

I wasn't really the jealous type and didn't torture myself wondering if Christine would dump me. After our intense two-year relationship and her constant assurance of love and loyalty, her ever dumping me was inconceivable to me.

My second semester was getting to be depressing. I was still smarting from my poor first semester academic performance. Tentatively exploring psychology as a possible major, I soon felt discouraged when the introductory course on perception turned out to be dry and boring. Wrestling and my involvement at the fraternity house were easy excuses not to study. The more guilt I carried for not studying, the worse I felt, and the more I thought about Christine. I looked forward to seeing her at the intra-fraternity weekend which would mark my official membership into the Chi Phi brotherhood after the tortuous hell week initiation.

Then I got a phone call.

"Hey Bruce," Christine hesitated. "How's it going?"

"Fine, I'm really looking forward to seeing you this weekend, I'm tired of studying and I just really want to see you."

"Well that's why I'm calling... I don't think I'm coming."

"What do you mean?"

"Well Kenny invited me to the big weekend that's being held at his fraternity."

"Yeah, but this is a big deal at our fraternity, I really want you to come."

"I'm sorry, but I want to go with Kenny. Let's talk about this when I see you in a couple of weeks at spring break."

"Are you breaking up with me?"

"Not exactly. I still love you, but I'm sort of confused and would rather talk about it when we see each other. I'm sorry."

"Yeah," I replied and hung up, looking at the wall, feeling like I had just been punched in the stomach. I stood there for a long time trying to compose myself as my throat tightened and the tears flowed. I kept breathing, trying to keep myself from crying.

Over spring break, I drove to Christine's house. In a shaky voice she apologized for having hurt me, explaining that she felt torn. When we were together she still loved me, but we were a five-hour car ride apart and only got to see each other every couple of months. On the other hand, Kenny was right there. Christine was making friends in college, gaining more confidence, and didn't want to depend on any one person for her self-esteem any more. Our relationship continued in limbo throughout the summer and then she officially broke up with me when the fall semester began. She and Kenny married immediately after their college graduation.

62

I WAS UNHAPPY ACADEMICALLY AND HAVING ABANDONED MY dreams of going to West Point, couldn't decide on a career path. Though I had been disappointed by my first psychology class, I hoped the second class would be better.

My father's advice was to pursue a passion and success and financial rewards would follow. Coming of age during the Depression, my father witnessed a stagnant construction business and the diminishing demand for architects. Yet despite lack of support from his father, he pursued architecture, loved to go to work every day and never regretted his decision.

After abandoning my dream of a career in the military, I started to wonder if maybe there was an architectural gene lying dormant somewhere and with a little coaxing or stimulation it would surface. However, I suspected that by now I would have discovered it. I didn't particularly like to draw and hadn't displayed much talent in my art or mechanical drawing classes.

The summer between my freshman and sophomore years I decided to give it one last shot and worked on one of my father's building projects. I.M. Pei and Partners had designed a complex of apartment buildings in Greenwich Village for New York University students and faculty.

My boss, Ted Amberg, was a young architect fresh out of school.

He monitored the construction of several thirty-story towers and was responsible for ensuring that the construction company was complying with the architectural specifications. One of my duties was climbing stairs to the concrete floor that was poured every couple of days, and determine if there were grooves thirty inches from the floor that would accommodate the air conditioning units. I spent hours in the trailer office when Ted wasn't around, staring out the window, reading or talking on the phone. I found my work pretty boring but loved spending time in the city where I would meet friends, go on dates, and wrestle at the New York Athletic Club. Ultimately my stint at the construction site confirmed my suspicion that a career as an architect wasn't in my future.

***

When my mother spent most of the summer between my freshman and sophomore year in the hospital, we began to suspect that she wasn't going to be able to beat this terrible disease. My father called me with the dreaded news on September 16, 1965 and I returned home from F&M to attend her funeral, surrounded by family from both sides. The past four years had been difficult. My mother was only forty-three when she passed away. For my remaining years in college, my relationship with my father became significantly closer as I tried to support him in his efforts to parent my difficult brother.

63

MY SOPHOMORE YEAR, I BROKE INTO THE STARTING VARSITY LINEUP by beating football player Tom McBee at 177. The coach moved Dave Lehman down to 177 and in my first varsity match weighing about 170, I wrestled at 191 and was crushed 7-0 by Columbia's captain. The next match was against Harvard and, still wrestling at 191, I won 10-2. When Johnson injured his knee I was able to wrestle at 167 and moved down to 160 when Kaufman hurt his shoulder.

The highlight of my season was a match against Lehigh's Muir. In December, Muir, a former Pennsylvania high school state champion, won the prestigious Wilkes Open tournament against college and post-college competitors. Lehigh was rated fifth in the country and second to Navy in the East. Lehigh boasted two returning national college champions: Caruso at 123, and Stuart at 137. Peritore had been runner up to Utake, a Japanese Olympian at 130.

Our gym was full of die-hard wrestling fans from both the college and the Lancaster community. After a single-leg attack, the freckled, muscular redhead picked up my right leg. I prevented the takedown by pushing against his head with one hand and dancing around on my opposite leg for a full minute and a half. He effectively rode me for the next three minutes and we entered the third period with a scoreless match. I knew I would exceed expectations if I could salvage a tie by riding this superior wrestler the third period. For the first two minutes of the period I managed to trap his left ankle with my right leg and prevented most of his attempts to escape or reverse.

With a minute left, the referee inexplicably penalized me a point for riding Muir's legs. Behind by a point, I could only win the match by the unlikely possibility of putting Muir on his back. With twenty seconds left, he sat out and I lunged over his shoulder and put him in the cradle pinning combination by locking my hands around his neck and under his knee. I rocked him to his back and as the buzzer sounded, announcing the end of the match, the crowd hesitated in unsure silence. The referee raised his hand, displaying two fingers. I won the match 2-1. The crowd roared as I was mobbed by my teammates. This was significant. I was one of three on our team to win a match, the others being our senior co-captains, Saul Shimansky at 123 and heavyweight Bill Schneiderman.

In the Easterns tournament at the end of the season, I wrestled Seaman from Penn State, who was the strongest competitor I could ever remember wrestling. He was a farm boy with a few missing teeth, his hands were the size of skillets, and his fingers looked as thick as sausages. When he gripped my wrists, his fingers seemed to wrap around twice. He never turned me over but I spent most of the match paralyzed flat on my stomach. I finished the year with a 6-6 record.

The summer between my sophomore and junior years, I worked at a wrestling camp in the Pennsylvania's Pocono Mountains operated by the brother of one of my F&M friends, Jim Saltzman. John Reese, the Wilkes College coach, was one of the co-operators of the camp and he brought in Dick Cook, one of his wrestlers who became a friend and workout partner. He taught me two wrestling moves that contributed to my winning junior year record. I perfected a Russian one-arm drag, which forced an opponent to step back and allow me to attack the opposite side to secure a single-leg takedown. I led the team in reversals by perfecting the Peterson Roll, which required gripping the wrist of the arm around my waist, looping my other arm around the opponent's thigh, rolling over onto my hip, scissoring my legs, and emerging on top with the guy on his back.

Ron Gray became the head coach my junior year. He had been a two-time national Iowa State champion. Jimmy Clair and I were selected as co-captains of the team. We had a very successful 9-1-1 dual meet season with a loss to University of Pittsburg and a tie with Temple. Among our outstanding wrestlers were Steve Sinatra, Dave Cricklair, Stan Berlin, and Jake Homiak. I had a successful dual meet record of 8-3. Jimmy Clair won a third place and Jake Homiak took a fourth in our end-of-season Easterns Wrestling Tournament.

That summer I once again worked out at the New York Athletic Club, wrestled with Dick Cook at the Pocono Mountain wrestling camp and had high hopes for a successful senior year winning season and placing in the Easterns Tournament. Our season did not turn out to be as successful as our last, with several wrestlers getting injured, including Dave Criklair. I had a disappointing season, winning seven and losing six.

One of my most memorable matches was against first-seeded Kent from Navy in the Eastern Tournament, which was being held at the University of Pittsburgh. After a mediocre season, I realized this tournament would be my last wrestling experience in college and I was determined to wrestle my heart out in hopes that I might be able to place in the tournament. Even though Kent had beaten me the previous year, I wrestled with a go-for-broke determination.

I immediately took him down to his back, with an arm drag leg trip. After the first period I was leading 4-0. There was a shifting in the stands and spectators moved to our mat to watch a possible upset. In the second period I was in the down position, and successfully reversed Kent with my reliable Peterson Roll. I was beating the first-seed in my weight class 6-0 and the crowd was going crazy. I was wrestling with total confidence and I felt invincible.

With what appeared to be an insurmountable lead, it looked like my dream of placing in the Easterns was about to be realized. All I had to do to win the match was to ride Kent out the third period or not give up 6 points. Kent and I had similar long, slim builds and were both six-feet tall. As I rode Kent he sat out and I sat under him, administering the crab ride. He pushed back into me and though he was on top of me I was technically in control and felt comfortable. I was determined to maintain my control but was so preoccupied that I didn't realize the position of my back. He knew what he was doing.

Suddenly I heard the referee slap the mat. The crowd groaned. While sitting in my lap, Kent kept pushing back into me until my shoulders were touching the mat. I was now the victim of wrestling's worst nightmare: I literally pinned myself. As quoted in the New York Times sports page, "John Kent, Navy's top-seeded 160-pounder, overcame a 6-0 deficit to pin Bruce Leonard of Franklin and Marshall and avoid a major upset."

This kind of loss was a devastating end to my college wrestling career. Kent went on to lose to Kline from Penn State in the finals, and then placed second in the nationals to Wayne Wells from Oklahoma, who won the 1968 Mexico City Olympics. My only comfort was witnessing my co-captain and four-year wrestling partner Jim Clair become the first Franklin and Marshall Eastern Champion in 11 years and only the fourth in the school's history.

64

I WAS A FRUSTRATED STUDENT AND FINDING A MAJOR TO COMMIT to was difficult. After completing a second psychology course and earning a D, I took classes in math, government, and history, in my ongoing search for a subject that interested me. Economics seemed practical and could provide me a foundation to pursue business or law. I was being practical, but wasn't especially interested in those careers or that subject.

Fortunately, I was having enough fun with wrestling and my social life that I was determined to persevere in college. With any luck, a cosmic switch would be pulled sometime in the future and illuminate the path to my academic or professional future.

In high school I was an adequate student. I've always loved to read, especially biographies, but I'm slow at it and retaining information requires a lot of effort. It always seemed that I couldn't write fast enough to capture the essence of lectures, and unless the instructor was an entertaining speaker, I spent most classes daydreaming. I probably had Attention Deficit Disorder, and somehow made it out of college by the skin of my teeth.

Many of my classmates recall the story of how college president Keith Spalding told us at orientation that school was going to be tough. He said to take a good look at the students sitting on either side of us; if we made it to graduation, there was a strong likelihood that neither of those students would still be in school. F&M had a very high attrition rate and many of my friends flunked out, though most returned after a semester and eventually graduated. I wasn't completely irresponsible. I attended most of my classes, and completed my coursework, but I was pretty much a C student.

On reflection I regret that I didn't find study partners. The concept of different learning styles was unknown to me at the time. Some individuals learn best by listening and others by hearing or seeing or doing. Through experience, I've found that I retain information best by learning it and then teaching it to someone else. Unfortunately, many of our exams were graded on a curve, which ultimately discouraged students from helping each other. The worse your classmates did on an exam, the better your grade would be.

Many of my close friends in the fraternity were mediocre students like me. Jimmy Clair and Rick Jarashow were the exceptions, both graduating as members of the Black Pyramid Honor Society.

Living in the fraternity house my junior and senior year didn't help. I was surrounded by fellow procrastinators. After a grueling wrestling practice, Jimmy and I would drag our asses to the fraternity house to eat dinner. If we were trying to make weight, our meals might consist of a piece of meat and some fruit. Afterwards Jimmy would immediately grab his books and head to the library to study. Thwarted by my need to interact and entertain, I would linger at the fraternity house, seduced into playing cards, watching TV, or pondering where we were getting dates for the upcoming weekend. We held a perverse admiration for those students who never studied or showed up for class and yet passed their courses and even excelled in some cases. My situation was just the opposite. I'd go to class, complete the work and still get C's.

Graduating from F&M was tough enough, but many majors, including economics, required that seniors pass comprehensive exams in order to graduate. We had the option to take the exam in January, and then, if we didn't pass, we could take it again in May. The comprehensives included a three-hour written exam followed by a thirty-minute faculty interview. The exam covered the total required micro and macro-economics coursework. Sitting for the exam was unbearably stressful.

I was not one of the star students of the department. As a matter of fact, I had received a letter from Department Chairman Will Lyons over the summer before my senior year, encouraging me to change majors. I had failed one of my macro-economics courses my junior year, when I foolishly went on a road trip to Vassar College with fraternity brothers Dyke Hendrickson and Rob Mendel instead of studying. Upon receiving the letter, I immediately hopped in our Chevy II and drove the four hours to Lancaster, set up an appointment with Chairman Lyons and groveled for a second chance. He relented, but I knew that I was going to be scrutinized closely and was extremely anxious about graduating.

I had heard horror stories of honor students with enough credits to graduate, who had been admitted to graduate school, but flunked their comprehensives and were denied diplomas.

I decided to take my comprehensive exam in January to alleviate the stress hanging over my head. I returned to school early, before our Christmas break was over, and stayed at the fraternity house and studied frantically. I flunked my first attempt at the exam, and would have one last chance to pass it in May. Rarely in my life have I ever experienced such exhilaration as when I learned I finally passed.

65

SUSAN SUTLIFFE, WHO HAD BEEN DATING LARRY POLLINS, SET UP Rick Mesard with one of her Skidmore College classmates, Lenna Warner. For whatever reasons, they didn't hit it off and Susan mentioned that Lenna was interested in going out with me. I was dumbfounded. She was gorgeous, with a regal presence accentuated by shoulder-length blond hair, light blue eyes, and a willowy stature of about five-foot-eight. Why would she want to go out with me? I considered Mesard to be one of the most attractive of my fraternity brothers and couldn't figure out what she saw in me. Apparently during Lenna's weekend with Mesard she had seen me wrestle and told Susan she was interested.

I had not had a serious relationship since the break-up with Christine. As vice president of the fraternity and co-captain of the wrestling team I'd finally attained my high school dream of respect and popularity. It was disappointing that I couldn't share one of the best years of my life with a girlfriend.

The weekend I was set up with Lenna fell on my twenty-first birthday and the first wrestling match of the season. I was no longer able to mask my receding hairline with my lame comb-over since I'd just gotten a haircut to comply with our coach's short-hair policy. I was certain that she'd take one look at me, turn around, and walk away.

When I saw her, I stared tongue-tied, having forgotten how beautiful she was. After regaining my composure and making some small talk, I suggested that we walk over to the gym and watch the freshman wrestling match. I took her hand under the pretense of ensuring a safe walk in the icy conditions. We slipped into easy conversation about our families and schools. Fortunately, she responded to my playful teasing, and as our senses of humor synchronized, my insecurity faded.

Our fraternity parties were always fun. In the basement was always a keg of beer and a jukebox that played a rotation of great Motown, Beatles, Cream, and Rolling Stones music. I'll never forget the amazing feeling of walking in with Lenna and receiving a standing ovation: everyone there had witnessed my winning wrestling match against Columbia.

Lenna and I spent time together over the Christmas holiday when I returned early for wrestling practice to study for my senior comprehensive economic exam. Our relationship continued to flourish as we saw each other on occasional weekends and talked often on the phone. Lenna was self-assured and smart. She could be a little loopy but she was never defensive when I'd tease her. My fraternity brothers loved her, and having a beautiful girlfriend elevated my self-esteem. I was completely smitten and had not felt this way about a girl since Christine. Both politically conservative, we supported the Vietnam War, and were critical of the drugs and hippies that were starting to surface. We would often find ourselves in heated discussions with friends who had more liberal views.

Lenna met me in Pittsburgh at the end of the wrestling season when I lost my match to Kent, and we watched Jimmy Clair win the Easterns. The following weekend she called, saying she needed to take a break from the relationship. I was stunned. I asked her if she was splitting up with me and she replied with a non-committal "sort of."

We had never had a fight or disagreement. At the time, I was convinced that she was the girl of my dreams, and the fact that I didn't see this break-up coming shook me to the core. I was mired in grief and self-doubt.

I missed a week of classes, my despair compounded by the profound disappointment at having lost my chance at the Easterns because of the devastating loss to Kent. My career as a college wrestler was over. All that lay in my future was the agony of writing my senior thesis and the unbearable pressure of passing my economics comprehensive exams. After a week preoccupied with wondering why she dumped me, I broke down and called her roommate Debbie Kelly for a possible explanation.

Lenna answered the dorm phone. I awkwardly asked for Debbie and she recognized my voice and asked me how I was doing, as if nothing had happened. She invited me to come meet her father at Skidmore College's father-daughter weekend. As we said good-bye, my heart pounded with elation, and I stared at the phone with disbelief. What the hell just happened?

The weekend went well. I met lots of her friends at the dance and got to tour the Skidmore campus. Her father was a former University of Pennsylvania football player and his demeanor reminded me of Christine's father. Though we continued to enjoy each other for the remainder of our relationship, I never completely trusted her and remained guarded.

A friend told me about a ten-buck a night hotel he had stayed at in Miami the previous spring vacation. Lenna and I flew down to Florida and I checked into the Kent Hotel. I requested the basement room that Roger had told me about and was able to sneak Lenna in the back entrance.

The hotel was located in the middle of a Jewish retirement community. Every morning we'd enjoy the thirty-five-cent breakfast at a kosher cafeteria. We were tall, blond Nordic kids surrounded by little old couples jabbering in Yiddish. They would glance over at us affectionately, as if their grandchildren's goyim friends had decided to visit. We were soon adopted by the Goldbergs and shared breakfast with them several times that week. Lenna took me aside after our first encounter with them and discreetly pointed out the faded numbers tattooed on Mrs. Goldberg's arm. We never inquired about it but we gained newfound respect for our elderly friends.

In the afternoon we would stroll out our back door and lay on the beach, conscientiously studying the textbooks we brought with us. We chowed down on kosher hot dogs and beer while watching episodes of the *Newlywed Game* at one of the beach bars. In the evening we got dressed up and took the Collins Avenue bus to any one of the appealing downtown restaurants for dinner. It was a spectacular vacation and it seemed like our relationship was back on track.

We returned to our respective schools for the final weeks of the semester and attended each other's graduation ceremonies. Within a couple of weeks Lenna moved to NYC with Debbie and began a career as a stockbroker. I flew to San Francisco for my VISTA training.

I knew I would miss Lenna, but I was excited about this next stage in my life. I was about to "come of age" in Hawaii.

Bruce Leonard with brother Craig with parents Jeanne and Eason.

Bruce with parents Eason and Jeanne Leonard

Bruce and Craig Leonard, Crucifer and acolyte at St. Mary's Episcopal Church, Scarborough, New York 1962

Bruce Leonard, 14 year old Eagle Scout, January 1961.

Bruce Leonard college sophomore 1965

Winning Lehigh wrestling match

Winning college wrestling match against Princeton at Franklin and Marshall College

I. M. Pei and managing partner, Eason Leonard at entrance to Louvre Pyramid 1990.

College graduation (from left to right) Eason Leonard, Bruce Leonard, Lenna Warner, grandmother Margaret Mason)

Chi Phi fraternity brothers from left to right (Top – Rick Mesard, Bruce Leonard, D. J. Korns, Jay Chittum, John Haass, Dennis Moriarty. Bottom – Doug Green, Dave Grayson, D. J. Shaffer, Fred Druck

EPILOGUE

*CAPTAIN ENERGY MANAGED TO SURVIVE THE SIXTIES/EARLY SEVEN-*ties with most of his faculties intact. He and Carol, Duke's girlfriend, married in Hawaii in 1978. After a 20-year career in the U.S. Public Health Service, they settled down and raised their children in Georgia where they currently reside.

ACKNOWLEDGEMENTS

*WRITING THIS COMING OF AGE SAGA WAS A JOURNEY THAT BENEFIT-*ed from the support of many people, including my wife Carol who patiently helped me edit the manuscript. I was also fortunate to connect with old friends who helped fill in details of some of the events.

These dear friends include Leo Dubois, Lenna Warner, John Stone, Larry Harrington, Bill Sutkus, Dick Brown, Neil Benedict, Cosmo Ohms, Gary Greenbaum, Rick Jarashow, Roc Caivano, and Charlie Smith. The following friends also helped with editing: Todd Frank, Enzo DiMaio Dennis Moriarty, Abigail Davis, Linda Hughes, and Ann Fisher. Though they didn't appear in the book, several friends encouraged me as they read early drafts and gave me feedback. Thanks to Bruce Buckbee, Dave Schaefer, and Sarah Harrington. This book would not have been possible without the Deeds/Babcock team of Bob, Jan, Mark, Matt, and editors David Ingle and Ashley Clarke.

I got significant moral support from many of my golfing and poker playing buddies that had to endure my book writing rantings; thanks to Bill Gue, Doug Deheck, and Spanky's Gang: Greg Eells, Robert Dennison, Michael Chafin, James LaRotonda, Brad Hoyt, Russ Wise, John Schultz, Jim Kramer, Ken Jewell, Dave Cloud, Cullen Horne, Rit Bouton, Tim Brown, Bill Hughes, Jim Wingo, George Patton, Parks Mann, Bob Donnan, Bob Morris, Tim Hamil, Stan Wilson, Vinnie Shemanski and Scott Barker.

I had been encouraged to write about Captain Energy by friends who had heard me relate portions of the story and wanted to hear more. It wasn't until I was encouraged by friends Holly Roberts and Ric Bothwell, I attended Natalie Goldberg's writing workshops, with friend Dave Hobler, in Taos, New Mexico 20 years ago that I began to put pen to paper. High school friend Butch Remmel and college fraternity brother Lee Browne encouraged me to finally commit to writing this book.

A special thanks to Georgia Gwinnett College colleague and fellow Deeds Author Linda Hughes who guided and encouraged me through the memoir writing process after I attended her Memoir Writing Workshop back in March 2015.

Thanks to all and love to Carol and our spectacular children Allison and Eason.

ABOUT THE AUTHOR

BRUCE LEONARD GREW UP IN SLEEPY HOLLOW, N.Y., GRADUATED from Franklin and Marshall College in Lancaster, PA. and served as a VISTA volunteer (Volunteers in Service to America) in Honolulu, Hawaii. He received a master's degree in public health from the University of Hawaii.

He retired as a Captain in the Public Health Service Commissioned Corps where he worked for both the Indian Health Service and the Centers for Disease Control and Prevention. He continues his career in health promotion as an instructor at Georgia Gwinnett College. He and his Hawaiian born wife Carol have been married since 1978 and have two children, Allison and Eason.